LES SECRETS QUE LES RICHES VEULENT TE CACHER

Les Secrets que les Riches Veulent te Cacher

-Le savoir qui rend riche

DEGBE J. GROUA

Copyright © 2025 by Degbe J. Groua.

All rights reserved. No part of this publication may be reproduced, distributed, or transmitted in any form or by any means, including photocopying, recording, or other electronic or mechanical methods, without the prior written permission of the author, except in the case of brief quotations embodied in critical reviews and certain other noncommercial uses permitted by copyright law.

Printed in the United States of America

ISBN 979-8-9933020-1-0 (sc)

Library of Congress Control Number: 2025921395

Remerciements

À ma famille

Je remercie du fond du cœur ma famille, qui a toujours cru en moi, même dans les moments où je doutais de tout. Votre soutien silencieux et constant a été ma plus grande force.

Aux amis et compagnons de route

À ceux qui, par leurs paroles, leurs conseils ou simplement leur présence, ont contribué à faire naître et mûrir ces idées : je vous suis redevable plus que je ne saurais l'exprimer. Et un remerciement special a toute l' equipe de Parchment Global Publishing pour votre brillant travail.

À mes lecteurs

Vous qui tenez ce livre entre vos mains, merci. Votre curiosité, votre ouverture et votre désir de grandir donnent vie à ces pages. Sans vous, ce travail ne serait qu'une voix perdue dans le silence.

LES SECRETS QUE LES RICHES VEULENT TE CACHER

Remerciements v

Introduction.. xiii
    Pourquoi ce livre ?

CHAPITRE 1 1
    Les deux piliers de la Vraie Richesse: Visible et invisible

CHAPITRE 2 17
    Ils ont une vision claire et chiffrée

CHAPITRE 3 29
    Ils maîtrisent des compétences rares

CHAPITRE 4 41
    Ils créent des systèmes de revenus multiples

CHAPITRE 5 47
    Ils maîtrisent l'art de l'argent

CHAPITRE 6 57
    Leur réseau vaut des millions

CHAPITRE 7 61
    Ils travaillent sur des projets à haut impact

CHAPITRE 8 69
    Ils n'ont pas peur du risque, mais le calculent

CHAPITRE 9 89
    TRANSFORMER LES PENSÉES
    NÉGATIVES EN FORCE MOTRICE

CHAPITRE 10 99
    Comment les grands riches exploitent l'IA pour dominer

CONCLUSION 105
    Active ton potentiel

Préface

C'est avec un immense plaisir et une profonde admiration que je vous présente « LES SECRETS QUE LES RICHES VEULENT TE CACHER » de Degbe Jean Groua. J'ai eu le privilège de connaître Degbe Jean Groua aussi bien sur le plan personnel que professionnel. En tant qu'expert certifié en cybersécurité, assurant la protection de systèmes critiques j'ai vu de nombreuses personnes tenter d'atteindre leurs objectifs. Mais rares sont celles qui incarnent la ténacité et la résilience comme le fait Degbe Jean Groua.

Dans ce livre percutant, Degbe Jean Groua emmène le lecteur dans un voyage révélateur, l'invitant à remettre en question les croyances limitantes qui freinent son potentiel, notamment en ce qui concerne l'argent, la richesse, et les mécanismes invisibles qui maintiennent tant de gens dans l'ignorance. « LES SECRETS QUE LES RICHES VEULENT TE CACHER » n'est pas simplement un livre de développement personnel : c'est une prise de conscience, un déclic, un appel à se réveiller et à agir.

L'histoire personnelle de Degbe Jean Groua illustre à merveille la puissance de la détermination. Parti d'un poste d'opérateur de machine, il aurait pu se contenter de cette voie toute tracée. Mais il a choisi de se dépasser, en consacrant d'innombrables heures d'étude pour décrocher la certification prestigieuse CISSP (Certified Information System Security Professional). Son parcours nous rappelle avec force que nos origines ou nos conditions actuelles ne définissent pas notre destinée – ce sont nos décisions et notre persévérance qui le font.

Au fil des pages, vous découvrirez des conseils concrets, des récits inspirants et des stratégies applicables immédiatement pour élever votre vie, sur les plans personnel, professionnel et financier. Ce livre s'adresse à toutes celles et ceux qui en ont assez de tourner en rond et qui veulent comprendre ce que les riches savent mais ne disent jamais, pour enfin prendre en main leur avenir.

Ce n'est pas seulement un guide, c'est une invitation urgente à reprendre votre pouvoir, à sortir des sentiers battus, à viser l'excellence. L'auteur y partage des années d'expériences personnelles, de lectures, d'efforts, et d'apprentissage acharné – condensés ici pour vous donner un accès direct à des clés de transformation.

À mesure que vous lirez ce livre, je vous invite à réfléchir à vos propres ambitions. Laissez-vous inspirer par le parcours de Degbe Jean Groua et osez faire le premier pas vers une vie meilleure, plus libre, et pourquoi pas, plus riche.

Souvenez-vous : les véritables limites sont celles que nous acceptons de croire. Rejetez-les. Ce que les riches savent peut vous libérer – à condition que vous soyez prêt à l'entendre.

Sincèrement,
Mickael Ben Ahmed Coulibaly
Certified Cybersecurity Expert

Dédicace

À ma très chère épouse,
Brou Epse Groua
Balefe Marie Asael

Ce livre t'est dédié, toi, l'amour de ma vie, ma source constante de force et ma plus grande bénédiction. Ton soutien indéfectible, ta patience infinie et ta sagesse profonde ont été mes étoiles guides, éclairant mon chemin à travers chaque défi et chaque victoire.

Tu n'as pas seulement été à mes côtés, tu m'as porté avec ta foi lorsque je ne pouvais avancer seul. Ton amour a été une forteresse, ton encouragement un phare, et ta confiance en moi un vent sous mes ailes.

Sans toi, ce voyage serait resté une histoire inachevée. Tu es la fondation sur laquelle reposent mes rêves et la lumière qui m'inspire à devenir la meilleure version de moi-même.

Merci d'être ma partenaire dans l'amour, ma confidente dans la vie et la muse de mon âme. Ta présence est le battement de cœur de mon existence, et pour cela, je t'en suis éternellement reconnaissant.

Avec tout l'amour de mon cœur,

Degbe Jean Groua

Introduction

Pourquoi ce livre ?

La richesse a toujours fasciné. Pourtant, mais pourquoi si peu de gens y parviennent ? Est-ce simplement une question de chance, de talent, ou y a-t-il autre chose ? Ce livre est une réponse à cette question. Il ne s'agit pas d'un énième guide rempli de conseils abstraits, mais d'une exploration concrète des secrets que les grands riches nous cachent, des principes simples mais puissants qui, s'ils sont appliqués, peuvent transformer votre vie et avant la conclusion, j' ai ajouté un bonus qui vous permettra de mieux vous organiser, de rendre votre processus rapide et vous faire gagner du temps. Vous étiez venu au monde pour dominer.

Pourquoi tant de gens échouent à atteindre la richesse ?

Il y a de nombreuses raisons pour lesquelles la majorité des gens ne parviennent pas à atteindre la liberté financière. Parmi ces raisons, nous pouvons citer une mauvaise éducation financière, des croyances limitantes héritées de la société ou de la famille et un manque de vision ou de plan concret pour y arriver. Au-delà de tout, il faut reconnaître qu' il y a aussi une vérité crue :

certains secrets sont volontairement gardés par les plus riches. Ils savent que leur réussite repose sur des principes que peu de gens comprennent ou appliquent. Ce livre a pour but de vous révéler ces secrets et de vous donner les outils nécessaires pour écrire votre propre histoire de succès. En réalité, j'ai passé la majorité de mes trois premières années aux USA en train d'acheter et lire des livres rares et puissants. Et je veux partager le résultat de mes nombreuses recherches avec vous.

MON HISTOIRE REELLE

Dehors de la classe, mais à l'intérieur du rêve

Au lycée, notre professeur de français nous avait demandé d'acheter un roman pour le cours. Malheureusement, comme certains de mes camarades, je n'avais pas les moyens d'acheter ce livre. À chaque séance, ceux qui ne l'avaient pas étaient invités à sortir de la salle, pendant que les autres restaient pour suivre le cours.

J'étais l'un de ceux qu'on laissait dehors. Je me souviens encore du moment où la porte se refermait derrière moi. Je faisais semblant que ça ne me dérangeait pas, mais au fond, j'avais honte. Honte d'être pauvre. Et une colère sourde que je ne comprenais pas encore

À force, j'en ai eu marre. Je me posais des questions comme :

Pourquoi nos parents ne sont-ils pas riches ?

Pourquoi devons-nous toujours rater les choses les plus importantes ?

Ces questions, nées de la frustration, ont été le point de départ de mon éveil.

Plus tard, en commençant une nouvelle vie aux États-Unis, j'ai pris une décision : je lirai autant de livres que possible. J'ai commencé à acheter des livres puissants sur Amazon, chez Goodwill et dans des boutiques d'occasion. Des livres sur l'argent, sur la façon dont les riches pensent, sur la croissance personnelle. Peu à peu, j'ai compris comment fonctionne l'argent, comment les millionnaires réfléchissent, et comment on peut partir de rien pour construire quelque chose de grand.

Mais une chose m'a marqué : la plupart de mes amis — que ce soit ici ou dans mon pays — n'ont pas toujours la possibilité d'avoir accès à de bons livres. Par manque de moyens ou simplement par absence de conseils.

C'est à ce moment-là que j'ai décidé d'écrire mon propre livre.

Un livre simple, puissant, et accessible.

Un livre qui résume tout ce que j'ai appris — le genre de livre que j'aurais aimé recevoir à l'époque, quand j'étais ce jeune élève resté dehors de la classe.

Ce livre sera disponible sur Amazon. La deuxieme édition sera en anglais, pour toucher un public plus large, mais le message reste universel :

Tu n'es pas condamné à rester là où tu es né.
Tu n'es pas limite.
Tu peux changer ta vie.

Et surtout :

Il est temps de découvrir ce que les riches savent... mais que personne ne t'a jamais dit.

Une histoire de transformation

Permettez-moi de vous raconter l'histoire de Jacob. Jacob était un jeune homme né dans une famille modeste, vivant dans un petit village. Etant enfant, il rêvait de grandes choses : construire des écoles, voyager à travers le monde, offrir une vie meilleure à sa famille. Mais le chemin semblait impossible.

À 20 ans, Jacob travaillait comme ouvrier dans une usine. Les journées étaient longues, et l'espoir s'amenuisait. Pourtant, un jour, tout a changé. Jacob est tombé sur un livre qui parlait de la puissance des habitudes et de l'éducation financière. Inspiré, il a décidé de se donner une mission : consacrer les cinq prochaines années de sa vie à apprendre tout ce qu'il pouvait sur la création de richesse.

Au début, ce fut difficile. Jacob lisait des livres empruntés à la bibliothèque, regardait des vidéos gratuites en ligne, et notait chaque centime qu'il gagnait et dépensait. Il a fait des sacrifices, travaillant de longues heures tout en investissant dans des petites idées. Lentement mais sûrement, ses efforts ont commencé à porter leurs fruits. À 35 ans, Jacob avait non seulement payé ses dettes, mais il avait aussi investi dans des biens immobiliers et lancé une entreprise prospère. Aujourd'hui, il vit la vie dont il rêvait, et il consacre son temps à aider d'autres personnes à atteindre leurs objectifs.

Pourquoi je ne prétends pas tout savoir

Avant d'aller plus loin, je tiens à être transparent : je ne suis pas encore riche. Cependant, je suis sur le chemin, et les leçons contenues dans ce livre m'ont profondément transformée.

Il y a quelques années, ma propre vie était loin d'être idéale. Je vivais avec des doutes, des peurs, et cette impression constante que la réussite était réservée aux autres. Puis, j'ai commencé à chercher des réponses, à lire des dizaines de livres achetés en ligne ou a (Goodwill), et aussi à observer les personnes qui réussissent. Ce que j'ai découvert a allumé une étincelle en moi. Ces 7 secrets m'ont montré que je n'étais pas impuissant; oui je n'étais pas destiné à vivre une vie minable sans joie. Aujourd'hui, ma vie est plus heureuse, plus ambitieuse, et surtout remplie d'espoir. Je partage ces idées non pas en prétendant être arrivé, mais en vous invitant à marcher à mes côtés sur ce chemin de transformation.

Un engagement mutuel

Ce livre est bien plus qu'un guide : c'est une invitation à repenser votre relation avec l'argent et le succès. Mon objectif est de vous transmettre ces principes de manière claire, accessible, et pratique. Cependant, il y a une condition : ces secrets ne fonctionneront que si vous êtes prêt à agir. Êtes-vous prêt à réécrire votre histoire ? Si oui, prenez une profonde inspiration et plongez dans cette aventure. Comme le dit si bien Jim Rohn : *"Le succès n'est pas à poursuivre, mais à attirer par la personne que l'on devient."*

Bienvenue dans votre transformation.

CHAPITRE 1

Les deux piliers de la Vraie Richesse: Visible et invisible

La richesse matérielle et immatérielle : Une distinction approfondie

La richesse peut être envisagée sous deux aspects fondamentaux : matériel et immatériel. Ces deux formes de richesse sont interconnectées, mais elles diffèrent dans leur nature et dans les moyens d'atteindre ces formes de richesse. Ce chapitre nous permettra de voir l'image réelle de la richesse pour que dans la suite nous puissions bien distinguer les types de stratégies à adopter pour en acquérir en abondance. Mais bien avant ca, voici ce qui a ouvert mes yeux:

Le jour où j'ai vu ce que les riches voyaient

C'était en septembre 2018. Pour la première fois de ma vie, je montais dans un avion.
Moi, qui avais passé toute mon enfance à lever les yeux vers le ciel pour regarder les avions passer au-dessus de moi, je me

retrouvais enfin à l'intérieur. Et pas pour un petit trajet : j'étais en route pour les États-Unis.

Ce jour-là, j'étais heureux. Vraiment.
Plein d'espoir.
Je ne savais pas exactement ce que l'avenir me réservait, mais j'étais convaincu que quelque chose de grand m'attendait.

Tout allait bien, jusqu'à un moment banal : j'ai eu envie d'aller aux toilettes.
Nous étions quelque part entre l'Éthiopie et les États-Unis, et bien sûr, tout à bord était en anglais. Je ne parlais pas bien cette langue à l'époque, alors je me suis levé timidement de mon siège, sans trop réfléchir, et j'ai commencé à chercher les toilettes. En marchant, j'ai ouvert un rideau... un simple rideau.

Mais ce n'était pas n'importe lequel.
C'était le rideau qui séparait la *classe économique*... de la *classe affaires*.

Et là, j'ai été frappé.
Devant moi, tout était différent : de grands sièges confortables, des lumières douces, des passagers détendus, servis comme des rois.
C'était un autre monde.

Mais je n'ai pas eu le temps de regarder longtemps. Une hôtesse m'a crié dessus :
« *Eeeeh, tu vas où ? Tu cherches quoi ? Les toilettes ? C'est pas ici !* »
Elle m'a finalement indiqué la bonne direction, mais l'image était déjà gravée dans mon esprit.

Ce jour-là, **quelque chose s'est réveillé en moi.**

Je me suis dit : *Un jour, moi aussi je m'assoirai dans cette partie-là de l'avion. Pas parce que je veux impressionner qui que ce soit. Mais parce que je sais que c'est possible, et que je le mérite aussi.*

Mais la réalité m'a vite rattrapé.

Malgré mes efforts, malgré mon courage, je me suis rendu compte qu'avoir un simple travail, même honnête et régulier, **ne suffit pas pour devenir riche.**
C'est à ce moment-là que j'ai commencé à chercher des réponses.
J'ai commencé à lire. Beaucoup.
Des livres sur l'argent. Sur l'investissement. Sur les habitudes des riches. Sur les mentalités qui créent la richesse.

Et c'est tout ce que j'ai découvert, appris, expérimenté, que je partage aujourd'hui dans ce livre :

« LES SECRETS QUE LES RICHES VEULENT TE CACHER ».

Parce que ce rideau, entre les riches et le reste du monde, n'est pas fait que de tissu. Il est aussi fait **d'ignorance, de croyances limitantes et de secrets bien gardés.**

Et maintenant que j'ai vu ce qu'il y a de l'autre côté, je veux t'y emmener aussi.

I. La richesse materielle

La richesse matérielle est la forme de richesse la plus facilement visible et quantifiable dans notre société. Elle est souvent associée au succès financier et se traduit par des biens tangibles comme de belles voitures, des duplexes, des grandes sociétés de production prospères et des revenus mesurables. Cependant, derrière cette apparente simplicité se cachent des mécanismes complexes nécessitant des connaissances et des stratégies adaptées.

Composantes de la richesse matérielle :

1. **Argent et revenus :**
    - **Les salaires** : Ils représentent la principale source de revenus pour une grande partie de la population, obtenue grâce à un emploi ou une prestation de service. **Les dividendes** : Ces paiements réguliers, issus d'investissements dans des entreprises, offrent un flux passif et stable pour les investisseurs. **Les bénéfices d'une entreprise** : Être propriétaire ou actionnaire d'une entreprise rentable constitue une source de revenus active ou passive. **Autres sources de revenus** : Royalties, rentes, ou encore revenus de location immobilière.

2. **Actifs :**
    - Les actifs sont des éléments qui non seulement conservent leur valeur mais peuvent aussi s'apprécier au fil du temps. **Biens immobiliers** : Maisons, appartements, terrains ou bâtiments commerciaux. Ces actifs génèrent souvent des revenus locatifs et

prennent de la valeur à long terme. **Objets de valeur** : Des biens comme des œuvres d'art, des bijoux, ou des collections (montres, voitures rares) peuvent aussi représenter une forme d'investissement. **Investissements financiers** : Actions, obligations, fonds communs de placement ou cryptomonnaies offrent des rendements financiers, souvent plus élevés que l'épargne traditionnelle.

3. **Propriétés physiques :**
   - Cela inclut tout ce que l'on possède physiquement et qui peut être échangé ou vendu sur un marché, comme des véhicules, des équipements, ou des biens personnels ayant une valeur.

Comment atteindre la richesse matérielle ?

Accumuler de la richesse matérielle ne repose pas sur le hasard, mais sur une planification minutieuse et des actions cohérentes. Voici les stratégies clés détaillées :

1. **L'éducation financière :**
   - L'éducation financière est essentielle pour comprendre les mécanismes qui régissent l'argent et les investissements. Dans le but de vous donner une idée claire sur certains aspects clés, essayons de comprendre d'abord c' est quoi l'éducation financière: plusieurs livres en parlent mais la définition claire reste toujours un tabou. L'éducation financière, c'est l'ensemble des connaissances et des compétences nécessaires pour gérer efficacement son argent et prendre des décisions financières éclairées tout au long de sa vie. Elle englobe

plusieurs aspects clés qui permettent de mieux comprendre et maîtriser les mécanismes financiers, évitant ainsi les erreurs courantes et maximisant les opportunités de croissance. Voici Les piliers de l'éducation financière :

2. **La gestion de budget :**
   - Qu'est-ce que c'est ?
   La capacité de suivre ses revenus et ses dépenses pour éviter les déséquilibres financiers. Pourquoi est-ce important ?
   Cela permet de vivre en fonction de ses moyens, d'épargner régulièrement et d'éviter les dettes inutiles. C'est effectivement l'un des points les plus importants pour ceux qui veulent réellement amener leur vie financière à un niveau supérieur.
   - Comment le faire ? Suivre ses dépenses via des outils comme une feuille Excel ou des applications (par ex. Mint, YNAB). Catégoriser ses dépenses (fixes, variables, non essentielles). Appliquer la règle 50/30/20 : 50 % pour les besoins, 30 % pour les envies, 20 % pour l'épargne/investissement. Parler de besoins, ici, il s'agit des choses qui vous permettent de vivre. C'est - a- dire le loyer, l'électricité, la nourriture, et autre

3. **Les bases des investissements :**
   - **Qu'est-ce que c'est ?**
   Investir consiste à utiliser votre argent pour acquérir des actifs (comme des actions, de l'immobilier, ou des obligations) dans le but de le faire croître. Contrairement à l'épargne simple, où votre argent reste immobile, l'investissement vise à le multiplier sur le long terme.
   - Pourquoi est-ce important ?

Laisser votre argent sur un compte courant le fait perdre de sa valeur avec le temps, car l'inflation réduit son pouvoir d'achat. Par exemple, ce que vous pouvez acheter avec 100 € aujourd'hui coûtera plus cher demain. C ' est l'une des raisons pour lesquelles vous devez trouver un moyen qui vous sied pour faire fructifier votre argent : Investir permet de créer une source de revenus supplémentaire ou d'atteindre vos objectifs financiers plus rapidement, comme acheter une maison, financer l'éducation de vos enfants ou préparer votre retraite.

Exemple concret :
Si vous investissez 1 000 € dans un actif qui rapporte 5 % par an, au bout de 10 ans, cet argent peut devenir 1 628 €, sans que vous n'ayez rien fait de plus. Mais sur un compte courant, ces 1 000 € pourraient ne valoir que 850 € à cause de l'inflation. Si l'on veut résumer cette phase qui vous ouvrira assez de portes pour que l' argent ne vous manque plus jamais, l'on dira que' investir, c'est mettre votre argent au travail pour qu'il vous rapporte davantage. Cela vous protège de la perte de valeur due à l'inflation et vous rapproche de vos objectifs financiers.

- Investir permet de générer des rendements à long terme. **Comment débuter ?** Étudier les différents types d'actifs (risqués et moins risqués). Commencer par des investissements simples, comme un fonds indiciel ou un compte épargne. Comprendre le concept des rendements composés (l'effet boule de neige des intérêts sur les intérêts)

4. **La gestion des dettes :**
   - **Qu'est-ce que c'est ?**
   Savoir emprunter intelligemment et gérer les remboursements pour éviter l'endettement excessif.

Pourquoi est-ce important ? Les mauvaises dettes (cartes de crédit, prêts à la consommation) freinent la capacité d'épargner et d'investir. Comment bien gérer ?
- Prioriser le remboursement des dettes à taux élevé (comme les crédits à la consommation).

5. **Éviter de vivre au-dessus de ses moyens**
   - Qu'est-ce que ça veut dire ?
   C'est dépenser moins que ce que l'on gagne. Cela permet d'éviter les problèmes financiers et de mettre de l'argent de côté pour ses projets ou imprévus. Et les dettes ? Toutes les dettes ne sont pas mauvaises. Une dette intelligente est un emprunt qui vous aide à investir dans quelque chose qui peut rapporter plus tard, comme : Un prêt immobilier pour acheter une maison ou un appartement. Un crédit pour financer un projet rentable, comme lancer une petite entreprise. Donc ne dépensez pas plus que ce que vous gagnez. Utilisez les emprunts pour des projets qui augmentent votre richesse, pas pour des choses inutiles

6. **L'épargne et la planification financière :**
   - Qu'est-ce que c'est ?
   Mettre de l'argent de côté pour des objectifs à court, moyen et long terme. Pourquoi est-ce important ? L'épargne constitue une sécurité (en cas d'urgence) et un tremplin pour investir. Comment épargner efficacement ? Automatiser les versements sur un compte épargne. Constituer un fonds d'urgence (3 à 6 mois de dépenses). Définir des objectifs financiers précis (acheter une maison, épargner pour la retraite, voyager).

7. **La compréhension des produits financiers :**
   - Qu'est-ce que c'est ?
   Connaître les outils financiers disponibles (assurances, placements, crédits, etc.) pour choisir ceux qui correspondent le mieux à ses objectifs.Pourquoi est-ce important ?
   Cela évite de tomber dans des pièges, comme des investissements trop risqués ou des produits financiers coûteux. Exemples courants :Les assurances (vie, habitation, santé). Les placements (fonds indiciels, actions, obligations). Les crédits (hypothèque, prêt étudiant).

8. **Les avantages de l'éducation financière :**

Indépendance financière : Tu deviens maître de tes décisions et évite de dépendre des autres pour des conseils financiers. Réduction du stress : Une meilleure gestion financière réduit les angoisses liées aux dettes ou aux imprévus. Opportunités de croissance : En comprenant l'argent, tu peux saisir les opportunités de faire fructifier ton patrimoine. Préparation à long terme : Elle t'aide à planifier pour des étapes clés de la vie (achat immobilier, retraite, éducation des enfants).

Comment acquérir une éducation financière ?

1. **Lire des livres** :
   - *Père riche, père pauvre* de Robert Kiyosaki.
   - *L'investisseur intelligent* de Benjamin Graham.

2. **Suivre des formations en ligne** : Des plateformes comme Coursera, Udemy ou Skillshare proposent des cours sur les bases financières.

3. **Consulter des ressources gratuites** : Blogs, podcasts, ou vidéos sur YouTube pour apprendre à gérer ton argent et investir.

4. **Pratiquer** : Commence petit (par exemple, suivre ton budget ou investir dans un fonds indiciel) et apprends au fur et à mesure.

L'éducation financière est donc la clé pour maîtriser ton argent au lieu de laisser l'argent te contrôler. Plus tu apprends tôt, plus tu seras en mesure de construire une base solide pour atteindre tes objectifs financiers et, pourquoi pas, la liberté financière que tu recherches !

Gestion budgétaire : Apprendre à suivre ses revenus et ses dépenses, établir un budget, et identifier les priorités financières. **Connaissance des produits financiers** : Comprendre les outils comme les actions, obligations, comptes d'épargne à intérêts, et comment ils fonctionnent. **Planification fiscale** : Réduire légalement ses impôts pour maximiser ses revenus nets. **Exemple concret :** Une personne qui investit dans un fonds indiciel à faible coût peut, grâce aux rendements composés, faire fructifier son capital sur plusieurs années, même avec un revenu moyen.

1. **Les investissements judicieux :**

Investir, c'est faire travailler son argent pour qu'il génère des revenus supplémentaires ou qu'il prenne de la valeur. Immobilier : Acheter une propriété pour la louer ou la revendre avec une plus-value. Actions et obligations : Développer un portefeuille diversifié pour réduire les risques tout en maximisant les rendements. Entreprises ou startups : Prendre des parts dans des entreprises à fort potentiel de croissance peut offrir des retours exceptionnels, bien que risqués. Astuce : Diversifie tes investissements. Par exemple, n'investis pas uniquement dans l'immobilier ; explore les marchés boursiers, les cryptomonnaies ou même les matières premières.

2. La discipline financière :

La discipline est cruciale pour éviter les pièges de la consommation excessive et garantir une progression régulière. Épargner régulièrement : Automatiser une partie de son revenu vers un compte épargne ou un plan d'investissement. Réduire les dépenses inutiles : Identifier les fuites financières (comme les abonnements inutilisés ou les achats impulsifs). Planifier ses dépenses : Établir des objectifs financiers à court, moyen et long terme (par exemple, acheter une maison dans 5 ans). Exemple : Mettre de côté 20 % de son revenu mensuel pour des investissements ou des projets futurs.

3. L'entrepreneuriat ou l'innovation :

Créer une entreprise ou développer une idée innovante peut être un levier puissant pour atteindre la richesse matérielle. Entrepreneuriat : Identifier un besoin ou un problème sur le marché et y répondre avec une solution unique. Multiplication des sources de revenus : Diversifier ses activités pour ne pas dépendre d'une seule source de revenus. Par exemple, cumuler un emploi principal avec une activité secondaire (freelance, vente en ligne). Innover dans un secteur : Les industries en plein essor, comme la technologie ou l'énergie verte, offrent d'énormes opportunités de croissance. **Idée inspirante :** Elon Musk a utilisé son innovation dans plusieurs domaines (paiements numériques, voitures électriques, exploration spatiale) pour bâtir une fortune impressionnante. En un mot, atteindre la richesse matérielle nécessite un mélange d'éducation, de discipline et de prise de risques calculée. Mais au-delà de l'accumulation de biens matériels, il est essentiel de s'assurer que ces richesses contribuent à une vie équilibrée et épanouissante. Après tout, la richesse matérielle n'est qu'un outil pour atteindre une plus grande liberté et un bien-être global.

II. La richesse immaterielle

La richesse immatérielle fait référence à des éléments non physiques mais qui ajoutent une valeur immense à la vie d'une personne. Cela inclut des aspects qui, bien que non mesurables en termes financiers immédiats, ont un impact profond sur le bien-être et la satisfaction : Les compétences et les connaissances : l' apprentissage continu, la maîtrise de compétences spécifiques, et le développement personnel. La valeur des connaissances s'apprécie au fil du temps, car elles peuvent ouvrir des portes dans la vie professionnelle, sociale et personnelle. Les relations et le réseau social : Les relations humaines, qu'elles soient familiales; (par exemple la présence de votre conjoint ou conjointe qui vous encourage, vous motive et qui vous accorde son attention est une inestimable richesse) amicales, ou professionnelles, sont essentielles. Le réseau social peut être un atout puissant pour ouvrir des opportunités et obtenir du soutien. Le bien-être émotionnel et spirituel : La capacité à être en paix avec soi-même, à cultiver la gratitude, la résilience et une vision positive de la vie. Cela peut inclure des pratiques telles que la méditation, la pleine conscience ou le développement personnel. L'impact social : La contribution à des causes sociales, environnementales ou humanitaires. Le fait d'apporter une valeur à la communauté ou de laisser un héritage spirituel ou social peut être une forme de richesse que beaucoup considèrent comme essentielle.

Comment atteindre la richesse immatérielle ?

Atteindre la richesse immatérielle nécessite une approche différente de la richesse matérielle, car elle repose sur des aspects moins tangibles. Apprentissage continu : Investir du temps dans l'acquisition de nouvelles compétences et dans l'expansion de ses connaissances. Lire, se former, assister à des séminaires, ou même rechercher un mentor peuvent être des étapes clés. Équilibre émotionnel et spirituel : Prendre soin de sa santé mentale, cultiver la gratitude, apprendre à gérer ses émotions et trouver une source de paix intérieure. Réseautage et relations humaines : Bâtir un réseau de personnes inspirantes, bienveillantes et qui partagent des valeurs similaires. Investir dans des relations de qualité, même si cela prend du temps et demande un engagement. Contribuer à des causes : Se trouver un but plus grand que soi, qu'il soit dans des projets sociaux, environnementaux, ou communautaires. Cela peut renforcer la sensation de richesse intérieure et de satisfaction durable.

Quelle mentalité adopter pour réussir à atteindre la richesse matérielle et immatérielle ?

1. Mentalité de croissance et abondance

La meilleure manière ici est d' avoir une mentalité de croissance, c'est croire que les capacités, les compétences et les opportunités peuvent se développer au fil du temps par l'effort, l'apprentissage et la persévérance. Cela implique :

Apprentissage continu : Ne jamais se contenter de ce que l'on sait. Chercher à se former, s'instruire et évoluer. Résilience : Accepter les échecs comme des étapes d'apprentissage, et non comme des obstacles définitifs. La persévérance dans l'adversité est un élément clé. Proactivité : Agir plutôt que d'attendre que les opportunités viennent à soi. Chercher à initier des projets, investir dans des idées, et prendre des initiatives dans son propre développement. Juste apres cette crutiale etape, il faut commencer par adopter une mentalité d'abondance, c'est-a-dire croire qu'il y a suffisamment de ressources et d'opportunités pour tout le monde. Cette mentalité : Favorise la collaboration plutôt que la compétition : Cela peut conduire à une coopération et à un réseautage plus efficaces, où l'on s'entraide mutuellement pour progresser. Valorise la gratitude : Se concentrer sur ce que l'on a déjà, plutôt que de se focaliser uniquement sur ce qui nous manque. Générosité : Partager son temps, ses connaissances, ou ses ressources pour aider les autres, ce qui peut également se retourner positivement sur soi.

2. Mentalité de discipline et de patience

Imaginons qu'une Université de renom vous propose de vous former en trois semaines pour que vous deveniez un grand Ingenieur en electricite ou en reseau informatique ou meme dans n'importe quel domaine, allez vous accepter ? super! juste une manière de dire que la richesse, qu'elle soit matérielle ou immatérielle, ne se construit pas du jour au lendemain. Une discipline et une patience constantes sont nécessaires pour : Suivre une stratégie à long terme : Éviter les raccourcis et rester concentré sur ses objectifs. Gérer les finances et les investissements avec prudence : Ne pas succomber à la tentation de la consommation immédiate, mais plutôt investir dans des projets à long terme. Construire progressivement :

Comprendre que chaque petit pas compte et qu'il faut du temps pour accumuler de la richesse, tant matérielle qu' immatérielle.

Conclusion

Atteindre la richesse matérielle et immatérielle requiert une combinaison de compétences, de mentalités et de stratégies. La richesse matérielle demande une approche stratégique de gestion des finances et des investissements, tandis que la richesse immatérielle repose sur le développement personnel, les relations humaines et le bien-être émotionnel. Pour réussir, il est essentiel d'adopter une mentalité de croissance, d'abondance, de discipline et de patience, tout en poursuivant un équilibre entre les deux types de richesse.

CHAPITRE 2

Ils ont une vision claire et chiffrée

« Tant de choses sont possibles, tant que tu ne sais pas qu'elles sont impossibles. »
— *Mildred D. Taylor*

Les grands riches ne se contentent pas de rêver vaguement de succès ou de fortune. Ils cultivent une vision claire, chiffrée et précise de ce qu'ils souhaitent accomplir. C'est leur boussole, leur guide dans toutes leurs décisions. C' est effectivement ce que les livres ont essayé de nous résumer en ces termes suivants: JOB 22:28 " A tes résolutions répondra le succès; Sur tes sentiers brillera la lumière."

Une course sans destination : l'histoire d'un homme sans vision

Un jour, un homme pressé s'approche d'un taxi. Il ouvre la portière, s'installe à l'arrière, et dit simplement au chauffeur :
— *Allez-y. Conduisez.*

Le conducteur, un peu surpris, lui demande :
— *Très bien, mais… où allons-nous ?*

L'homme répond sans réfléchir :
— *Peu importe. Roulez juste. Faites-moi avancer.*

Alors le chauffeur démarre. Il tourne à gauche, puis à droite, roule quelques kilomètres… mais sans destination précise, il finit par revenir au point de départ. Le compteur tourne, l'essence diminue, et l'homme commence à s'impatienter.
— *Mais on tourne en rond ! On n'avance pas !*

Le chauffeur se retourne et dit calmement :
— *Monsieur, vous ne m'avez jamais dit où vous vouliez aller.*

Silence.

Cette scène peut sembler absurde… mais elle ressemble à la vie de beaucoup de gens.

Ils veulent "réussir", "devenir riches", "vivre mieux", mais quand on leur demande *où exactement ils vont*, ils ne savent pas répondre. Pas de plan, pas d'objectif chiffré, pas de cap.

> C'est exactement ça, le danger de vivre sans vision.
> Tu es en mouvement… mais tu ne progresses pas.
> Tu dépenses ton énergie, ton temps, ton argent —
> sans jamais arriver quelque part.

Les grands riches, eux, ne prennent jamais le taxi de la vie sans donner une adresse claire.

Ils savent ce qu'ils veulent.

Ils ont une vision précise, mesurable, planifiée.

C'est ce que les livres, les mentors et même la sagesse ancienne nous enseignent :

> "A tes résolutions répondra le succès ; sur tes sentiers brillera la lumière." — Job 22:28

La réussite n'est pas le fruit du hasard. C'est le résultat d'une vision consciente, nourrie de chiffres, d'objectifs et de décisions assumées.

Alors pose-toi la question :
As-tu donné une adresse claire au conducteur de ta vie ?

Pourquoi une vision claire est essentielle ?

L'une des raisons principales pour lesquelles tant de gens échouent est qu'ils naviguent sans but précis. Avoir une vision floue, comme "je veux être riche", ne suffit pas. Les riches, en revanche, savent exactement ce qu'ils veulent :

- Ils fixent des objectifs chiffrés (combien veulent-ils gagner, investir ou économiser ?).
- Ils définissent un délai (quand souhaitent-ils atteindre cet objectif ?).
- Ils précisent les étapes nécessaires pour y arriver.

Une vision claire transforme les rêves en projets concrets. C'est cette clarté qui pousse à agir avec discipline et persévérance. En réalité, ceux qui savent exactement ce qu'ils veulent l'obtiennent plus rapidement. Le saviez-vous ?

En un mot, quelqu'un qui arrête un taxi, monte, s'assoit et dit au chauffeur : *"Conduisez, mais je n'ai pas de destination précise."* Que va-t-il arriver selon vous ? Le taxi ne bougera pas, ou pire, il avancera au hasard, gaspillant du temps et de l'énergie sans jamais atteindre de destination satisfaisante. C'est exactement ce qui se passe dans la vie lorsque vous n'avez pas d'objectif clair : vous bougez, mais vous n'avancez pas. La clarté, elle, donne une direction précise et transforme chaque action en un pas vers votre réussite. Alors, où voulez-vous aller ? Quelle est votre destination ? Décidez, car la route ne s'ouvre que pour ceux qui savent où ils vont.

C'est tres important de le souligner encore, les riches ne se lèvent pas chaque matin en espérant que « les choses s'améliorent ». Ils commencent l'année avec une vision écrite, précise et chiffrée de ce qu'ils veulent atteindre. Ils définissent leurs projets dès le départ : revenus visés, entreprises à lancer, livres à publier, partenariats à construire, niveaux de vie à franchir. Ce ne sont pas de simples rêves dans leur tête — ce sont des plans concrets, notés noir sur blanc, qu'ils suivent de près. Et même s'ils ajustent le plan en cours de route, ils savent exactement où ils vont. C'est cette clarté qui crée le mouvement, l'action et finalement les résultats.

Je ne t'écris pas cela par théorie. Cette méthode m'a permis d'écrire ce livre que tu tiens entre tes mains. En début d'année, j'ai inscrit deux objectifs sur papier : publier ce livre et devenir certifié en cybersécurité. J'ai gardé ces objectifs devant mes yeux, jour après jour. Et devine quoi ? Aujourd'hui, non seulement ce livre existe, mais je suis aussi devenu analyste certifié en cybersécurité. Pas parce que je suis meilleur que toi — mais parce que j'ai appris ce que les riches savent : un objectif clair, chiffré, écrit et suivi change tout.

Méthode pour clarifier ta vision (comme les riches le font)

1. Décide exactement ce que tu veux

Ne dis pas "je veux être riche" ou "je veux réussir", car ce n'est pas une vision, c'est un souhait vague. Pose-toi les bonnes questions :

- Combien veux-tu gagner par mois dans 5 ans ? Quelle vie veux-tu concrètement vivre ? (appartement ? maison ? pays ? emploi du temps ?) Combien d'argent veux-tu avoir investi ? Sur quels supports ? Quel métier, quelle entreprise, quel mode de vie ?

  Exemple : "Je veux générer 10 000 $/mois d'ici 5 ans avec un business en ligne, avoir 200 000 $ investis en bourse et vivre en Floride."

2. Chiffre ta vision

La richesse aime la précision.

Prends une feuille ou ton téléphone et commence à écrire des chiffres :

> Revenu mensuel visé Montant total à épargner/investir. Nombre de clients ou ventes nécessaires si tu as un business. Combien de temps par semaine tu veux travailler
>
> Les riches pensent toujours en valeurs mesurables. Si tu ne peux pas mesurer ta vision, tu ne peux pas l'atteindre.

3. Fixe un délai réaliste mais ambitieux

Un rêve sans date reste un rêve.
- Fixe une échéance précise pour chaque objectif. Découpe les étapes : dans 6 mois, 1 an, 3 ans…
  Exemple : "Dans 12 mois, je veux déjà générer 2 000 $/mois en revenus passifs."

4. Écris ta vision et relis-la tous les jours

Cela peut sembler simple, mais c'est une arme mentale ultra puissante. Ce que tu relis chaque jour finit par s'ancrer dans ton subconscient.
- Écris une version claire de ta vision en quelques phrases. Relis-la matin et soir. Visualise-toi déjà en train de vivre cette vie. Tu ne dois pas juste "penser" à ta vision, tu dois la vivre mentalement avant qu'elle devienne réalité.

En un mot, pas de vision claire est egal a pas de destination.
Les riches savent où ils vont. Ils planifient leur succès comme un architecte planifie une maison : chaque brique, chaque mur, chaque chiffre compte.Oui, reussir, c est seulement avoir une certaine somme d' argent, mais c est aussi ce donner un objectif et tout faire pour l' atteindre. Ils doit inclure aussi ces trois cles: reussite financiaire, familiale et sante physique.

Alors toi aussi, deviens l'architecte de ta vie financière.
Ce que tu ne vois pas clairement aujourd'hui, tu ne construiras jamais demain.

L'exemple inspirant de Steve Jobs

Prenons Steve Jobs, cofondateur d'Apple. Bien avant qu'Apple devienne un géant mondial, Jobs avait une vision précise : il voulait mettre un ordinateur dans chaque foyer. À une époque où les ordinateurs étaient des machines massives réservées aux entreprises, cette idée semblait folle. Mais Jobs ne s'est pas contenté d'un rêve. Il a détaillé cette vision :

1. Créer des ordinateurs accessibles en termes de prix.
2. Les rendre esthétiquement plaisants et simples à utiliser.
3. Les commercialiser comme des outils indispensables, et non comme des gadgets pour techniciens.

Sa vision était non seulement claire mais aussi mesurable. Chaque produit que Apple lançait était un pas concret vers cet objectif. Aujourd'hui, Apple est l'une des entreprises les plus prospères de l'histoire, grâce à une vision claire et bien définie.

Il n'est jamais trop tard pour changer ta vie
Maintenant que tu sais ces choses, ne baisse plus jamais les bras, peu importe la situation.
Tu vas peut-être entendre des voix autour de toi — ou même à l'intérieur de toi — te dire :

> « C'est trop tard pour moi. Je suis trop vieux. C'est plus possible. »

À ça, je te réponds simplement :
Tu te trompes.

L'histoire est remplie d'hommes et de femmes qui ont changé leur destin bien après ce que le monde appelle "l'âge de réussir". L'un des exemples les plus incroyables de cette vérité s'appelle le Colonel Harland Sanders, fondateur de la chaîne mondiale KFC (Kentucky Fried Chicken). Son histoire dépasse le courage ordinaire.

▶ Une vie marquée par les échecs et les recommencements

Harland Sanders n'a pas eu une jeunesse facile. Son père meurt alors qu'il est encore enfant, et il quitte l'école dès la 7e année. Il enchaîne les petits boulots : ouvrier agricole, conducteur de tramway, vendeur d'assurance…

Et la plupart de ses tentatives professionnelles ? Des échecs.

▶ Le déclic à 40 ans

À 40 ans, il commence à cuisiner pour les voyageurs dans une petite station-service, à Corbin, dans le Kentucky. Puis il ouvre un petit restaurant. Son poulet frit commence à faire parler de lui, mais ce n'est qu'à l'âge de 62 ans qu'il décide de franchiser sa recette.

Là encore, ce n'est pas facile.

Il prend sa voiture, traverse les États-Unis, dort dans son véhicule, et se fait refuser des centaines de fois.
Mais il n'a pas abandonné.

▶ La réussite enfin

Finalement, il trouve un restaurateur qui accepte de franchiser son concept.
Le reste appartient à l'histoire.
À 73 ans, le Colonel Sanders vend son entreprise pour 2 millions de dollars (l'équivalent de plus de 16 millions aujourd'hui) tout

en continuant à représenter la marque KFC jusqu'à la fin de sa vie.

Pourquoi cette histoire dans ce livre ?

Parce qu'elle brise l'un des mensonges que les riches ne veulent surtout pas que tu comprennes :

> Il n'est jamais trop tard.
> Ce n'est pas ton âge qui te bloque,
> c'est ton ignorance de ce que les riches savent.

Le Colonel Sanders n'était pas un surhomme. Il n'avait pas de fortune familiale, pas de diplôme prestigieux, pas de connexion politique. Il avait une idée, une vision claire, et une détermination inébranlable.

Et surtout : il a compris que tant que tu respires, tu peux encore bâtir quelque chose de grand

Une histoire de transformation personnelle : Amadou

Amadou est un jeune homme d'Afrique de l'Ouest. Enfant, il vivait dans une maison sans électricité ni eau courante. Malgré les défis, il avait un rêve : devenir ingénieur et bâtir une entreprise qui offrirait des solutions technologiques accessibles à son pays.

À 18 ans, Amadou a décidé de transformer son rêve en vision claire. Il s'est posé trois questions clés :

1. *Que veux-tu précisément ?* Il voulait devenir ingénieur en télécommunications et lancer une startup technologique.
2. *Combien cela coûtera-t-il ?* Il a calculé qu'il aurait besoin de 15 000 $ pour ses études et 10 000 $ supplémentaires pour démarrer son entreprise.
3. *Quand veux-tu y arriver ?* Son objectif était de devenir ingénieur à 25 ans et de lancer sa startup avant ses 30 ans.

Avec cette vision chiffrée, Amadou a commencé à travailler : Il a obtenu des bourses et travaillé comme technicien pour financer ses études. Il a économisé chaque centime, réinvestissant dans des petits projets. Aujourd'hui, Amadou dirige une entreprise prospère qui fournit des solutions numériques à des milliers de personnes. Sa vision claire l'a guidé à chaque étape.

Exercice pour vous : Définissez votre vision

À votre tour de réfléchir. Prenez un moment pour répondre honnêtement aux questions suivantes :

1. *Quel est votre rêve ?* Décrivez-le avec le plus de précision possible.
2. *Combien cela coûtera-t-il ?* Faites une estimation chiffrée réaliste.
3. *Quand voulez-vous l'atteindre ?* Fixez une échéance claire.

Exemple :
- Rêve : Acheter une maison.
- Coût : 500 000 $.
- Échéance : Dans 5 ans.

Maintenant, écrivez votre vision et affichez-la quelque part où vous pourrez la voir tous les jours. Souvenez-vous : une vision claire est le premier pas vers la réalisation de vos objectifs. Avec ce premier secret, vous commencez à construire les fondations d'une réussite durable. Êtes-vous prêt à passer au secret suivant ?

CHAPITRE 3

Ils maîtrisent des compétences rares

Une des clés de la richesse durable réside dans la maîtrise de compétences rares et précieuses. Les riches ne se contentent pas de compétences ordinaires, car ils comprennent un principe simple mais puissant : ce qui est rare a de la valeur. Ils appliquent à leur carrière et à leurs compétences la loi de l'offre et de la demande.

(Et ils veulent que tu continues à croire que le talent suffit…)

Voici un secret que les riches ne crient pas sur tous les toits :
Ce qui fait la vraie différence entre eux et les autres, ce ne sont pas leurs diplômes. Ce ne sont pas leurs relations au départ. Ce n'est même pas la chance.

C'est ce qu'ils savent faire, et que 90 % des gens n'ont jamais pris la peine d'apprendre.

Je vais être direct avec toi :
Les riches deviennent riches parce qu'ils ont appris des compétences que peu de gens osent apprendre.

Ils ont maîtrisé des choses compliquées, techniques, stratégiques, pendant que d'autres regardaient Netflix ou scrollaient sur TikTok.

Pendant que tu hésitais à suivre une formation à 100 $, ils payaient 5 000$ pour apprendre quelque chose que personne ne pouvait leur enlever. Et le plus beau dans tout ça ? Personne ne naît avec ces compétences.
Elles s'acquièrent. Elles s'apprennent. Elles se méritent. Ce que les riches savent (et que toi aussi tu dois savoir)

Dans les cercles fermés, il existe une vérité que personne ne veut vraiment t'expliquer :
Celui qui possède une compétence rare contrôle le jeu.
Il a le pouvoir de dire NON, de fixer ses prix, de lancer un projet, de quitter un patron, de vendre à grande échelle.

Les riches investissent constamment dans ce genre de compétences. Pas dans la distraction. Pas dans la dernière tendance inutile.

> « J'habite dans la possibilité. »
> — *Emily Dickinson*

Le savoir est la base de toute richesse

Ce n'est ni la chance, ni le privilège, ni même les circonstances qui forgent un destin : ce sont les compétences que tu développes et la manière dont tu les mets en pratique. La vraie différence entre ceux qui deviennent grands et ceux qui stagnent, c'est leur engagement profond à apprendre continuellement et à évoluer.

Pourquoi les compétences, et non la chance, dessinent ton avenir

Beaucoup pensent que les riches ont eu de la chance. Mais c'est la maîtrise de compétences précieuses qui ouvre les vraies portes. Regarde Elon Musk. Ce n'est pas le hasard qui l'a amené à bâtir Tesla ou SpaceX. Il n'avait aucune formation officielle en ingénierie aérospatiale. Il a appris tout seul, en lisant des livres de haut niveau et en s'entourant des meilleurs. Résultat : il a bousculé toute une industrie.

Ce principe vaut pour tous les domaines. Que tu rêves de devenir entrepreneur, expert dans ton métier ou innovateur, c'est ta capacité à acquérir et utiliser les bonnes compétences qui fera la différence. La chance peut peut-être t'ouvrir une porte... mais seul le savoir te permet d'y rester.

Une leçon simple mais puissante : le savoir est un levier

Imagine : tu es prêt à prendre un taxi pour l'aéroport. Le chauffeur arrive, souriant, mais t'annonce que c'est la première fois de sa vie qu'il conduit une voiture. Es-tu prêt à lui confier ta sécurité ? Bien sûr que non.

Pourquoi ? Parce que l'expérience et la compétence comptent. C'est la même chose dans la vie. Plus tu apprends, plus tu deviens compétent — et plus tu es en position de force. Tu n'es plus limité. Tu te démarques, tu gagnes en confiance, en influence et en succès.

Le monde ne récompense pas l'ignorance. Si tu veux réussir, il faut apprendre, t'exercer, et évoluer. C'est là que réside le vrai pouvoir.

Comment acquérir un savoir transformateur

1. Deviens un apprenant à vie

Le monde change trop vite pour que tu restes sur tes acquis. Engage-toi à apprendre constamment : lis des livres, suis des formations, cherche des mentors. Si Elon Musk peut apprendre la science des fusées seul, toi aussi tu peux devenir expert dans n'importe quel domaine.

2. Apprends en pratiquant

Lire, c'est bien. Faire, c'est mieux. Musk n'a pas seulement lu des livres, il a construit et testé des fusées. C'est la pratique qui crée l'excellence. Que ce soit dans l'investissement, la tech, ou l'entrepreneuriat, mets tes apprentissages en action.

Entoure-toi de ceux qui savent

Ton environnement détermine ton niveau. Le savoir, c'est comme une flamme. Plus tu es entouré de gens brillants, plus ta propre lumière s'intensifie.

Essaye d'apprendre seul un domaine complexe, sans mentor ni discussion… ce sera long, frustrant, plein d'erreurs. Maintenant, imagine que tu sois entouré d'experts. Chaque discussion est un raccourci. Chaque conseil te fait gagner des années.

Musk ne travaille pas seul. Il s'entoure des meilleurs. Il pose des questions, il absorbe leur savoir, et il accélère son évolution. Fais comme lui. Rejoins des communautés, lis les livres des meilleurs, participe à des événements, parle avec des gens qui te challengent.

Tu ne peux pas évoluer en restant entouré de personnes limitées. Tu deviens la moyenne des gens que tu fréquentes. Alors choisis bien.

Adapte-toi. Ou disparais.

Apprendre une fois ne suffit pas. Ce que tu sais aujourd'hui peut devenir obsolète demain. Le monde change. Vite.

Regarde Blockbuster. Ils ont refusé de s'adapter à Netflix. Résultat : disparus. Kodak ? Même chose. Ils ont ignoré le passage au numérique. Résultat : oubliés.

En revanche, ceux qui réussissent acceptent d'évoluer constamment. Bezos, Musk, Jobs... tous ont bâti leur empire non pas sur leurs connaissances du passé, mais sur leur capacité à rester curieux et flexibles.

Apprends. Désapprends. Réapprends. C'est la seule manière de rester en avance.

Mets en pratique ce que tu apprends

Apprendre juste pour savoir, ça ne suffit pas. Le but final du savoir, c'est la transformation. Résoudre des problèmes. Créer de la valeur. Impacter le monde. Musk a utilisé son savoir en physique, en ingénierie et en affaires pour bâtir des entreprises qui ont transformé le monde. Toi aussi, tu peux utiliser ce que tu sais pour changer ton avenir, aider les autres, et créer ta propre richesse.

Tu n'es pas limité. Tu n'es pas limité. Pas tant que tu choisis d'apprendre. Ta capacité à apprendre, t'adapter et appliquer ce que tu sais détermine ton avenir. Le succès n'est pas une question de chance, mais de préparation et de compétences. Tu tiens ton destin entre tes mains. Apprends. Applique. Répète. Et surtout, n'arrête jamais d'évoluer. Non, eux, ils vont droit à l'essentiel : **ils apprennent à vendre, à négocier, à coder, à diriger, à convaincre.**

Et pendant ce temps, le reste du monde se plaint, rêve, espère… mais n'agit pas.

Elon Musk ne s'est pas contenté de rêver

Laisse-moi te donner un exemple réel que les gens admirent sans jamais creuser.

Avant de lancer Tesla et SpaceX, **Elon Musk s'est enfermé des nuits entières à apprendre** :
- La programmation.
- L'ingénierie.
- La physique appliquée.

Il ne s'est pas contenté d'engager des experts. Il **est devenu lui-même un expert**. Parce qu'il a compris une chose que toi aussi tu dois comprendre maintenant : **Celui qui sait faire ne dépend de personne et celui qui sait faire est libre.**

Ce que TU dois faire maintenant (si tu veux vraiment changer de vie)

Tu veux devenir riche ? Commence par penser comme les riches.

Et **les riches pensent toujours en termes de compétences à fort impact.**

Voici ce que tu dois faire **dès aujourd'hui** :

Choisis une compétence à haute valeur économique.
- Vente, marketing digital, négociation, copywriting, cybersécurité, trading, intelligence artificielle, création de contenu, gestion de projet...
- Peu importe d'où tu pars, ce qui compte c'est où tu vas.

Engage-toi pendant 6 à 12 mois. Sérieusement.
- Lis, regarde des vidéos, suis des formations, pratique.
- Même une heure par jour change une vie entière.

Mets-toi en action rapidement.
- N'attends pas d'être parfait. Propose tes services, fais un stage, vends un petit produit, rejoins un projet.
- C'est dans l'action que la compétence devient richesse.

Entoure-toi de gens qui veulent aussi évoluer.
- Fuis les gens qui se moquent, qui doutent, qui critiquent sans rien construire.
- Cherche des groupes, des communautés, des mentors.

Le vrai pouvoir, c'est de savoir faire ce que les autres ne savent pas faire.

Retiens bien cette phrase. Le monde n'a pas besoin de plus de rêveurs. Il a besoin de **faiseurs compétents**. Et si tu deviens cette personne-là, crois-moi :

L'argent viendra.
Les opportunités aussi.

Et tu n'auras plus jamais à mendier quoi que ce soit.

Ce que les riches ne veulent pas que tu saches ?

C'est que toi aussi, tu peux apprendre ce qu'ils ont appris.
Tu peux te former, t'élever, maîtriser une compétence rare et changer de niveau .Mais ils préfèrent que tu restes distrait. Que tu crois que c'est une question de chance ou de piston. Parce que pendant ce temps, ils gardent l'avantage. Aujourd'hui, tu sais. Alors que vas-tu faire de ce savoir ?

Comment ? C'est simple :

Quand une compétence est rare (faible offre), elle devient précieuse. Les entreprises ou clients sont prêts à payer cher pour l'obtenir de meme quand tout le monde possède la même compétence (forte offre), elle perd de sa valeur. La concurrence est forte, et les opportunités se font plus rares. Les plus riches le savent : pour gagner gros, il faut offrir ce que peu de gens peuvent proposer. Ils se spécialisent, développent des talents uniques ou maîtrisent des connaissances recherchées. Résultat ? Ils se placent en position de force, attirant naturellement les meilleures opportunités et les plus grandes récompenses. En bref, les riches créent leur richesse en respectant cette règle : soyez l'expert rare dans un domaine demandé, et le monde sera prêt à vous récompenser généreusement.

Pourquoi les compétences rares sont-elles essentielles ?

Dans un monde compétitif, être moyen ne suffit pas. Les riches comprennent que les compétences courantes sont facilement remplaçables, alors que les compétences rares créent une demande irrésistible. Voici pourquoi :

1. **Elles augmentent votre valeur sur le marché** : Plus une compétence est difficile à acquérir, plus elle est recherchée.
2. **Elles ouvrent des opportunités uniques** : Ces compétences permettent d'accéder à des rôles et des projets réservés à une élite.
3. **Elles assurent une croissance continue** : Investir dans des compétences rares est un actif qui prend de la valeur avec le temps.

Les domaines comme la finance, la technologie, le leadership, et l'entrepreneuriat sont particulièrement prisés, car ils combinent expertise, influence, et potentiel de revenus élevés.

L'exemple inspirant d'Elon Musk

Prenons l'exemple d'Elon Musk, l'un des entrepreneurs les plus emblématiques de notre époque. Avant de fonder Tesla et SpaceX, Musk a investi massivement dans lui-même :

- **Programmation** : Dès son adolescence, il a appris à coder, une compétence rare à l'époque. Cela lui a permis de lancer Zip2, une de ses premières entreprises technologiques.

- **Génie industriel et physique** : Musk s'est spécialisé dans des domaines complexes pour comprendre les bases des fusées et des véhicules électriques.
- **Autodidacte acharné** : Il a lu des centaines de livres techniques pour maîtriser des sujets comme l'aérospatiale, une industrie où il n'avait aucune formation formelle.

Grâce à sa soif d'apprendre et à ses compétences rares, Musk a pu construire des entreprises innovantes qui dominent leurs marchés.

Une histoire personnelle : Amina, la gestionnaire transformée

Amina, une jeune femme vivant dans une petite ville, travaillait comme assistante administrative. Son travail était stable, mais ses revenus étaient limités, et ses opportunités d'évolution presque inexistantes.

Un jour, elle a décidé qu'elle ne voulait plus se contenter de ce qu'elle avait. Elle a analysé le marché du travail et a remarqué une forte demande pour les compétences en marketing numérique. Amina a alors décidé de se spécialiser dans ce domaine.

Voici ce qu'elle a fait :

1. **Investissement personnel** : Elle a suivi des cours en ligne abordables, regardé des tutoriels gratuits et lu des livres spécialisés.
2. **Pratique constante** : Elle a créé un blog personnel pour appliquer ses connaissances, et a offert ses services gratuitement à des petites entreprises locales.

3. **Certifications** : Elle a obtenu une certification en publicité sur les réseaux sociaux et en référencement (SEO).

En moins d'un an, Amina est passée d'assistante administrative à consultante en marketing numérique, triplant ses revenus. Aujourd'hui, elle travaille à son compte et aide des entreprises à booster leur visibilité en ligne.

Action pour vous : Identifiez une compétence à maîtriser

À présent, c'est à votre tour de réfléchir. Quelle compétence rare pourriez-vous développer dans les 6 à 12 prochains mois ?

1. Analysez votre marché : Regardez les secteurs qui vous intéressent et identifiez les compétences les plus demandées.
2. Choisissez une compétence : Voici quelques suggestions selon les domaines : Entrepreneuriat : Apprenez les bases de la vente ou de la gestion d'équipe. Technologie : Maîtrisez le codage, l'analyse de données, ou l'intelligence artificielle. Finance : Spécialisez-vous dans l'investissement ou la gestion de patrimoine. Communication : Développez des compétences en négociation ou en prise de parole en public. Agissez dès maintenant : Inscrivez-vous à une formation en ligne, lisez un livre, ou trouvez un mentor dans votre domaine choisi.

Exemple d'objectif personnel :
- Compétence : Apprendre à coder.
- Temps : 6 mois.

- Ressources : Cours en ligne gratuits comme Codecademy ou FreeCodeCamp.

Votre engagement au succès

Rappelez-vous : les riches investissent constamment en eux-mêmes. Choisir de développer une compétence rare est un pas décisif vers votre propre réussite. Alors, quelle compétence allez-vous choisir aujourd'hui pour devenir inarrêtable demain ?

CHAPITRE 4

Ils créent des systèmes de revenus multiples

Secret 4 : Ils créent des systèmes de revenus multiples

Les riches savent qu'une seule source de revenus est risquée. Contrairement à la classe moyenne qui dépend généralement d'un salaire unique, ils bâtissent des systèmes qui génèrent de l'argent même lorsqu'ils dorment.

Pourquoi diversifier ses revenus est essentiel ?

Dépendre d'un seul revenu, c'est comme marcher sur une corde raide sans filet de sécurité. Si cette source venait à disparaître (licenciement, crise économique, ou faillite), tout s'écroulerait. Les riches, eux, adoptent une approche différente : Ils multiplient les flux de revenus : Ils ne mettent jamais tous leurs œufs dans le même panier. Ils réduisent les risques : Si une source de revenus échoue, les autres continuent de fonctionner. Ils maximisent leurs opportunités : Plus ils diversifient, plus ils augmentent leurs chances de créer des richesses significatives.

Imagine un ingénieur aux États-Unis. Il gagne en moyenne 100 000 $ par an. C'est respectable. Mais voyons la réalité mathématique : Après impôts, dépenses, assurances, obligations familiales, il lui reste environ 30 000 $ par an. Pour atteindre 1 000 000 $ en épargne, il lui faudra plus de 33 ans de travail. Et encore… ça suppose :

- Aucun accident de vie.
- Aucune pause.
- Une discipline financière militaire.

Maintenant regarde bien ceci :

Quelqu'un écrit un livre à 20 $. Il le vend à 50 000 personnes en ligne, sur Amazon, sur TikTok, dans des conférences…

⇒   1 000 000 $ générés. En 1 ou 2 ans de vente

Sans patron. Sans plafond. Avec une idée transformée en produit. Ce n'est pas de la magie. C'est le pouvoir de créer une source de revenu qui ne dépend pas du temps.

Les riches ne comptent pas uniquement sur leur salaire,ils construisent des systèmes.Des mécanismes qui tournent même quand ils dorment, voyagent ou sont malades. Et surtout : Des sources diversifiées : immobilier, livres, services, business, licences, plateformes… Des idées utiles transformées en valeur pour les autres.

Pourquoi c'est important ?

Parce que le travail salarié ne suffit plus. Oui, parce qu'un seul revenu est trop risqué dans un monde instable. Mais surtout… Un bon système peut changer la société. Les grandes fortunes du monde viennent souvent de la résolution d'un problème collectif. Un livre qui éclaire des milliers de jeunes, une plateforme qui connecte des artisans à leurs clients, une application qui facilite la vie des familles...

Quand tu bâtis un système qui aide les gens, tu fais plus que gagner de l'argent : Tu crées de la valeur réelle;Tu fais avancer la société. Et en retour... tu deviens riche. La richesse vient alors quand tu arrêtes de vendre ton temps... et que tu commences à résoudre des problèmes. C'est ce que les riches ont compris — et qu'ils ne veulent surtout pas que tu saches.

Les trois piliers des revenus multiples

Investissements

Les riches investissent leur argent pour qu'il travaille à leur place. Cela peut inclure : L'immobilier : Acheter des biens pour les louer ou les revendre à profit. La bourse : Investir dans des actions, obligations, ou fonds indiciels. Les startups : Devenir investisseur dans des entreprises émergentes. Entreprises: Beaucoup de riches créent ou possèdent des entreprises générant des revenus récurrents : Business en ligne : E-commerce, blogs monétisés, ou abonnements numériques. Franchises : Posséder une franchise permet de profiter d'un modèle d'affaires éprouvé. Produits passifs : Livres, cours en ligne, ou applications. Autres sources passives Droits d'auteur : Écriture de livres, création de musique ou d'applications. Partenariats et affiliations : Promouvoir des produits en échange de commissions.

Exemple inspirant : Warren Buffett

Warren Buffett est l'un des hommes les plus riches au monde grâce à sa capacité à diversifier ses sources de revenus. Sa stratégie repose sur deux principes clés : Investissements intelligents : Buffett possède des participations dans des centaines d'entreprises, allant de Coca-Cola à Apple. Ses investissements sont soigneusement choisis pour leur potentiel de croissance à long terme. Revenus passifs : Grâce à ses placements, Buffett génère des milliards chaque année, sans avoir à gérer directement ces entreprises. Son mantra célèbre résume bien cette stratégie : *"Ne mettez pas tous vos œufs dans le même panier."*

Une histoire personnelle : Sofia, entrepreneuse créative

Sofia travaillait comme enseignante, mais ses revenus limités ne lui permettaient pas de réaliser ses rêves. Inspirée par l'idée de diversifier ses revenus, elle a décidé de commencer petit, mais stratégiquement : Première source : Sofia a lancé un blog sur l'éducation, qu'elle a monétisé avec des publicités et des cours en ligne. Automatisation : Une fois son blog stabilisé, elle a engagé un assistant virtuel pour gérer les tâches quotidiennes. Diversification : Avec les revenus de son blog, elle a investi dans l'immobilier, achetant un petit appartement à louer. Aujourd'hui, Safia génère des revenus grâce à son blog, son bien immobilier, et même un cours en ligne qu'elle a créé pour aider d'autres enseignants à diversifier leurs revenus. Astuce : Commencez petit et automatisé. Créer plusieurs sources de revenus ne signifie pas tout faire en même temps. Voici une méthode simple pour commencer : Identifiez une première source : Par exemple, un business en ligne ou une petite activité secondaire. Faites-la fonctionner : Consacrez du temps et de l'énergie à la rendre rentable. Automatisez ou déléguez : Une fois qu'elle génère des revenus constants, déléguez les tâches ou utilisez des outils d'automatisation. Passez à une nouvelle source : Utilisez vos premiers revenus pour en créer une autre.

Exemple d'objectif pour débuter :

- Créez une boutique en ligne en vendant des produits numériques.
- Une fois automatisée, investissez les profits dans un fonds indiciel.

Action pour le lecteur : Concevez votre premier système de revenus multiples Évaluez vos compétences et ressources : Que pouvez-vous offrir ou investir dès aujourd'hui ? Choisissez un domaine : Immobilier, business en ligne, ou partenariats. Établissez un plan : Définissez vos objectifs pour les 6 à 12 prochains mois. Agissez : Faites le premier pas, même si c'est petit. Avec ce secret, vous commencez à poser les bases d'un empire financier. Vous êtes prêt pour le prochain secret ?

CHAPITRE 5

Ils maîtrisent l'art de l'argent

Secret 5 : Ils maîtrisent l'art de l'argent

Les riches comprennent que l'argent n'est pas seulement un outil d'échange, mais aussi un levier puissant pour créer davantage de richesse. Leur maîtrise des principes financiers fondamentaux leur permet de transformer chaque euro ou dollar en une opportunité de croissance. Mais avant de rentrer dans les détails, je souhaite préciser certains points importants pour que nous soyons tous à la même page; notamment la définition de l'art de l'argent et les conséquences de la personne qui voudrait l'ignorer.

Le terme art de l'argent fait allusion à la maîtrise des principes et des stratégies qui permettent non seulement de gagner de l'argent, mais aussi de le gérer, de le faire fructifier et de l'utiliser pour créer une vie équilibrée et épanouie. C'est une combinaison de vision, de discipline et de décisions intelligentes pour transformer l'argent en un outil au service de nos objectifs et de notre liberté. cela ayant été bien clarifié, nous allons explorer ensemble ce qui peut arriver à la personne qui va vouloir négliger l'art de l' argent.

Négliger ou mépriser l'art de l'argent peut entraîner des conséquences profondes, tant dans la vie actuelle que dans l'avenir d'une personne. Voici quelques-unes des principales répercussions :

Conséquences dans la vie actuelle :

1. Stress financier constant : Une mauvaise gestion de l'argent peut entraîner des dettes, des retards de paiement et une instabilité économique. Opportunités manquées : Sans épargne ni investissements, il devient difficile de saisir des opportunités (formation, voyage, entreprise, etc.). Relations affectées : Les tensions financières sont une cause majeure de conflits dans les couples, les familles et les relations sociales. Manque de sérénité : L'insécurité financière peut générer un sentiment permanent d'incertitude et d'anxiété.

Conséquences pour l'avenir : Absence de sécurité : Une absence de planification financière peut laisser une personne vulnérable face aux imprévus (maladie, chômage, etc.). Retraite difficile : Sans investissements ou épargne, il devient impossible de maintenir un niveau de vie décent après l'arrêt du travail. Transmission limitée : Une mauvaise gestion financière empêche de bâtir un patrimoine à léguer à ses proches ou de contribuer à des causes importantes. Dépendance aux autres : Négliger l'argent aujourd'hui peut forcer une personne à dépendre de ses enfants, de l'État ou d'autres soutiens dans le futur.

Les trois habitudes financières des riches

1. Épargner une part de chaque revenu (10-30 %)

Les riches savent qu'il est essentiel de *payer à soi-même en premier*. Avant de dépenser, ils épargnent un pourcentage fixe de leurs revenus.
- Cette discipline leur permet de constituer un capital de sécurité.
- Ils priorisent toujours leurs objectifs financiers à long terme sur les plaisirs immédiats.

Exemple pratique : Si vous gagnez 2 000 € par mois, épargnez 20 % (400 €) systématiquement. En un an, vous aurez économisé 4 800 €, sans compter les intérêts.

1. Qu'est-ce que l'épargne ?

Définition :
L'épargne, c'est la partie de vos revenus que vous mettez de côté au lieu de la dépenser immédiatement. Elle peut servir à :
- Réaliser des projets futurs (acheter une maison, créer une entreprise).
- Faire face à des imprévus (pannes, maladies, urgences).
- Préparer la retraite ou assurer une sécurité financière.

Contexte psychologique :
Dans le système économique, les riches utilisent l'épargne comme un outil de liberté et de pouvoir. Plus vous épargnez, plus vous créez des opportunités pour générer de la richesse.

2. Pourquoi épargner ?

A. La sécurité financière
Sans épargne, une simple urgence peut entraîner un endettement. L'épargne agit comme un filet de sécurité.

B. La liberté d'agir
Elle vous permet de prendre des décisions sans être limité par vos finances, comme changer de carrière, voyager ou investir dans des opportunités lucratives.

C. L'effet boule de neige
En épargnant, vous accumulez des ressources qui, lorsqu'investies, génèrent des revenus passifs grâce à des intérêts, des dividendes ou des rendements.

D. Rôle dans l'accumulation de richesse
Les riches ne dépensent pas tout ce qu'ils gagnent ; ils utilisent une partie pour investir et faire fructifier leur capital. C'est leur secret principal.

3. Comment épargner efficacement ?

A. Adoptez une mentalité d'épargnant
- Priorité : se payer en premier. Dès que vous recevez un revenu, mettez un pourcentage de côté avant toute dépense.
- Connaître vos objectifs : Épargnez avec une vision claire (court, moyen ou long terme).

B. Analysez vos finances actuelles
1. Identifiez vos revenus et dépenses.
2. Classez vos dépenses en :
    - Essentielles (logement, nourriture).
    - Non essentielles (abonnements, loisirs).

C. Créez un budget
- Suivez la règle des 50/30/20 :
- 50% pour les besoins.
- 30% pour les envies.
- 20% pour l'épargne et les investissements.

D. Utilisez des outils d'épargne. Comptes bancaires spécifiques : Un compte épargne distinct vous évite de toucher à vos économies. Investissements à faible risque : Livrets d'épargne, obligations. Automatisez vos épargnes : Configurez des virements automatiques pour simplifier la discipline.

E. Réduisez les dépenses inutiles. Apprenez à différencier les besoins des envies. Négociez vos contrats (assurance, forfaits téléphoniques). Achetez en gros ou en promo pour économiser.

F. Diversifiez vos épargnes. Gardez une épargne d'urgence facilement accessible (3-6 mois de dépenses). Investissez dans des actifs qui génèrent des rendements sur le long terme.

2. Investir intelligemment

Les riches ne laissent pas leur argent dormir. Ils le mettent au travail, en l'investissant : Avec une recherche approfondie : Avant chaque investissement, ils étudient les risques et les rendements potentiels.

Dans des actifs diversifiés : Immobilier, bourse, entreprises ou matières premières. *Exemple d'intelligence financière* : Investir dans un fonds indiciel qui suit les marchés boursiers peut rapporter des rendements réguliers sur le long terme.

3. Éviter les dettes inutiles

Les riches ne s'endettent pas pour acheter des biens de consommation comme des voitures luxueuses ou des gadgets.

Ils utilisent les dettes comme un outil stratégique, pour financer des actifs générateurs de revenus, comme l'immobilier locatif ou une entreprise. *Astuce :* Avant de prendre une dette, demandez-vous : Va-t-elle me rendre plus riche ou plus pauvre ?

L'effet cumulé : La magie des intérêts composés

Imaginez que vous investissiez 200 € par mois dans un portefeuille générant un rendement annuel moyen de 8 %. Grâce aux intérêts composés, voici ce qui se passerait : En 10 ans : Vous auriez environ 36 000 €. En 20 ans : Cette somme atteindrait environ 120 000 €. En 30 ans : Vous auriez près de 450 000 €. L'effet cumulé transforme des petits efforts réguliers en résultats massifs avec le temps. Ce principe est l'un des secrets les mieux gardés des riches.

Exemple inspirant : José, le boulanger visionnaire

José travaillait comme boulanger avec un salaire modeste. À 30 ans, il a décidé de changer sa relation avec l'argent. Voici ce qu'il a fait : Épargne systématique : José a commencé à mettre de côté 20 % de son revenu chaque mois. Investissement réfléchi : Il a étudié l'immobilier et acheté un petit studio qu'il a mis en location. Endettement stratégique : Il a pris un prêt pour un deuxième appartement, remboursé grâce aux loyers perçus. À 45 ans, José possédait plusieurs biens immobiliers et gagnait plus avec ses investissements qu'avec son métier de boulanger.

Exercice : Créez votre plan d'épargne-investissement mensuel

Déterminez votre objectif à 10 ans

Que voulez-vous atteindre financièrement ? (Par exemple, épargner 100 000 € ou acheter un bien immobilier.)Chiffrez cet objectif.Fixez votre part d'épargne mensuelle Décidez d'un pourcentage fixe à mettre de côté chaque mois (10 %, 20 %, ou plus). *Astuce* : Automatisez votre épargne pour qu'elle soit transférée dès que vous recevez votre salaire.Choisissez vos investissements Étudiez les options disponibles : bourse, immobilier, fonds d'investissement, etc. Diversifiez pour réduire les risques. Appliquez et ajustez régulièrement. Revoyez votre plan tous les 6 mois pour vérifier votre progression. Exemple de plan simple : Objectif : Avoir 50 000 € pour un apport immobilier dans 10 ans. Épargne mensuelle : 300 €.Investissement : Fonds indiciels à rendement moyen de 7 %. Résultat attendu : Grâce aux intérêts composés, votre capital atteindra environ 52 000 € au bout de 10 ans.L'argent,pour conclure, bien qu'il ne soit pas une fin en soi, est un levier essentiel pour construire une vie stable, libre et épanouie. Ceux qui ignorent cet art risquent de vivre avec des regrets, une perte d'indépendance et une lutte perpétuelle pour joindre les deux bouts. En maîtrisant ces trois habitudes, vous transformerez votre gestion de l'argent et poserez les bases de votre indépendance financière. Le pouvoir de l'argent réside dans votre capacité à le gérer avec intelligence et discipline.

Vendre, vendre, vendre

Un jour, j'ai compris une vérité que personne ne m'avait jamais clairement dite : les riches ne gagnent pas de l'argent par magie. Ils appliquent une loi puissante et immuable : la loi de cause à effet, Chaque effet visible dans leur vie maisons luxueuses, liberté financière, entreprises florissantes est le résultat d'une cause invisible mais intentionnelle.

L'une de ces causes, que beaucoup sous-estiment, c'est la capacité à vendre. Pas forcément vendre dans un bureau climatisé ou avec un costume-cravate. Non. Vendre au sens profond : proposer une solution a un besoin reel et recevoir en échange une rémunération.

Je pense à un jeune homme que j'ai rencontré lors d'un webinaire. Sans diplôme prestigieux ni capital, il a commencé à acheter des petits objets électroniques en liquidation écouteurs, chargeurs, cafetières, montres connectées qu'il revendait ensuite sur des plateformes comme Facebook Marketplace et OfferUp. En moins de deux mois, il générait plus de 1 000 dollars par mois, Ce n'était que le début, mais il venait d'activer une cause puissante : le service. Et l'effet ? L'argent a suivi.

Beaucoup veulent devenir riches sans jamais activer la cause. Ils rêvent de résultats sans action concrète. Mais tant que tu ne passes pas à l'action, la loi de cause à effet travaille contre toi, pas pour toi.

Pose-toi cette question : qu'est-ce que je peux proposer aujourd'hui qui résout un problème chez quelqu'un d'autre ? Tu serais étonné de voir à quel point ton talent, tes objets inutilisés, ton savoir-faire peuvent devenir une source de revenu. Les riches ne se contentent pas de consommer. Ils créent, ils proposent, ils négocient. Ils vendent, La richesse n' est pas un fruit du hazarre ou de negligence. Elle répond à une cause. Et le jour où tu apprends à vendre même de façon simple et directe tu déclenches une réaction en chaîne que tu peux contrôler. Vendre, c'est déclencher un effet puissant : l'abondance.

Le Secret du Temps

Beaucoup de gens entendent cette phrase sans vraiment la comprendre : « Le temps, c'est de l'argent. » Pourtant, c'est l'un des plus grands secrets qui separent les riches des pauvres. Le temps est une richesse invisible que tout le monde possede, mais que seules peu de personnes savent utiliser. Chaque jour, nous recevons tous vingt-quatre heures, ni plus, ni mains. Ce que tu fais avec ces heures determine ce que tu deviendras demain. J'ai decide de faire un bref resume mais tres tres important ici car plus tard dans ce meme livre, je vais mieux developper l' importance de tes 8 heures.

Le pauvre pense qu'il a tout le temps du monde. Il se dit: « J'ai encore demain », ou « je ferai ca plutard. » Alors il passe des heures a regarder la television, a discuter pour rien, a scroller sur son telephone. A la fin de la journée, il n'a rien cree, rien appris, rien gagne. Il a perdu du temps, sans meme s'en rendre compte. Et ce temps perdu ne revient jamais.

Le riche, lui, voit le temps comme de l'or. Il sait que chaque minute peut lui rapporter quelque chose. Quand il apprend une nouvelle competence, quand il lit, quand il planifie son avenir ou cree un projet, il investit son temps et plus tard, cet investissement produit de l'argent, du succes, ou des opportunites. Le riche comprend que le temps bien utilise devient une source de liberte, tandis que le temps gaspille devient une prison.

La difference entre le riche et le pauvre n'est pas seulement dans l'argent qu'ils ant, mais dans la valeur qu'ils donnent a leur temps. Le riche protege ses heures comme un tresor. Le pauvre les depense sans reflechir. Voila pourquoi on dit: les riches achetent du temps, les pauvres le vendent sans le savoir.

Si tu veux changer ta vie, commence par regarder comment tu utilises ton temps. Chaque heure peut soit te rapprocher de ton reve, soit t'en eloigner. La cle, c'est de comprendre que le temps n'est pas gratuit : il te rend riche ou pauvre selon ce que tu en fais.

CHAPITRE 6

Leur réseau vaut des millions

Secret 6 : Leur réseau vaut des millions

Les riches comprennent qu'un réseau de qualité est l'un des actifs les plus précieux. Ils ne réussissent pas seuls, mais grâce à des connexions stratégiques avec des mentors, partenaires, et personnes influentes.

Un réseau, dans ce contexte, représente l'ensemble des relations que les riches construisent et entretiennent pour avancer dans leur vie personnelle et professionnelle. Ce n'est pas seulement une liste de contacts, mais un cercle dynamique de personnes influentes, inspirantes et complémentaires qui ajoutent de la valeur à leurs objectifs.

Qu'est-ce qu'un réseau et pourquoi est-il si important ?

Un réseau efficace est un écosystème où chaque membre partage des ressources, des idées, et des opportunités. Pour les riches, le réseau ne se limite pas à des amis ou des collègues, mais inclut : Mentors : Des personnes expérimentées qui les conseillent et les guident. Investisseurs et partenaires : Des individus prêts à financer ou à collaborer sur des projets. Influenceurs et pairs : Ceux qui les inspirent et les poussent à se surpasser.

Les riches bâtissent leur réseau pour trois raisons clés

1. Accéder à des opportunités

Beaucoup d'occasions cruciales, comme des projets lucratifs ou des introductions stratégiques, passent par des relations, pas par des annonces publiques.

Exemple : Une conversation informelle avec un contact peut vous mener à un partenariat commercial ou à une nouvelle carrière. Apprendre plus rapidement

Les riches s'entourent de personnes qui possèdent des compétences ou des expériences qu'ils n'ont pas. Ils apprennent en observant, en posant des questions, et en écoutant les conseils. Ce processus réduit leur courbe d'apprentissage et leur évite de commettre des erreurs coûteuses. Créer une dynamique de soutien

Un bon réseau offre un environnement positif où l'ambition et la créativité sont encouragées. Les membres s'aident mutuellement à surmonter les défis. Exemple inspirant : Oprah Winfrey et son réseau stratégique Oprah Winfrey a grandi dans la pauvreté, mais elle a construit un empire en s'appuyant sur un réseau solide Mentors comme Maya Angelou : Oprah attribue une grande partie de sa résilience et de sa vision à des figures inspirantes qui l'ont guidée. Partenaires influents : Elle a collaboré avec des producteurs, des investisseurs et des écrivains pour transformer son talk-show en une plateforme mondiale. Soutien mutuel : Oprah entretient des relations authentiques, basées sur l'échange et le partage, ce qui lui a permis de garder un cercle d'amis et de partenaires fidèles.

Comment construire un réseau puissant ?

Commencez par comprendre vos besoins Avez-vous besoin d'un mentor pour développer vos compétences ? Souhaitez-vous entrer en contact avec des investisseurs ou des entrepreneurs ? Identifiez les bonnes personne. Cherchez des leaders dans votre domaine. Rejoignez des communautés pertinentes en ligne (LinkedIn, Meetup) ou dans votre région. Créez de la valeur pour les autres Offrez quelque chose avant de demander : une information utile, un contact mutuel, ou même simplement du soutien par e*xemple* : Si vous voulez apprendre d'un entrepreneur, proposez-lui d'aider bénévolement sur un projet en échange de son expertise. Entretien et authenticité Ne cherchez pas uniquement à "prendre". Investissez dans vos relations en restant en contact et en montrant un intérêt sincère. Un simple message de remerciement ou un suivi peut renforcer une connexion durable. Exercice pour le lecteur : Construisez votre réseau Définissez un objectif précis Exemple : Rencontrer trois experts dans votre domaine ou trouver un mentor dans les six prochains mois. Dressez une liste de cinq cibles Choisissez des personnes ou des groupes qui peuvent vous aider à atteindre vos objectifs. Rejoignez des événements et des communautés Participez à des conférences, inscrivez-vous à des clubs ou engagez des discussions sur des plateformes comme LinkedIn. Engagez-vous à apporter de la valeur Faites un premier pas en offrant votre aide, en partageant vos idées, ou en créant une introduction utile. Suivez et mesurez vos progrès Notez les connexions établies et les retours obtenus. Réévaluez votre stratégie tous les trois mois. Astuce : Ne sous-estimez jamais la puissance des petites actions Un réseau ne se construit pas du jour au lendemain. Chaque petite action – un e-mail, une conversation, ou un café – peut mener à de grandes opportunités. Soyez constant et authentique dans vos efforts. Un réseau est bien plus qu'un simple carnet d'adresses. C'est un levier puissant pour atteindre vos rêves et vos ambitions. Construisez-le avec intention, nourrissez-le avec authenticité, et il deviendra l'un de vos atouts les plus précieux.

CHAPITRE 7

Ils travaillent sur des projets à haut impact

Secret 7 : Ils travaillent sur des projets à haut impact

En 2021, un événement a profondément bouleversé ma vie.

Une femme m'a contacté via un réseau social. Elle paraissait gentille, sûre d'elle, et parlait de trading comme si c'était la clé d'un avenir meilleur. Elle m'a convaincu de lui confier de l'argent pour qu'elle l'investisse à ma place. Tout ce que je devais faire, c'était lui envoyer de l'argent sur son compte Bitcoin.

J'étais nouveau dans ce domaine, plein d'espoir, et je ne connaissais presque rien aux arnaques.
Alors je lui ai envoyé plus de 1 000 dollars.
Et puis... plus rien.

Elle a disparu. Elle ne répondait plus à mes messages ni à mes appels.
L'argent était perdu.
Ce moment a été un choc. J'étais en colère, perdu... et je me sentais complètement limité.

Mais au lieu de rester dans cette douleur, j'ai pris une décision radicale :
j'allais apprendre.

Pas seulement pour moi. Mais pour protéger ma communauté, pour que d'autres ne tombent pas dans le même piège.

Et quelques années plus tard, me voici :
Je suis aujourd'hui analyste en cybersécurité certifié, étudiant en informatique, et je poursuis un objectif ambitieux : devenir consultant en cybersécurité et décrocher la prestigieuse certification CISSP.

Mais ce n'est que le début.

Pourquoi je partage cette histoire dans ce livre ? Parce que le savoir est un pouvoir que les riches utilisent chaque jour pour changer leur destin. Ils travaillent sur des projets à haut impact, souvent basés sur l'information, la technologie, et l'anticipation des problèmes des autres.
Ils ne subissent pas la vie. Ils l'étudient, la comprennent, et agissent en conséquence.

Et toi aussi, tu peux faire de même.

C'est pour cela que j'ai écrit ce livre.
Tu n'es pas limité, ni par ton passé, ni par ton origine, ni par tes échecs.
Tu peux apprendre. Tu peux devenir plus fort. Tu peux utiliser les mêmes armes que les riches utilisent : la connaissance, les compétences, et des projets porteurs de sens.

Ce chapitre te rappelle que la richesse commence par une décision :

celle de ne plus subir... mais d'agir.
Celle de te former, de créer, d'oser voir plus grand.
Et surtout, de transformer ta douleur en pouvoir.

Parce que les riches ne sont pas riches par accident.
Ils sont riches parce qu'ils savent.
Et maintenant, toi aussi, tu peux savoir.
Ne sois pas comme la majorité des gens. Tu n'en fais pas partie.

Oui, tu m'as bien entendu. Je parle à toi, personnellement. Certains penseront peut-être que j'exagère, mais je dois le répéter encore une fois : tu n'en fais pas partie. Tu ne fais pas partie de ces gens qui abandonnent dès que c'est difficile, qui enterrent leurs rêves dès les premières tempêtes. Non. Toi, tu es différent. Et quand tu veux quelque chose avec assez de force, tu ne peux pas abandonner. Tu ne peux pas accepter que ta réalité actuelle soit ton futur permanent. Impossible.

Tu vaux mieux que ça. Tu es plus grand que ce que tu crois, plus fort, plus intelligent. Alors laisse-moi te dire quelque chose : garde cette colère en toi, cette énergie brûlante, jusqu'à ce que tu atteignes ton objectif de vie. Ton vrai rêve. Parce que je sais que tu peux y arriver, si tu le veux vraiment.

Je te le dis avec certitude, car avant d'accéder à ce nouveau niveau de ta vie, tu devras quitter ta zone de confort. Oui, mentalement d'abord. Il faut que tu décides de quitter cette petite vie, ce petit salaire, cette petite vision, ce petit entourage, ce petit appartement... Dans Genèse 12, Dieu dit à Abraham : *"Quitte ton pays, ta parenté et la maison de ton père, et va dans le pays que je te montrerai."* C'est tout ce que Dieu lui a demandé s'il voulait une vie meilleure. Aujourd'hui encore, cette stratégie fonctionne. Tu dois partir, sortir, t'élever.

Souviens-toi toujours de cela : tu n'es pas comme les autres. Tu ne peux pas accepter ta réalité actuelle comme ton avenir final. Tu es né comme un lion, tu as cette puissance en toi. La puissance de surmonter, d'aller au-delà, de bâtir, d'inspirer, de dominer.

Alors, par où commencer pour changer ta vie et travailler enfin sur quelque chose qui a du poids, de l'impact, du sens ?

Arrête d'être négligent avec ta vie financière.

Les riches ne sont jamais négligents avec leur argent. Qu'est-ce que ça veut dire ? Ça veut dire que tu dois compter tout ce qui peut contribuer à tes finances, à ton bonheur, à ton bien-être. Parce que si tu agis comme si l'argent n'avait pas d'importance, la vie va t'envoyer des situations qui confirment exactement ça : le manque.

Parfois, je cite des versets simples de la Bible. Pas pour te convertir, mais parce que c'est vérifiable et concret. Regarde ceci : *Ecclésiaste 10:19 — "On prépare des festins pour rire, le vin rend la vie joyeuse, et l'argent répond à tout."* En mots simples : un festin = rire. Le vin = la joie. Et l'argent ? L'argent est la réponse à tout.

C'est pour cela que je dis : tu ne peux pas être négligent avec l'argent qui nourrit ta famille, paie tes soins, soutient tes projets, et élève ta vision. Si tu l'es, c'est comme si tu étais négligent avec ta propre vie.

Travaille sur des projets qui comptent. Pas seulement pour faire joli. Pas juste pour "être occupé". Travaille sur des choses qui peuvent changer ta vie et impacter le monde. Les riches ne perdent pas leur énergie sur des activités sans direction. Ils investissent leur temps, leur force, leur mental sur des projets à haut rendement, à haute valeur, à haut impact.

Ce n'est pas réservé à une élite. Toi aussi tu peux. Tu dois juste décider. Le lion ne demande pas la permission pour rugir. Il rugit, et le monde écoute.

Tu es un lion. Ne l'oublie jamais.

Les riches ne dilapident pas leur énergie sur des tâches inutiles. Ils appliquent la règle du 80/20, aussi appelée le principe de Pareto : 80 % des résultats proviennent de 20 % des efforts. Cela signifie qu'ils identifient les tâches essentielles qui créent le plus de valeur et concentrent leur énergie dessus, tout en éliminant ou déléguant les tâches secondaires. Pourquoi se concentrer sur l'essentiel est crucial ? Maximiser le temps et l'énergie : Vous avez un nombre limité d'heures par jour. Travailler sur des projets qui génèrent les meilleurs résultats est le chemin vers l'efficacité. Créer un impact durable : Les grandes réussites viennent d'efforts ciblés sur des objectifs ambitieux et stratégiques. Exemple inspirant : Jeff Bezos et Amazon: Au début d'Amazon, Jeff Bezos a concentré tous les efforts sur deux aspects critiques :

1. **L'expérience client** : S'assurer que les clients puissent trouver ce qu'ils cherchent rapidement et facilement.
2. **La logistique** : Créer un système de livraison rapide et fiable.

En se concentrant uniquement sur ces priorités, il a transformé Amazon en un géant mondial.

Comment appliquer ce principe dans votre vie ?

Identifiez vos tâches à haut impact

Prenez quelques minutes pour réfléchir : quelles sont les 20 % d'activités dans votre journée qui produisent 80 % des résultats ? Par exemple : si vous êtes entrepreneur, vos activités principales pourraient être la vente ou la création de produits. Si vous êtes étudiant ou salarié, cela pourrait être l'apprentissage de nouvelles compétences ou la gestion de projets importants.

Éliminez ou déléguez les distractions

Les réseaux sociaux, bien qu'apparemment inoffensifs, sont parmi les distractions les plus insidieuses de notre époque. Ils ne se contentent pas de voler notre temps : ils s'infiltrent dans chaque aspect de notre vie, sapant notre santé mentale, physique et financière. Ils représentent un vrai désastre pour votre santé mentale. Passez trop de temps à faire défiler des contenus soigneusement filtrés et vous commencerez à ressentir une pression invisible : celle de toujours vouloir plus. Les réseaux sociaux exploitent notre besoin d'approbation en nous exposant à une avalanche de « vies parfaites » qui peuvent éroder notre confiance en nous. Cette comparaison constante peut entraîner des sentiments de dévalorisation, d'anxiété ou même de dépression. Chaque « like » que vous attendez devient une validation externe, vous privant de votre propre capacité à vous estimer. Une menace pour votre santé physique. Ce que plusieurs personnes ne savent pas est que les heures passées à scroller signifient des heures d'inactivité. Les réseaux sociaux encouragent un mode de vie sédentaire, associé à des problèmes de posture, des douleurs cervicales et des troubles du sommeil. Les écrans perturbent également notre rythme circadien : plus vous restez exposé à la lumière bleue avant de dormir, plus votre sommeil est perturbé, affectant votre énergie, votre concentration et votre productivité. ils sont aussi un piège financier déguisé. Les réseaux sociaux ne se contentent pas de voler votre attention : ils influencent subtilement vos décisions financières. Les publicités ciblées, les promotions d'influenceurs et le sentiment de « manquer quelque chose » (FOMO) vous poussent à dépenser sur des choses dont vous n'avez pas besoin. Une simple session sur Instagram ou TikTok peut vous faire sortir votre carte bancaire pour acheter une tenue, un gadget ou une expérience que vous auriez ignoré autrement. Posez-vous cette question : combien d'heures et combien d'argent avez-vous déjà sacrifiés aujourd'hui pour des plateformes qui exploitent votre attention ? Il est donc temps de passer à l' action. Agissez maintenant La solution ? Réduisez le temps passé sur les réseaux sociaux, voire éliminez-les complètement si possible. Déconnectez-vous pour mieux vous reconnecter à vos objectifs. Si vous trouvez que certaines tâches ou interactions en ligne sont incontournables, déléguez-les à des outils automatisés ou à des personnes compétentes. Chaque minute que vous récupérez est une opportunité d'investir dans ce qui compte réellement pour vous. Ne laissez pas les réseaux sociaux saboter vos ambitions. Ils ne vous donneront jamais la richesse, la paix intérieure ou la liberté que vous recherchez. C'est à vous de reprendre le contrôle.

Créez une liste de priorités quotidiennes. Chaque matin, notez les 3 tâches les plus importantes de la journée. Concentrez-vous d'abord sur ces tâches avant de passer à autre chose. Action pour vous : Mettez en pratique Prenez une feuille de papier ou ouvrez une note. Listez toutes vos tâches actuelles. Notez tout ce que vous faites dans une journée ou une semaine. Classez-les par impact. Quelles tâches ont le plus grand effet sur vos résultats ou vos objectifs Supprimez celles qui semblent inutiles, déléguez celles que vous pouvez ou automatisez les tâches peu importantes. Exemple : Si vous gérez un business en ligne, vous pouvez automatiser l'envoi d'e-mails via un logiciel. Si vous passez trop de temps à faire des recherches, déléguez à un assistant ou limitez votre temps. Astuce : La délégation est une compétence Si vous avez du mal à déléguer : Commencez petit, en confiant une tâche simple. Donnez des instructions claires pour garantir que la tâche soit bien faite. Faites confiance et concentrez-vous sur ce que vous seul pouvez faire.

Conclusion

En appliquant la règle du 80/20, vous pourrez accomplir plus avec moins d'efforts. Identifiez ce qui a le plus de valeur dans votre vie, concentrez-vous dessus, et éliminez ce qui vous ralentit.

CHAPITRE 8

Ils n'ont pas peur du risque, mais le calculent

Secret 8 : Ils n'ont pas peur du risque, mais le calculent

Dans le voyage de la vie, on regarde souvent vers ceux qui ont atteint un succès extraordinaire. Pas seulement pour leur richesse, mais pour **la sagesse qu'ils ont récoltée en chemin**. Devenir milliardaire n'est presque jamais une ligne droite. Mais les leçons apprises, les mentalités adoptées, et les stratégies mises en œuvre par ces géants peuvent **guider n'importe qui vers une version plus grande et plus puissante de lui-même**.

Voici ce que certains des titans de notre époque ont appris et appliqué. Des principes qui peuvent transformer ta trajectoire si tu oses les intégrer.

Pense grand, commence petit – Jeff Bezos

Jeff Bezos, le fondateur d'Amazon, nous enseigne qu'il faut rêver en grand, tout en commençant avec des étapes maîtrisables. Il a dit un jour : « Je savais que si j'échouais, je n'allais pas le regretter, mais je savais que la seule chose que je pourrais regretter, c'est de ne pas avoir essayé. » Il a commencé Amazon comme une simple librairie en ligne, mais sa vision a toujours été immense. Il n'a pas attendu d'avoir tout pour commencer. Il a juste commencé.

Leçon : aie une vision grandiose, mais découpe-la en petites étapes que tu peux exécuter dès maintenant.

Innove sans relâche – Elon Musk

Elon Musk, le cerveau derrière Tesla et SpaceX, est reconnu pour sa capacité à repousser les limites. Il croit que lorsque quelque chose est vraiment important, **tu dois le faire, même si les chances sont contre toi**. On s'est souvent moqué de ses projets, mais son engagement envers l'innovation l'a mené à redéfinir plusieurs industries.

Leçon : ose innover. Et surtout, persévère même quand personne ne croit en toi.

Fais de l'échec un allié – Sara Blakely

Sara Blakely, fondatrice de Spanx, attribue sa réussite à sa relation avec l'échec. Son père lui demandait chaque semaine ce qu'elle avait raté, et s'il n'y avait rien, il était déçu. Cette approche l'a libérée de la peur d'échouer. Elle a osé plus. Pris plus de risques. Et ça a payé.

Leçon : ne fuis pas l'échec. Utilise-le comme une rampe de lancement.

Reste affamé, reste audacieux – Steve Jobs

Steve Jobs, le cofondateur d'Apple, répétait : « Stay hungry, stay foolish. » Ce n'était pas une phrase vide. C'était un appel à **rester curieux, affamé de savoir, et prêt à explorer sans peur du ridicule.** Jobs n'a jamais cessé de chercher de nouvelles idées, de nouveaux produits, de nouvelles façons de penser.

Leçon : ne perds jamais ta curiosité. C'est l'une de tes plus grandes armes.

Valorise les gens – Richard Branson

Richard Branson, fondateur du groupe Virgin, place **les êtres humains au cœur de tout**. Il a dit : « Les clients ne passent pas en premier. Les employés passent en premier. Si vous prenez soin de vos employés, ils prendront soin des clients. » Branson nous rappelle que le succès durable est toujours lié à la qualité de nos relations humaines.

Leçon : traite bien ceux qui t'entourent. Le capital humain est la richesse la plus précieuse.

Sois résilient – Oprah Winfrey

Oprah a traversé l'humiliation, les abus, la pauvreté, les rejets. Elle aurait pu s'effondrer mille fois. Elle a choisi de **transformer ses blessures en sagesse**. C'est cette force mentale qui l'a élevée au sommet, et qui fait d'elle un symbole de puissance et de grâce.

Leçon : transforme ta douleur en puissance. Ta plus grande force peut venir de ta plus grande blessure.

Ne cesse jamais d'apprendre – Warren Buffett

Warren Buffett est peut-être l'investisseur le plus respecté au monde, mais il reste un étudiant. Il lit plusieurs heures par jour. Il dit : « Plus tu apprends, plus tu gagnes. » Son succès ne vient pas juste de l'argent, mais **de sa discipline à apprendre en permanence.**

Leçon : engage-toi à apprendre toute ta vie. Ton esprit est ton meilleur actif.

Suis ta passion – Mark Zuckerberg

Mark Zuckerberg croit profondément à la puissance de la passion. Il dit : « Trouve ce qui te passionne profondément. » Son amour pour les connexions humaines est ce qui a donné naissance à Facebook. Il a bâti une entreprise planétaire en suivant ce feu intérieur.

Leçon : suis ce qui te passionne. C'est ce feu qui te portera quand tout semblera s'effondrer.

Oui, le risque fait partie intégrante de la réussite. Pourtant, contrairement aux idées reçues, les riches ne se lancent pas dans l'inconnu sans préparation. Ils évaluent, mesurent et planifient avant de prendre des décisions audacieuses. Ils savent que chaque risque calculé peut ouvrir la porte à des opportunités extraordinaires.

Pourquoi les riches prennent-ils des risques mesurés ?

Si vous aspirez à la réussite et à la liberté financière, il est crucial de comprendre une vérité fondamentale : les riches ne deviennent pas riches par hasard. Ce n'est ni un coup de chance ni une série de bonnes fortunes ; c'est une manière de penser et d'agir, où les risques mesurés jouent un rôle central. Voici pourquoi ils osent là où d'autres hésitent :

1. Pour grandir et évoluer

Rester dans sa zone de confort peut sembler sécurisant, mais c'est en réalité un piège invisible. Imaginez une graine plantée dans un pot : tant qu'elle reste dans cet espace restreint, elle ne pourra jamais devenir un arbre majestueux. Les riches l'ont compris : pour grandir, il faut briser les limites et oser explorer l'inconnu. Prendre des risques ne signifie pas se jeter aveuglément dans le vide. C'est un acte calculé. Par exemple, investir dans un nouveau secteur ou lancer une entreprise innovante peut sembler risqué, mais les riches s'entourent d'experts, font des recherches et prennent des décisions basées sur des données solides. **Leçon : Chaque fois que vous osez sortir de votre zone de confort, vous élargissez votre champ de possibilités.**

2. Pour transformer les échecs en apprentissages

La peur de l'échec est l'un des plus grands obstacles au succès. Mais pour les riches, l'échec n'est pas une fin : c'est un tremplin. Chaque erreur est une opportunité d'apprendre, de s'améliorer et de se rapprocher du succès. Prenez l'exemple de Thomas Edison. Lorsqu'on lui a demandé ce qu'il ressentait après avoir échoué 1 000 fois avant d'inventer l'ampoule, il a répondu : « Je n'ai pas échoué 1 000 fois. J'ai trouvé 1 000 façons qui ne fonctionnent pas. » Les riches adoptent cette mentalité. Au lieu de fuir les échecs, ils les accueillent comme des maîtres enseignants. **Leçon : Chaque échec vous rapproche d'une version plus forte et plus résiliente de vous-même.**

3. **Pour saisir les opportunités invisibles aux autres**

Là où la majorité voit des risques et des dangers, les riches voient des opportunités uniques. C'est ce qui les différencie. Ils savent que les plus grandes récompenses se trouvent souvent là où les autres ont peur d'aller.Prenons l'exemple d'Elon Musk. Lorsqu'il a investi dans SpaceX, Tesla et d'autres projets révolutionnaires, beaucoup pensaient qu'il prenait des risques insensés. Mais il voyait au-delà des obstacles immédiats : il voyait l'opportunité de transformer des industries entières. Aujourd'hui, ces « risques » ont fait de lui l'un des entrepreneurs les plus influents de notre époque.Les riches comprennent que l'incertitude est inévitable. Mais plutôt que de la craindre, ils l'étudient, l'embrassent et l'utilisent à leur avantage. Leçon : Les opportunités les plus précieuses sont souvent cachées derrière un voile d'incertitude. Ayez le courage de les chercher.

Comment appliquer cette mentalité à votre vie ?

Changez votre vision de l'échec : Voyez chaque défi comme une opportunité de grandir. Prenez des risques intelligents et apprenez de vos erreurs. Investissez dans vous-même : Acquérez des connaissances et des compétences qui vous aideront à prendre des décisions éclairées. Entourez-vous des bonnes personnes : Apprenez des mentors, des experts et des modèles de réussite. Ils vous guideront dans la prise de risques mesurés. Passez à l'action : Ne laissez pas la peur de l'échec vous paralyser. Faites le premier pas, aussi petit soit-il. Souvenez-vous : Ce n'est pas l'absence de risque qui garantit le succès, mais votre capacité à le gérer intelligemment. Prenez des risques mesurés et préparez-vous à récolter les fruits de votre audace. Exemple inspirant : Richard Branson et l'art de l'audace Richard Branson, le célèbre entrepreneur et fondateur du groupe Virgin, est l'incarnation de ce principe. Il a pris son premier grand risque en lançant Virgin Records à 22 ans, malgré un capital limité et une industrie très compétitive. Plus tard, il a diversifié son empire avec des entreprises audacieuses comme Virgin Atlantic et Virgin Galactic. Échecs ? Oui, il en a connu, comme Virgin Cola ou Virgin Cars. Mais à chaque fois, il a tiré des leçons et est revenu plus fort. Branson résume son approche : "Le plus grand risque est de ne jamais en prendre.

Comment prendre des risques calculés comme les riches ? Analysez les avantages et les inconvénients Quels sont les gains possibles si tout se passe bien ? Quels sont les pires scénarios ? Pouvez-vous les surmonter ? Faites de petits essais Ne pariez pas tout dès le départ. Testez vos idées à petite échelle pour minimiser les pertes en cas d'échec. *Exemple* : Investir un montant modéré (comme 1 000 €) dans un projet ou un placement pour apprendre les bases et comprendre les dynamiques. Préparez un plan de secours Ayez toujours une stratégie pour limiter vos pertes. Cela vous donnera la confiance nécessaire pour avancer. Développez votre tolérance au risque Prenez des risques progressivement. Chaque succès (même modeste) renforcera votre confiance et vous préparera à des projets plus ambitieux. Action : Votre premier pas vers l'audace Identifiez un petit risque que vous pouvez prendre cette semaine Cela peut être un investissement, la création d'un blog, ou même une conversation importante avec un mentor potentiel. Évaluez les scénarios et faites une liste des bénéfices et des obstacles potentiels. Réfléchissez à la manière de gérer les imprévus. Passez à l'action Fixez une échéance pour franchir le pas. Le vrai apprentissage vient de l'expérience, pas de la réflexion. Astuce pour progresser. Entourez-vous de personnes audacieuses : Leur énergie et leurs expériences vous inspireront à voir le risque autrement. Célébrez vos avancées : Chaque petit pas est une victoire qui vous rapproche de votre potentiel.

Conclusion : Le courage est la clé

Ces milliardaires ne sont pas des superhéros. Ils ont simplement fait des choix différents. Ils ont appris à calculer les risques au lieu de les fuir. Ils n'attendent pas que tout soit parfait pour agir. Ils avancent. Ils corrigent. Ils recommencent. Et surtout, ils n'ont jamais abandonné leurs principes.

Toi aussi tu peux emprunter ce chemin. Tu n'es pas limité. Pas tant que tu continues à penser grand, à apprendre, à oser, à échouer avec intelligence, et à te relever. Ce sont là les secrets que les riches ne veulent pas que tu comprennes. Parce que le jour où tu les appliques, tu deviens inarrêtable.

Retiens bien ceci : les risques ne sont pas faits pour te faire peur. Ils sont faits pour être maîtrisés. Et c'est à ce moment-là que tu entres dans une autre dimension. Celle des bâtisseurs. Des conquérants. Des lions.

Prendre des risques mesurés est un trait commun à toutes les personnes qui réussissent. Ce n'est pas une question d'être imprudent, mais d'être suffisamment audacieux pour aller au-delà de vos limites. En osant avec intelligence, vous découvrirez que les opportunités les plus gratifiantes se trouvent souvent juste de l'autre côté de la peur. Vous êtes prêt ? Alors, faites votre premier pas aujourd'hui.

Félicitations ! Vous avez maintenant en main les secrets que les plus grands riches utilisent pour transformer leur vie et bâtir un avenir extraordinaire. Vous êtes désormais armé(e) des principes essentiels pour tracer votre propre chemin vers la réussite. Mais votre voyage ne s'arrête pas là.

Le miracle mathematique de l'existence humaine

Lors d'un seul rapport sexuel, un homme éjacule entre 100 à 300 millions de spermatozoïdes.

Parmi cette armée microscopique, un seul atteindra et fécondera l'ovule de la femme pour donner naissance a un être humain. Taux de chance pour qu'un spermatozoïde devienne un être humain : {1 sur 100 millions à 300 millions}. Soit entre 0,000001 % et 0,00000033 % de chances,

Super important, Tu es donc littéralement un miracle statistique vivant. Tu as battu des centaines de millions d'autres candidats pour arriver en premier. Tu n'étais pas une erreur : tu es le résultat d'un combat cosmique que tu as gagné dès ta conception.Tu es une victoire vivante,oui !

En de termes tres simple et scientifiques, lors d'un rapport sexuel, entre 100 et 300 millions de spermatozoïdes sont libérés. Ils se lancent dans une course folle, brutale, et impitoyable vers l'ovule, Et sur ces centaines de millions de prétendants, un seul gagne. Un seul réussit à franchir tous les obstacles, à survivre dans un environnement hostile, à battre tous les autres pour donner naissance à un être humain.

Ce vainqueur, c'était toi.

Tu n'étais pas une erreur. Tu n'étais pas un accident. Tu étais la victoire au bout d'un combat biologique que presque aucun spermatozoïde ne gagne.

Tu as été choisi par la vie, par la nature, par le destin - peu importe ton point de départ, tu as déjà prouvé que tu avais en toi ce qu'il faut pour vaincre,

Quand on comprend ça, on ne peut plus se permettre de vivre à moitié, On ne peut plus s'autoriser à traîner dans l'autosabotage, dans la peur des autres, dans l'esprit de complexe ou de comparaison,

Tu es né avec un avantage énorme : la preuve vivante que tu peux surmonter la concurrence, les obstacles, et réussir même quand les chances sont contre toi. Alors refuse toute voix intérieure ou extérieure qui te dit que tu es "moins que". Refuse de vivre comme si tu n'avais pas de valeur, Refuse de t'excuser d'exister.

Tu es le résultat d'un exploit biologique, un miracle statistique vivant. Tu dois maintenant honorer cette victoire - en vivant pleinement, en croyant en toi, en osant rêver grand, et en laissant ton empreinte sur cette Terre. N'accepte pas la médiocrité, ne t'agenouille pas devant les opinions, et surtout, n'oublie jamais qui tu es.

Sources fiables :
- **Mayo Clinic et American Pregnancy Association** estiment l'ejaculat moyen entre 100 et 300 millions de spermatozoïdes.
- **Harvard Medical School et Cleveland Clinic** confirment que seul un spermatozoïde parvient généralement à féconder l'ovule.
- Le livre "**The Selfish Gene**" de Richard Dawkins explique aussi la selection drastique dans le processus de reproduction.

ET SI TU ETAIS NE POUR ETRE UN LEADER ?

Et si toutes les épreuves que tu as traversées étaient en réalité des preuves ? Des preuves que tu es destiné à bien plus que ce que tu vis aujourd'hui. Un leader ne naît pas pour une vie tranquille et ordinaire. Il est appelé à se battre, à rêver plus grand que les autres, à supporter des douleurs que la majorité fuirait. C'est pourquoi ta vie n'a pas été facile. Parce qu'elle te préparait. Te forgeait. Te formait pour une mission plus haute, Si tu t'es toujours senti à part, différent, ce n'est pas un hasard c'est un appel. Celui du leadership. La comprehension de cette etape est tres importante pour toi qui veut aller au dela de la vie normale. Il y a des personnes qui ne sont pas nes pour suivre les autres, mais pour devenir un vrai leader. Ces personnes la portent une energie rare, forte et meme on peut aller plus loin pour dire independante donc ne sois pas etonne si tu es souvent incompris, tu sais pourquoi? La raison est tres simple; un leader a une vision, il voit dans le future, il utulise beaucoup son imagination, il parles des choses qui n' exite pas encore ce qui fait que les cytoyens moyens ne le comprennent pas toujours.

Donc mon message ici pour toi est que tu n' es pas vennu dans ce monde pour etre comme les autres, tu es ne pour briser des plans, des chema, Peu importe le type, tu as une mission a accomplir c est pourquoi tu ne dois jamais etre etonne de te sentir souvent seul meme si tu es entoure physiquement des personnes, Un leader est un independent, un createur, un vrai pionnier, Un leader est une personne qui fait les choses a sa propre maniere meme si cela peu deranger les autres, Un leader suit son instin, sa vision et plus precisement un feu interieur qui blule en lui, oui ce vaillant feu qui te pousse a aller plus loin, a donner le meilleur de toi. Le seul probleme est que est tu dois juste savoir te maitriser, maitriser ton EGO interieur a chaque fois que tu sens une pression, celle de faire quelque chose de grand, d'extraordinaire, de precieux voire meme de haut niveau. Tu es celui ou celle qui veut apporter un changement, A ce niveau la, tu pourrais commencer a remaquer que seulement peu de gens te tendront la main. C est souvent normal, car tu es different des 75% des personnes qui n' ont meme pas de journal, leur journees dependent de celles des autres. C' est un peu comme" une feuille seche que un petit vent peut trimballer la ou il veut, et cela est vraiment minable. Mais toi, tu as un plan, tu sais ce que tu veux, tu es exceptionnel.

Regarde Elon Musk. Aujourd'hui, il est l'un des hommes les plus riches du monde, à la tête de Tesla, SpaceX, et d'autres entreprises révolutionnaires, Mais peu de gens savent qu'il a été victime de harcèlement à l'école, battu au point d'être hospitalisé. Il a quitté son pays natal, l'Afrique du Sud, avec presque rien. Il a dormi sur des canapés, vécu dans l'incertitude, pris des risques fous. Il a été critiqué, rejeté, même traité de fou. Mais il a tenu bon. Il a transformé chaque rejet en carburant, Chaque douleur en détermination, Pourquoi ? Parce qu'il a compris qu'il n'était pas né pour suivre, mais pour créer. Pour innover. Pour inspirer.

Et toi ? Tu crois que tu souffres sans raison ? Tu crois que tes difficultes veulent dire que tu es condamné ? Détrompe-toi. Tu es en cours de transformation. Tes cicatrices ne sont pas des preuves de faiblesse- elles sont les marques de ta préparation. Tu as survécu à la tempête, maintenant tu es prêt à guider d'autres vers la lumière. Tu n'es pas petit. Tu es simplement en construction.

Alors lève-toi. Garde la tête haute. Aie confiance en toi. Ce monde a besoin de voix fortes, de cœurs solides, de leaders vrais, Tu es né pour ça. Et si tu étais né pour être un leader ... il est temps d'embrasser ta destinée.

NE GASPILLE PAS TES 8H- Chaque jour te donne une chance en or

Chaque être humain sur cette terre reçoit 24 heures dans sa journée. Ni plus, ni moins. Toi aussi, tu as ces 24 heures chaque jour, En général, on utilise 8 heures pour travailler ou aller à l'école, 8 heures pour dormir et reposer notre corps, et il reste encore 8 heures libres. Ces 8 heures sont très importantes, même si beaucoup de gens ne s'en rendent pas compte,

Ces 8 heures sont les plus précieuses, parce que ce sont les heures où tu es libre de choisir ce que tu veux faire. Tu peux les utiliser pour t'amuser, bien sûr, mais aussi pour construire ton avenir. Imagine que chaque jour, tu utilises seulement 2 ou 3 heures pour apprendre quelque chose de nouveau, lire un livre, écrire, t'exercer à un talent, ou même créer un petit projet.

Imagine que tu fais ça chaque jour pendant 1 an, 2 ans, 5 ans … Tu serais surpris de tout ce que tu serais capable d'accomplir !

Beaucoup de gens disent qu'ils n'ont pas le temps. Mais en vérité, ils gaspillent leurs 8 heures en regardant trop la télé, en jouant trop à des jeux, ou en restant sur les réseaux sociaux sans but. Pendant ce temps-là, d'autres personnes utilisent leurs heures pour devenir meilleures, plus intelligentes, plus fortes. Et dans quelques années, ces personnes deviennent riches, libres, heureuses … tout ça parce qu'elles ont bien utilisé leurs 8 heures par jour.

Toi aussi, tu peux commencer aujourd'hui. Même si tu n'as que 10 ou 12 ans, tu peux faire des choses grandes, Tu peux apprendre à programmer, à dessiner, à cuisiner, à créer des vidéos, à inventer des histoires, ou à aider les autres. Tu n'as pas besoin d'attendre d'être adulte pour commencer à bâtir ta vie. Utilise bien ton temps.

Souviens-toi : les 8 heures restantes de ta journée sont ton trésor secret. C'est comme si la vie te donnait chaque jour un coffre rempli d'or, mais que tu ne l'ouvrais jamais, Ce livre, veut te réveiller. Il veut te dire : "Ne perds pas ton temps ! Tes 8 heures peuvent te rendre très très riche, heureux et libre, si tu sais les utiliser avec intelligence et courage."

COMMENCE PETIT, commence aujourd'hui

Quand tu fais un rêve, un vrai rêve, grand, fort, qui brûle en toi; c'est déjà un acte de rébellion. Pourquoi ? Parce que rêver, c'est refuser la vie qu'on veut t'imposer. C'est dire au monde : "Je sais ce que je vaux, et je ne me contenterai pas de survivre, Je veux vivre pleinement."

Mais rêver ne suffit pas. Il faut agir, Et souvent, ce qui bloque les gens, ce n'est pas le rêve … c'est le début.

Beaucoup attendent le moment parfait. Ils disent : "Je commencerai quand j'aurai plus d'argent", "quand j'aurai plus de temps", "quand j'aurai tout compris." Mais la vérité, c'est que ce moment parfait n'existe pas. Et si tu attends trop longtemps, ton rêve risque de mourir en silence. C'est pour cela que tu dois commencer petit, mais commencer aujourd'hui.

Pas besoin d'avoir tout en main. Si tu veux écrire un livre, commence par écrire une page, Si tu veux lancer un petit business, commence avec ce que tu as, même si c'est peu. Si tu veux devenir un expert en quelque chose, commence par apprendre 10 minutes par jour. L'important, ce n'est pas de faire grand au début. L'important, c'est de mettre ton rêve en mouvement.

Commencer petit, c'est comme planter une graine. Tu ne vois pas l'arbre tout de suite, mais tu sais qu'il va pousser si tu t'en occupes chaque jour, Et plus tu avances, plus tu deviens fort, plus tu gagnes en confiance, et ton rêve deviant peu à peu une réalité. Ne laisse pas la peur du "pas assez" t'arrêter. Personne ne commence avec tout. Mais ceux qui osent faire un petit pas aujourd'hui auront bientot parcouru un grand chemin.

Ce chapitre du livre est là pour te secouer et te dire : tu n'as pas besoin de tout pour commencer. Mais tu dois commencer. Aujourd'hui. Maintenant. Parce que chaque jour où tu n'agis pas, c'est un jour où ton rêve recule, Et chaque petit pas que tu fais, c'est une victoire contre la peur, la paresse, et les excuses. Commence petit. Commence aujourd'hui. Et ne t'arrête pas.

LE MONDE APPARTIENT A CEUX QUI NE SE CONTENTERONT JAMAIS

Il y a deux types de personnes dans ce monde, Ceux qui disent : "C'est deja bien comme ça … ", et ceux qui disent : "Je peux faire mieux."

Le premier groupe accepte la vie qu'on lui donne.

Il s'adapte, il se résigne, il baisse les bras. Il ne dérange personne, il ne rêve pas trop grand. Il travaille, il dort, il recommence, Et il finit par croire que c'est ça, la vie, Mais le second groupe … ah, ce second groupe ! Ce sont ceux qui ne se contentent jamais.

Même s'ils vivent dans un petit quartier, dans une maison modeste, avec peu de moyens, ils ont quelque chose en eux que rien ni personne ne peut éteindre : une faim. Une soif de mieux. Un feu intérieur qui leur murmure chaque jour : "Tu es né pour plus que ça."

Ce sont ces gens-là qui construisent les entreprises, écrivent les livres, inventent les idées, bâtissent des écoles, sauvent des vies, inspirent des nations. Ils ne sont pas meilleurs que toi. Ils n'avaient pas tout au debut. Mais ils avaient ce refus silencieux dans le cœur :

"Je ne vais pas juste survivre, Je vais vivre pleinement, Je vais oser, je vais apprendre, je vais échouer, recommencer, mais je ne vais pas m'arrêter tant que je n'aurai pas changé ma vie."

Ne te laisse pas endormir par la routine. Ne te laisse pas endormir par les "c'est déjà pas mal." Tu n'es pas venu sur cette Terre pour juste "tenir bon jusqu'au vendredi". Tu es ici pour laisser une empreinte, pour inspirer, pour bâtir quelque chose que même la mort ne pourra pas effacer. Tu n'as pas besoin d'être riche aujourd'hui. Tu n'as pas besoin d'etre parfait. Tu dois juste refuser la médiocrité. Refuser la petite vie que la peur veut t'imposer.

Le monde, ce monde dans lequel tu vis, il appartient à ceux qui n'abandonnent pas. À ceux qui rêvent grand, qui commencent petit, mais qui ne se contentent jamais. Je sais que certains vont se demander est-ce que moi-meme je mets toutes ces bonnes idees en practique? Et a cette question, ma reponse est oui. Le simple fait que tu tiens ce livre en main en ce moment est une preuve vivante que a un moment de la vie j ai ose dire non a une vie normale, Oui, j ai voulu quelque chose de mieux, quelque chose de superieur qui me permettrait de voyager dans le temps et dans l'espace pour motiver et inspirer des personnes dans le monde entier, Et en plus de cela, En Mai 2022 je pense, j ai perdu onze milles Dollars en une semaine dans crypto monnaie. Bien sur que pour certain cette somme est inssignifiant mais pour moi, en tout cas, c etait une nuit blanche. Je voulu essayer ce domaine et bref le reste n' est qu' une histoire. Donc je t' encourage toi aussi a ne pas te contenter de ce que tu as. Vas et demande a la vie ce que tu merites, Et si tu lis ce livre, c'est que toi aussi, tu fais partie de ceux-là. Alors prouve-le. Pas aux autres. À toi-même.

Ton role sur terre

L'homme n'est pas ne pour ramper, mais pour regner.

Dès les premières pages de la Bible, en Genèse 1:26-28, Dieu révèle Son intention :"Faisons l'homme à notre image ... et qu'il DOMINE ..."

Le mot hébreu utilisé ici est radah, ce qui signifie exercer une autorité royale, diriger, gouverner avec puissance et responsabilité. Dieu a donc créé l'homme pour être un leader naturel, un gestionnaire de la terre, un représentant de Sa grandeur.Tu n'es pas né pour te contenter du minimum. Tu n'es pas venu sur cette terre pour survivre, mais pour conquérir. Tes rêves doivent être à la hauteur de ta nature divine,

Rêver petit, c'est trahir l'image de Dieu en toi. Tu as été conçu pour voir grand, penser grand, construire grand, vivre avec impact, Chaque fois que tu te limites, chaque fois que tu abandonnes tes rêves, tu refuses le mandat divin de dominer. Tu n'es pas une erreur, tu es une autorité en mission. Tu es venu pour gouverner dans ton domaine, pour exceller, pour élever les autres, pour créer de la Valeur et inspirer le monde.

Regarde les plus grands. Ils n'ont pas commencé avec des diplômes prestigieux ou des comptes bancaires pleins. Ils ont commence avec une vision. Quelque chose qu'ils voyaient en eux alors que personne n'y croyait.

Nelson Mandela, dans sa cellule de prison, rêvait d'un pays libre, alors même qu'il etait enchaîne. Martin Luther King revait d'un monde ou sa fille ne serait pas jugée par la couleur de sa peau, alors que cette société le réduisait à l'état de menace. Elon Musk rêvait d'envoyer des fusées dans l'espace depuis un garage. Et tous les gens rationnels lui ont dit que c'etait de la folie. Mais le rêve n'a pas besoin d'autorisation. Il a juste besoin de foi, de discipline et de courage.

Tu crois que rêver, c'est un luxe ? Tu te trompes. Le rêve est une nécessité. Il est ce qui distingue ceux qui survivent de ceux qui vivent. Il est ce qui te tire du lit quand tu n'as aucune autre raison de continuer. Il est ce qui te pousse à apprendre, à oser, à tomber, à te relever, La pauvreté peut te voler ton confort, ton toit, tes repas ... mais elle ne peut rien contre un esprit qui rêve encore.

Tu dois proteger ton reve comme un tresor sacre. Parce que beaucoup essaieront de te le voler. Pas forcément par méchanceté. Mais parce qu'ils ont abandonne le leur. Ils veulent te ramener dans leur monde. Ils se sentient menacés par ta lumière. Ton rêve leur rappelle ce qu'ils ont laissé mourir en eux.

Alors protège-le. Nourris-le. Dessine-le. Écris-le. Parle-lui. Donne-lui une forme, même fragile, Même ridicule aux yeux des autres, C'est ton rêve, Et personne ne le vivra à ta place.

Et surtout, n'attends pas d'avoir tout pour commencer. Commence là où tu es. Avec ce que tu as. Ce n'est pas le lieu qui fait la grandeur. C'est la clarté de la vision, et la foi qui l'accompagne.

Tu crois que tu dois d'abord avoir de l'argent pour rever ? Faux. Le reve precede l'argent. Il attire les ressources. Il crée les connexions. Il donne naissance aux opportunités.

Tu crois que ton reve est trop grand ? Parfait. Il doit te faire trembler un peu. Sinon, ce n'est pas un rêve, c'est une tâche.

Tu crois que rêver ne change pas la réalité ? Dis ça à tous ceux qui, grâce à leur rêve, ont déplacé des montagnes, soigné des peuples, créé des empires ou sauvé des familles entières de la misère.

Rêver, c'est défier le destin fixé. C'est dire : « Peut-être que tout le monde autour de moi a échoué, mais moi, je vais essayer. »

Et si tu échoues ? Ce sera un échec digne. Un échec debout. Un échec de quelqu'un qui a osé, Pas de quelqu'un qui a abandonné.

Aujourd'hui, je veux que tu comprennes ceci : ton rêve n'est pas une option. Il est une responsabilité. Tu n'es pas venu sur cette terre pour reproduire une vie par défaut. Tu es venu pour créer quelque chose d'unique, Quelque chose qui commence dans ton imagination, mais qui finira par bénir le monde entier.

Rêver, c'est refuser la soumission. C'est dire : *Je ne suis pas ce qu'on m'a dit. Je suis ce que je décide de devenir.*

Alors rêve. Rêve comme un acte de guerre contre la résignation. Rêve comme un soldat silencieux. Rêve jusqu'à ce que ce que tu vois en toi devienne plus reel que ce que tu vois autour de toi.

Et surtout ... n'attends plus.

CHAPITRE 9

TRANSFORMER LES PENSÉES NÉGATIVES EN FORCE MOTRICE

Les riches ne sont pas moins confrontés à l'échec ou aux pensées négatives. Mais ils ont appris à transformer ces moments en moteurs de croissance, là où d'autres s'arrêtent, doutent ou fuient. Ce chapitre te montre comment tu peux, toi aussi, transformer chaque pensée négative, chaque échec, chaque rejet en énergie propulsive.

Échouer n'est pas la fin, c'est un message

Au lieu de voir l'échec comme une impasse, considère-le comme un retour d'information. Qu'est-ce qui n'a pas fonctionné ? Qu'est-ce que tu peux améliorer ? Chaque revers te donne une leçon que tu peux utiliser pour revenir plus fort, plus avisé et mieux préparé.

C'est une richesse que les riches savent exploiter : ils apprennent plus de leurs échecs que de leurs succès.

Adopte un état d'esprit de croissance

La psychologue Carol Dweck parle d'un concept fondamental : le "growth mindset", ou état d'esprit de croissance. Ceux qui le développent croient que l'intelligence, les compétences, la réussite s'apprennent et se construisent.

Ceux qui ont un état d'esprit figé, eux, pensent que leurs capacités sont limitées et immuables. Résultat ? Ils abandonnent plus vite, se découragent plus facilement. En développant un état d'esprit de croissance, tu verras les défis comme des opportunités, pas comme des barrières. Tu ne te définis plus par ton passé, mais par ton potentiel.

Cultive la résilience émotionnelle

Le rejet fait mal, c'est vrai. Mais il ne te définit pas. La plupart des figures emblématiques de la réussite ont été rejetées de nombreuses fois avant de percer. La différence ? Elles n'ont jamais permis à ce rejet de limiter leur valeur. La résilience émotionnelle, c'est cette capacité à séparer ton identité de tes échecs. Ce n'est pas parce que tu rates une étape que tu es voué à échouer. C'est une alerte, pas une condamnation. Utilise-la pour t'améliorer, pas pour t'arrêter.

Histoires vraies : Ils ont refusé d'abandonner

Voici quelques exemples de personnalités qui ont transformé les obstacles en tremplins :

Thomas Edison : 10 000 essais avant la lumière

Il disait : « Je n'ai pas échoué. J'ai juste trouvé 10 000 façons qui ne fonctionnent pas. »

Son invention de l'ampoule a changé le monde. Mais c'est sa persévérance, pas son génie, qui a fait la différence.

Oprah Winfrey : rejetée… puis reine des médias

Virée de son premier job à la télé parce qu'on la trouvait "inapte pour l'écran", elle aurait pu abandonner. Mais non. Elle a bâti un empire médiatique. Oprah est aujourd'hui l'une des femmes les plus influentes de la planète. Le rejet ne l'a pas brisée. Il l'a propulsée.

J.K. Rowling : au fond du trou avant de devenir milliardaire

Avant que *Harry Potter* ne devienne un phénomène mondial, elle était une mère célibataire, fauchée, rejetée par plusieurs éditeurs. Mais elle y a cru. Et elle a persisté. Une maison d'édition a fini par lui dire oui. Aujourd'hui, elle inspire des millions de lecteurs dans le monde.

Nelson Mandela : 27 ans de prison, pas de haine

27 ans derrière les barreaux. Il aurait pu en ressortir aigri, haineux. Mais Mandela a choisi la réconciliation, pas la vengeance. Sa force intérieure a permis la fin de l'apartheid et l'émergence d'une Afrique du Sud libre. Un exemple ultime de résilience et de grandeur.

Stratégies pratiques pour devenir plus résilient
- Accepte les épreuves comme partie intégrante de la vie. Ce sont des tests, pas des défaites.
- Entoure-toi bien. Ton entourage peut t'élever ou te tirer vers le bas. Choisis des gens qui te soutiennent.
- Sois flexible. Le succès n'est jamais linéaire. L'adaptabilité est une arme puissante.
- Prends soin de ta santé mentale et physique. Sans énergie ni clarté mentale, tu ne peux pas avancer loin.
- Concentre-toi sur ce que tu peux contrôler. Ne perds pas ton énergie sur ce qui est hors de ta portée.
- Célèbre les petites victoires. Chaque progrès, même minime, est un pas vers ta transformation.

Pensée finale : La résilience crée la réussite

La résilience est le pont entre l'échec et la réussite. C'est le secret que les riches utilisent pour ne jamais rester à terre. Chaque grand accomplissement repose sur la persévérance, l'apprentissage, et la capacité à rebondir.

Quand les obstacles se dressent—et ils viendront—rappelle-toi qu'ils sont temporaires. Si tu continues à avancer, à apprendre, à te relever, tu iras plus loin que tu ne l'aurais jamais imaginé.

Tu n'es pas limité. Tu as en toi une force immense. Il est temps de l'activer.

Le mythe du manque d'amour : Une illusion à déconstruire

"Le manque d'amour est souvent une perception, non une réalité. Ce sentiment découle de la comparaison, des attentes irréalistes, et parfois, d'une blessure émotionnelle non guérie. Mais voici la vérité : tu es déjà aimé, car l'amour commence en toi."Voici une stratégie simple et puissante pour éviter les pensées négatives et stressantes.

La stratégie des 3 R : Reconnaître, Remplacer, Répéter

1. **Reconnaître les pensées négatives**
   - Description : La première étape pour éviter les pensées négatives est de prendre conscience qu'elles existent. Beaucoup de gens ne réalisent même pas qu'ils s'autosabotent mentalement.
   - Action pratique :
   - Lorsque tu ressens du stress ou de l'anxiété, arrête-toi et demande-toi :
   "Quelle est la pensée qui cause cette émotion ? Est-elle réaliste ou exagérée ?"
   - Identifie les déclencheurs (situations, personnes ou événements qui provoquent ces pensées).

2. **Remplacer les pensées négatives par des pensées positives**
   - Description : Une fois que tu as identifié une pensée négative, remplace-la immédiatement par une pensée qui te redonne du pouvoir.
   - Astuce : Utilise des affirmations positives ou reformule la pensée négative en question constructive. Exemple : "Je n'y arriverai jamais" devient "Chaque jour, je m'améliore et je me rapproche de mon objectif."
   - "Tout va mal" devient "Ce moment est difficile, mais il ne durera pas éternellement."

3. Répéter cette habitude quotidiennement
   - Description : La clé pour éviter les pensées négatives sur le long terme est de transformer cette pratique en habitude. La répétition entraîne une reprogrammation du cerveau. Action pratique : Chaque matin, prends 5 minutes pour écrire 3 affirmations positives ou 3 choses pour lesquelles tu es reconnaissant. À la fin de chaque journée, note une réussite, même petite, pour ancrer une mentalité positive. Pourquoi cette stratégie fonctionne pour les grands riches

En réalité, les grands riches appliquent souvent cette stratégie inconsciemment : Ils ne perdent pas de temps à ruminer des pensées négatives. Ils se concentrent sur les solutions et non sur les problèmes.
   - Ils cultivent une discipline mentale qui leur permet de rester sereins et productifs face au stress. Par exemple, "Les riches ne se laissent pas dominer par leurs pensées. Ils les contrôlent. Chaque fois qu'une pensée limitante surgit, ils la remplacent immédiatement par une pensée qui les motive à avancer."

Message clé :

1. "Le vrai amour, celui qui transforme, commence par toi-même. Quand tu t'aimes pleinement, tu attires l'amour que tu mérites."
   - Exercice pratique :
   La lettre d'amour à soi-même : Écris une lettre dans laquelle tu te pardonnes pour tes erreurs, tu célèbres tes forces et tu te promets d'être toujours là pour toi-même. Relis cette lettre chaque fois que tu ressens un vide émotionnel. Exemple inspirant : "Imagine une femme entrepreneure, Marie, qui pensait qu'elle ne valait rien parce que ses relations ne duraient pas. Un jour, elle a décidé de s'aimer d'abord. Elle a commencé par prendre soin d'elle, valoriser ses talents, et trouver du bonheur dans ses propres actions. Quelques mois plus tard, elle a non seulement attiré une relation saine, mais elle a aussi gagné confiance pour développer son projet qui est devenu un succès."

2. Les doutes et l'échec : Des alliés déguisés

Rappelez-vous de l' histoire de Thomas Edison que nous avons citée dans le chapitre précédent, je l' ai cité ici encore pour montrer à quel point la patience joue un très grand rôle dans la vie de chaque grand riche. "Thomas Edison a échoué 1 000 fois avant d'inventer l'ampoule. Quand on lui a demandé ce qu'il pensait de ces échecs, il a répondu : 'Je n'ai pas échoué 1 000 fois. J'ai trouvé 1 000 façons qui ne marchaient pas.'" La patience : La clé que peu utilisent et surtoout quand le moment viendra que tout semble bizarre ou que tu penses que plus rien n' avance, rappelle toi que c est l' hyver.

L'HYVER VA PASSER !

Maintenant que tu sais exactement pourquoi tu étais né, et que tu as fait un plan bien dressé de ce que tu comptes faire a partir d'aujourd' hui, nous allons parler de l' une des étapes les plus importantes. Je sais que tu auras besoin de cette étape quand les vraies choses vont commencer. J' ai juste une suite de petite question a te poser: As tu une fois eu l'experience une nuit ou tu n'arrivais pas a dormir? Surement que tu pensais a plusieurs choses à la foi peut-être ou soit tu devais prendre une decision tres tres cruciale de ta vie .. bref. Et malgré tout ce tu as fait, tu avais l'impression de ne pas avoir sommeil ? super! Mais qu'as tu remarqué vers la fin? Malgré que tu ais constaté que la nuit semblait trop durer le jour a fini par arriver n' est-ce pas? Yes c' est de ça que nous allons parler. Parlant de l'hiver, je fais allusion à chaque temps pénible que tu traverses actuellement ou bien que tu vas traverser souvent dans la vie. De façon générale, la vie elle-même est faite de haut et de bas donc les temps durs où tout semble tomber sur toi seul, ou sur ta famille font partie de la vie. Oui tiens bon et reste fort (e) durant ce temps de réflexion. C' est justement pour cela que je t'encourage à garder ton vrai regard sur ton objectif, tes rêves, ta vision, tes ambitions parce que tôt ou tard. L'hiver va passer. Oui la sécheresse va passer, les pleurs vont passer et surtout rappelle toi qu'un seul appel téléphonique ou un simple mail peut changer tout à tout moment.!

"Dans un monde où tout va vite, beaucoup oublient que les grandes choses prennent du temps. La patience, c'est croire en tes efforts, même quand les résultats tardent à venir." Message clé : "Le bambou chinois ne pousse pas immédiatement. Pendant 5 ans, il ne montre aucun signe de croissance. Puis, en 6 semaines, il pousse de 30 mètres. Pendant ces 5 ans, il développait ses racines. Toi aussi, développe tes racines."

- Exercice pratique : Le rituel des racines : Chaque soir, note une action que tu as accomplie, même petite. Écris pourquoi cette action te rapproche de ton but, même si le résultat n'est pas encore visible. Relis ces notes chaque semaine pour voir ta progression. S'entourer des bonnes influences : Le pouvoir invisible de l'entourage• Introduction captivante :"Tu es la moyenne des 5 personnes avec qui tu passes le plus de temps. Si ces personnes te rabaissent, te critiquent ou ne croient pas en toi, tu porteras ce poids. Choisis des alliés, pas des saboteurs." Message clé : "Les personnes qui réussissent s'entourent de mentors, d'amis et de partenaires qui les inspirent, les soutiennent et les élèvent."

- Exercice pratique : L'audit social : Fais une liste des 5 personnes les plus proches de toi. Évalue leur impact sur ta vie : t'apportent-elles du soutien ou te drainent-elles d'énergie ? Engage-toi à passer plus de temps avec des personnes positives et à limiter les interactions toxiques.

Une histoire inspirante pour conclure

"Une jeune femme, Claire, pensait qu'elle n'était pas aimée et que rien ne marchait dans sa vie. Elle a suivi ces étapes : elle a appris à s'aimer, elle a transformé ses échecs en apprentissages, et elle a pris le temps de cultiver ses racines. Peu à peu, elle a retrouvé sa confiance, attiré l'amour qu'elle cherchait, et créé un projet qui reflétait sa vraie valeur. Aujourd'hui, Claire est une source d'inspiration pour des centaines de personnes." Conclusion motivante Termine cette section en rappelant que : "Les grands riches que j'ai étudiés ont tous traversé des périodes de doute et de solitude. Ce qui les différencie, c'est leur capacité à transformer ces moments en opportunités. Tu peux, toi aussi, créer une vie de gloire en partant de rien. Tout commence par ton esprit et tes actions."

CHAPITRE 10

Comment les grands riches exploitent l'IA pour dominer

Plongez dans le dernier chapitre pour découvrir comment les visionnaires et leaders mondiaux utilisent l'IA pour transformer leur business, multiplier leurs revenus et rester à la pointe de l'innovation. Vous apprendrez à intégrer cette technologie dans votre propre stratégie pour prendre une longueur d'avance sur la concurrence. Préparez-vous à entrer dans l'ère de la domination digitale. Le futur commence maintenant.

Normalement nous avons fini de citer et approfondir les sept secrets efficaces pour se bâtir une fortune en partant d'une vision simple et claire. Mais étant donné que je suis aussi un puissant en Informatique, je ne peux pas terminer cette œuvre sans vous décrire une idée géniale de la technologie actuelle et pour le monde futur. Il a pour rôle de faciliter votre vie, vous faire gagner du temps et vous permettre de dominer sur tous les plans. Il est le plus récent secret des nouveaux puissants riches de notre époque. La vraie réalité est que le mot richesse est adapté à chaque époque. Quand on prend par exemple les anciennes histoire des plus riches racontés dans les vieux livres comme la bible, et qu'analyse un peu leur moyen de richesse, on verra que c' est purement différent de ce qui donne réellement de la joie financière à tout homme de notre actuelle époque. Ce chapitre met en lumière comment les riches utilisent l'intelligence artificielle comme levier discret mais puissant pour amplifier leurs richesses et simplifier leur vie.

"L'argent n'est pas seulement une question d'effort, mais aussi de stratégie. L' IA est l'un des outils secrets des plus riches pour multiplier leur impact tout en réduisant leur effort."

Comprendre l'IA : L'arme secrète des élites

Pour une simple définition, l 'intelligence artificielle (IA) désigne les systèmes ou machines capables de simuler des processus cognitifs humains tels que l'apprentissage, le raisonnement, la résolution de problèmes, la perception et la compréhension du langage et même la création des images, vidéo et plus . Elle utilise des algorithmes et des données pour effectuer des tâches qui, traditionnellement, nécessitent une intelligence humaine. Elle est une technologie révolutionnaire en constante évolution. Depuis ses débuts théoriques dans les années 1950 jusqu'aux applications avancées d'aujourd'hui, elle continue de transformer la société et ouvre des possibilités immenses pour l'avenir. Les grands riches ne voient pas l'intelligence artificielle comme une simple mode technologique, mais comme un multiplicateur de ressources. Là où d'autres dépensent leur temps sur des tâches répétitives, les riches délèguent ces tâches à des systèmes d'IA, libérant ainsi leur esprit pour des décisions stratégiques.

Pourquoi l'IA ?

L'IA offre une capacité surhumaine d'analyse, d'anticipation et d'automatisation, permettant de prendre des décisions basées sur des données précises et en temps réel. Exemple : Jeff Bezos et Amazon utilisent l'IA pour prévoir les comportements d'achat des clients et optimiser leurs stocks, ce qui génère des milliards d'économies.

Automatisation financière : Faites travailler votre argent pour vous

Les riches utilisent l'IA pour faire croître leurs finances tout en minimisant les risques. Voici comment :
- Investissements guidés par l' IA : Les plateformes comme Wealthfront et Betterment utilisent l' IA pour recommander des portefeuilles d'investissement personnalisés, adaptés aux objectifs financiers individuels. Analyse des opportunités : Des outils comme Bloomberg Terminal AI permettent aux riches d'identifier des tendances et opportunités sur les marchés financiers avant tout le monde. Gestion automatisée des budgets : L' IA aide à surveiller les dépenses et à optimiser la trésorerie avec des applications comme YNAB ou Mint. En fait, le secret est que les riches ne laissent rien au hasard. Chaque euro ou dollar est optimisé grâce à l'analyse prédictive.

Productivité personnelle : Maximisez votre temps

La gestion du temps est un facteur clé de réussite pour les riches. C est en cela que l' IA leur permet de libérer des heures précieuses en automatisant les tâches quotidiennes : Assistants virtuels : Des outils comme Calendly, Notion AI, ou ChatGPT organisent leurs plannings, répondent aux emails et résolvent des problèmes simples en un instant. Apprentissage accéléré : Les riches investissent dans eux-mêmes en utilisant des plateformes d'apprentissage IA (comme Duolingo, Coursera, ou Khan Academy) pour acquérir de nouvelles compétences rapidement. Exemple : Elon Musk, l'un des hommes d'affaires les plus riches de notre temps, utilise des outils d' IA pour apprendre et s'organiser, ce qui lui permet de diriger plusieurs entreprises en même temps.

Développer des entreprises intelligentes avec l'IA

Les grands entrepreneurs exploitent l'IA pour créer et scaler leurs entreprises : Création de contenu automatisé : Avec des outils comme Jasper AI ou Canva, ils produisent des textes, des designs et des publicités en quelques minutes. Analyse de marché : Les riches utilisent des plateformes comme Google Trends ou Tableau AI pour repérer les besoins émergents sur lesquels bâtir leurs entreprises. Service client optimisé : Les chatbots IA réduisent les coûts tout en améliorant l'expérience client. Conseil : Adoptez ces outils pour maximiser vos revenus passifs et réduire vos coûts opérationnels.

Préparez-vous pour l'avenir avec l'IA

Les riches investissent dans l'IA non seulement pour aujourd'hui, mais pour dominer demain. Ils comprennent que l'IA n'est pas une option, mais une nécessité pour rester compétitifs. Investissez dans l'IA : Achetez des actions dans des entreprises technologiques ou lancez des projets axés sur l'IA. A cette allure où vont les choses, il est vivement recommandé de vous adapter au changement : Apprenez à collaborer avec l'IA et non à la craindre.Pour ceux qui aiment la pratique, voici un peu ma propre expérience. Durant mes temps de richesses pour pouvoir écrire cette immense œuvre, j'ai demandé a chatGPT, l'un des outils de l'IA connus et révolutionnaire, de me faire la liste des petites actions boursières qui ne valent pas vingt dollars chacune. Et j'ai investi environ mille dollars dans deux différentes. Imaginez ce qui s'est passé! J'ai fais deux milles trois cent dollars dans le trimestre suivant.Donc je sais de quoi il est question. La meilleure manière aussi de bien l'utiliser est de lui poser des questions précises et concrètes. Notez aussi qu'ils peuvent faire des erreurs, donc prenez le temps de bien réviser leur propositions et la décision finale doit venir de vous en tant qu'être humain. Bien que les grands États vont mettre des loi en place dans le future pour réglementer cette industrie pour protéger les droits d'auteur, l'IA reste un outil très important pour vous aider à avoir un avenir brillant. Une simple vision : "Ceux qui ignorent l'IA aujourd'hui seront dépassés demain."

Conclusion : Faites de l'IA votre serviteur, pas votre rival

Les riches savent que l'IA, bien utilisée, est une arme puissante pour bâtir des empires. "L'intelligence artificielle est le levier des visionnaires. Elle transforme les rêves audacieux en réalités inévitables." Elle peut vous aider à automatiser vos finances, maximiser votre productivité et développer des entreprises prospères.Les temps changent, et avec eux, de nouvelles opportunités révolutionnaires émergent. Les grands riches savent que pour rester en tête, ils doivent exploiter les outils les plus puissants de notre époque. Et aujourd'hui, **l'intelligence artificielle (IA)** est l'une des armes les plus redoutables pour dominer dans presque tous les domaines. Le secret est simple : adoptez une mentalité de croissance et exploitez les outils d'IA dès aujourd'hui.

CONCLUSION

Active ton potentiel

Conclusion : Active ton potentiel

Félicitations, tu as maintenant en main les meilleurs et grands **secrets** que les personnes riches utilisent pour transformer leur vie. Mais ces secrets ne resteront que des idées si tu ne les mets pas en pratique. L'action est ce qui fait la différence entre ceux qui rêvent et ceux qui réussissent. L'action est la clé du changement, tout ce que tu as appris dans ce livre ne sert à rien si tu n'agis pas. Les riches ne se contentent pas de planifier ou de rêver. Ils prennent des décisions, agissent rapidement, et ajustent leurs stratégies en fonction des résultats. Chaque petite action aujourd'hui te rapproche de la vie que tu désires. N'attends pas demain. Commence dès aujourd'hui. Le plus grand risque est de ne rien risquer. Si tu veux changer, tu dois oser faire ce que les autres n'osent pas. Chaque pas que tu fais dans la bonne direction, aussi petit soit-il, te rapproche de tes objectifs

Ton challenge : Applique es secrets puissants dès aujourd'hui

Le défi ? Choisis **une action clé** dans ces secrets et applique-la **dès aujourd'hui**. Cela peut être aussi simple que de commencer à épargner, d'identifier une compétence à développer ou de prendre contact avec une personne influente. L'importance est de ne pas remettre à demain ce que tu peux commencer maintenant.

"Le plus grand risque est de ne rien risquer." – **Oprah Winfrey**

Le véritable risque, c'est de ne jamais passer à l'action. L'opportunité est devant toi. Maintenant, c'est à toi de la saisir. Active ton potentiel et commence dès aujourd'hui à créer la vie que tu mérites.

www.ingramcontent.com/pod-product-compliance
Lightning Source LLC
Chambersburg PA
CBHW060518030426
42337CB00015B/1933

Intentional Influence

Harnessing Cultural Mapping to Build Commitment

Ben Johnson

Bobby Dodd

ConnectEDD Publishing
Hanover, Pennsylvania

Copyright © 2025 by Ben Johnson and Bobby Dodd
All rights reserved. No part of this publication may be reproduced, distributed, or transmitted in any form or by any means, including photocopying, recording, or other electronic or mechanical methods, without the prior written permission of the publisher, except in the case of brief quotations embodied in critical reviews and certain other noncommercial uses permitted by copyright law. For permission requests, contact the publisher at: info@connecteddpublishing.com

This publication is available at discount pricing when purchased in quantity for educational purposes, promotions, or fundraisers. For inquiries and details, contact the publisher at: info@connecteddpublishing.com

Published by ConnectEDD Publishing LLC
Hanover, PA
www.connecteddpublishing.com

Cover Design: Kheila Casas

Intentional Influence —1st ed. Paperback
ISBN 979-8-9933700-0-2

Praise for *Intentional Influence*

Intentional Influence is a refreshing guide to leadership built on strong principles—personal accountability, relationship-driven culture, and capacity-building within organizations. Dr. Johnson's approach is research-informed yet highly practical, offering tools leaders can put to work immediately. Through memorable stories and metaphors, he shows how intentional leadership can transform compliance into true commitment. As a state superintendent and nominee for U.S. Assistant Secretary, I found this book both deeply authentic and empowering—an invaluable resource for anyone entrusted with leading others."

–Kirsten Baesler | ND State Superintendent and US Education Assistant Secretary

Having spent the last fifteen years leading school systems, I've read my share of leadership books. Too many offer platitudes without a roadmap. This book is different. Ben Johnson and Bobby Dodd cut through the fluff and deliver a forward-thinking framework that respects the messy, human reality of school culture. The narrative of Ron's wake-up call sets the stage for why we need a new approach. Faced with survey data showing his staff felt unheard, he didn't look for a gimmick; he mapped his people, identified the true influencers and built a network of commitment. That level of candour about what it takes to move a culture resonated with me. It mirrors the challenges we face every day as superintendents when we discover that the public narrative about our schools doesn't match the lived experience of staff and students.

What makes this book stand out is its insistence that influence isn't tied to a title. Johnson and Dodd show how Cultural Mapping exposes the informal networks that actually drive change, allowing leaders to leverage committed staff to re-energize a culture. They explain, with practical examples, how to identify commitment levels, use spheres of influence, and create cascades of leadership that ripple through an organization. This isn't theory; it's a blueprint grounded in relationships and data.

As someone who has led districts through crises and change, I appreciate their blunt acknowledgement that transformation isn't linear, and it's often messy. They rightly point out that systemic issues may be the source of dysfunction, but the power to address them begins with us. If you're looking for a way to build a coherent culture where people feel seen and committed to the mission, *Intentional Influence* is it. Don't pick it up expecting an easy fix. Pick it up because you're ready to do the hard work of mapping relationships, investing in people, and leading with authenticity.

–Mike Lubelfeld | Superintendent, Author, and Consultant

School leaders working to create the learning outcomes for students' greatest success know that they need to build committed staff members, teams, and communities. Beyond identifying the importance of that culture, *Intentional Influence: Harnessing Cultural Mapping to Build Commitment*, provides the strategies and steps to guide leaders' actions. A great book study for school leadership teams mapping the path to continuous learning for everyone.

–Steve Barkley | Chief Learning Officer, PLS3rdLearning

In an era where educational change is both constant and critical, this book offers a much-needed compass for leaders seeking to transform their schools. It masterfully reveals that true influence extends far beyond a title, operating instead through the intentional cultivation of relationships and a deep understanding of your people. The strategic framework of Cultural Mapping offers a powerful and practical guide to building a resilient, collaborative culture that can sustain change and enhance outcomes for everyone. This is a must-read for any leader ready to move from simply managing a school to intentionally shaping its future.

—Eric Sheninger | Keynote speaker and best-selling author

Intentional Influence: Harnessing Cultural Mapping to Build Commitment is the essential roadmap for any leader struggling to move beyond compliance and cultivate genuine, sustainable commitment. Ben Johnson and Bobby Dodd deliver a powerful and practical framework centered on 'Cultural Mapping,' an actionable strategy that illuminates the hidden forces shaping team behavior. They redefine the concept of influence that is essential for leaders to possess for profound, lasting change. This book is a must-read for anyone serious about elevating their leadership, fostering deep dedication, and ensuring their vision translates into collective action.

—Neil Gupta | Superintendent, Oakwood Schools, Ohio

Intentional Influence: Harnessing Cultural Mapping to Build Commitment is a masterclass in understanding how true leadership begins from within and radiates outward to shape culture, inspire commitment, and transform organizations. Rooted in servant leadership and the power of intentionality, this book offers a practical roadmap for leaders to map influence, build trust, and re-engage the disengaged. Through a blend of research, reflection, and actionable strategies, it shows how culture isn't built by accident; it's cultivated by purpose-driven leaders who serve first and influence always. For anyone passionate about leading with heart, vision, and impact, this is essential reading.

—Glenn Robbins | Award-Winning Educational Leader, Best Selling Author, Speaker

Intentional Influence captures the essence of leading in today's schools—navigating complexity, fostering trust, and inspiring growth amid constant change. As a longtime principal, I know the strain of balancing accountability demands with protecting space for teachers to innovate and kids to thrive—a tension this book addresses with refreshing clarity. It is a timely, essential guide offering practical wisdom and perspective for anyone shaping the future of education.

>–Michael Acomb | Director of Business and Personnel, Solon (OH) City Schools; Veteran Principal and Career Educator

Intentional Influence is more than a leadership book. It's a roadmap for building cultures of trust, connection, and purpose. Ben Johnson and Bobby Dodd bring fresh insight into the often-overlooked networks of influence that shape organizations. Their Cultural Mapping framework equips leaders to build trust, re-engage teams, and multiply impact. This is a must-read for anyone serious about creating a thriving culture of commitment.

>–Dr. Winston Y. Sakurai | National Digital Principal of the Year & Hawaii State Principal of the Year

Intentional Influence by Ben Johnson and Bobby Dodd is a must-read for every educational leader who believes that relationships are at the heart of meaningful change. I was deeply moved by its blend of insight, authenticity, and practical strategies. The Cultural Mapping process is truly transformational. It helps leaders see the invisible threads of influence that shape a school's culture and shows how small, intentional actions can spark lasting impact. Johnson and Dodd remind us that leadership is less about position and more about purpose, connection, and heart. This book rekindles the joy of leading and inspires a renewed commitment to building schools where every person feels valued, empowered, and part of something extraordinary.

>–Dr. Robyn Jordan | K-12 Educational Administrator

How many times have you heard others attribute organizational success or failure to culture? And it's true!" Intentional Influence" explains and visualizes culture within the complex web of dynamics that exist in school buildings of relationships, behavior, and impact. As you read it, you can picture the ecosystem, understand the social architecture of people who work there, and more importantly - how a leader can positively harness collaboration from this knowledge to make their school a place where kids want to learn and teachers want to teach.

–Dr. Jim Mahoney | Executive Director, Emeritus, Battelle for Kids and Assistant Professor, Voinovich School of Leadership and Public Service, Ohio University

Intentional Influence: Harnessing Cultural Mapping to Build Commitment by Ben Johnson and Bobby Dodd is unlike any book on school culture I've encountered. The book offers a clear roadmap for understanding both the science and art of building thriving learning communities. The mapping instructions are so actionable and would be transformational for any leader who engages in the practice. In this book, you will learn how to visualize professional networks by identifying people and categorizing their influence, clarifying commitment levels, and mapping relational change. This structured approach will help you turn complex human dynamics into a clear, actionable strategic process. If you are seeking to better understand your own leadership, your team, and how to build collective efficacy, read this book and then take action.

–William D. Parker, Founder, Principal Matters, LLC

This book is unique in that within it, leadership philosophy bumps headlong into daily leadership challenges. Chapter by chapter, the authors offer a road map to improvement, complete with examples, tools, and guidance. Throughout, readers can envision how to build the kind of culture everyone wants, and moreover, how to maintain it.

–Dr. Tamara Uselman | Retired Superintendent, Leadership Consultant

In *Intentional Influence*, Dr. Ben Johnson and Dr. Bobby Dodd elevate culture mapping from idea to implementation. They begin with a global view—making visible the relationships, informal networks, and strengths that shape a school—then guide readers through a clear, step-by-step process to build their own culture map. Each step highlights what to consider (who's at the table, trust levels, key connectors, friction points, and evidence to gather), replacing assumptions with shared clarity. The result is a practical blueprint that helps leaders see people first, align strengths, and move the whole system forward with intention.

–Jim Wichman, EdS | Leadership Catalyst | Inspiration Architect

Intentional Influence is a powerful and timely work that shows how culture drives commitment and lasting change. Johnson and Dodd offer a practical, research-based framework for leading with purpose and authenticity. Their insights on Cultural Mapping remind us that real progress happens when leaders understand people, systems, and the influence that connects them."

–Dr. James Driscoll | Superintendent of Tempe Elementary Schools

Intentional Influence is a powerful exploration of how relationships and influence shape the heart of every school culture. Dodd and Johnson highlight that authentic leadership isn't confined to titles but flows through the invisible networks of trust and connection that exist within every team. Their framework for Cultural Mapping provides leaders with a practical approach to visualize and leverage these networks, identifying key influencers, collaboration gaps, and the 'invisible energy' driving momentum. By focusing on subcultures, critical connectors, and the social dynamics that make schools thrive, this work turns the abstract idea of culture into an actionable leadership practice. It's a must-read for anyone serious about leading change through connection, reflection, and intentional influence.

–Joe Sanfelippo, PhD. | Retired Superintendent, Author, Speaker

As someone who's spent years coaching leaders and building businesses from the ground up, I found *Intentional Influence* to be both a mirror and a map—a reflection of what great leadership looks like in practice, and a practical framework for cultivating it across any organization.

Ben Johnson and Bobby Dodd introduce "Cultural Mapping" as more than a diagnostic tool—it's a system for understanding how influence truly flows through an organization. As a coach, I often see teams mistake authority for influence. This book dismantles that assumption. Through the authors' narrative storytelling and case studies, particularly the story of "Ron," readers see how informal leaders—those without titles—often carry the greatest cultural weight.

What impressed me most was how the framework transcends education, where it's rooted, and applies directly to business, startups, and high-performing teams. In my own experience leading entrepreneurs and operators, I've learned that growth depends on one thing: commitment. Johnson and Dodd don't just talk about engagement—they map it. Their process helps you see who's committed, who's compliant, and who's quietly shaping the culture for better or worse. It's the kind of tool every leader wishes they had during periods of change or scale.

–Patrick Klein | Operating Partner in Vessel, LLC, and ex-college basketball coach

Intentional Influence is a reminder that cultural change must first take place internally, then externally through concentric circles of influence. Dr. Ben Johnson and Bobby Dodd provide research-based and practical strategies to help leaders implement a framework, such as their Cultural Mapping tool, for improving school culture by focusing on adult behavior, highlighting champions, and tapping into their influence to increase commitment to the school's mission, vision, and values. In these uncertain times, whether you are leading a struggling school turnaround or maintaining excellence in a high-performing building, this framework is exactly what aspiring, new, or veteran administrators need.

–Dwight Carter | award-winning K-12 school administrator, best-selling author, and Presenter

The process of Cultural Mapping—from leading oneself to leading others and organizations—profoundly motivated my experience as a district educational leader. Rooted in relational insight, the thought processes within each map continues to empower me to build people-first systems grounded in connection and purpose, allowing me to lead authentically while staying true to my passion for education.

–Tana Sukauskas | Executive Director, AVID Center

What struck me immediately about Ben Johnson and Bobby Dodd's *Intentional Influence* is the unique lens the authors provide to affect systemic change in schools. Strong school culture doesn't occur by happenstance; it is a purposeful reflection and reaction of the work, ethos, and attitude of your educational microcosm. The book inspires you to seize and recognize these powerful elements and then craft an individual roadmap. The book is filled with authenticity: I loved the real-school stories and anecdotes from the trenches that help personalize this book. *Intentional Influence* strikes the perfect balance between theory, strategy, and school-based application by showing the beneficial ripples from relationships and networking in action.

–Brian McCann | Principal Emeritus, Joseph Case High School, Swansea, Mass., Massachusetts High School Principal of the Year, NASSP Digital Principal of the Year

In *Intention Influence*, Dr. Johnson provides leaders an opportunity to strategically identify the influencers in an organization and community. His approach removes the guessing game and offers leaders an opportunity to not only think critically about their own leadership but to zero in on others who hold influence. By using a systemic cultural process, Dr. Johnson creates the condition for leaders to name the influential leaders as well as a guide on how to harness the potential that influence holds. This book serves the whole spectrum of leaders, from those serving in their first leadership roles to those seasoned veterans looking for ways to maximize their own influence and impact. A special thank you to Ben and Bobby for helping me to continuously improve!

–Matt Degner | Superintendent, Iowa City Community School District

Intentional Influence: Harnessing Cultural Mapping to Build Commitment is a practical resource designed to help leaders leverage influence and foster shared commitment to the challenging and purposeful work in our learning organizations. Through a mix of engaging narrative and a grounding framework embedded throughout the book, the authors convey an impactful message that enables readers to develop leadership acumen, as well as specific strategies for intentionally influencing culture within their organizations.

–Dr. Sarah Johnson | Senior Associate and Leadership Coach

The biggest challenge in schools tends to be EXECUTION. Johnson and Dodd detail in this book a unique but systemic process for successfully implementing educational initiatives. Rooted in decades of proven experience and change leadership, their emphasis on cultural mapping, networks of influence, and intentional organizational cascades is an extremely powerful combination and the focus on troubleshooting common problems is particularly useful. Simply put, this thoughtful and practical book helps school administrators do their work better.

–Dr. Scott McLeod | Professor of Educational Leadership, University of Colorado Denver; Founding Director, CASTLE

Intentional Influence is a powerful and timely resource for today's school and district leaders who understand that culture—not compliance—drives sustainable change. Ben Johnson and Bobby Dodd offer a thoughtful and actionable framework for transforming relationships into results through the art and science of cultural mapping. Their insights bridge leadership theory and real-world practice, showing how intentional influence can unite teams, elevate commitment, and amplify impact across an organization. Every educator serious about leading people—rather than programs—should read this book and apply its lessons to build the kind of culture where both staff and students thrive.

–Dr Matthew Friedman | Superintendent of Schools, Quakertown Community School District (PA)

Dedication

From Ben:

I thank my wife, Brigitte, and my daughters Isabella and Sophia for the love and support they have given me over the years of hard work and sacrificed family time. To my wife Brigitte, your love and faith in my work have carried me through the countless hours of writing. To Isabella and Sophia, I hope one day you will find your own passions, educational pursuits, and influence those in your personal and professional walks of life.

A special thanks to Jimmy Casas for encouraging me to be the best educational leader - one who focuses on building culture and relationships. I'm grateful not just for your guidance and advice over the years, but for your constant encouragement to grow into the best version of myself—so I can better serve fellow leaders, educators, and students.

I also thank my past professors, colleagues, and mentors: I'm grateful to all who have supported my growth - from a passionate teacher to a leader dedicated to cultivating culture and leading learning.

From Bobby:

To my beloved wife, Charity, and my wonderful daughters, Sydney, Kaitlyn, and Sophie – your love and support have been my greatest inspiration. To my parents, Bob and Mary, whose unwavering encouragement and belief in me have been the foundation of my journey.

To all the dedicated staff I have had the privilege of working with over the years – your unwavering care for students and colleagues, often equal the care you show your own families, is truly inspiring. Thank you for your steadfast commitment to making a difference every day.

Table of Contents

Foreword xxiii

SECTION I:
LEADING ONESELF

Introduction: *Intentional Influence: Harnessing Cultural Mapping to Build Commitment*. 1
    The Joy of the Work: The Power to Influence 6
    Cascades of Leadership 8

Chapter 1: *Leading Oneself: Building a Culture of Influence*. 13
    The Power of Leadership: Unleashing Cascades of Influence. ... 13
    Presence of Systemic Leadership 14
    Inner Leadership: Becoming the Leader Others Need 16
    Leading a Culture of Influence 19
    Cultivating the Culture and Leading the Learning 20
    Leading Change Across an Organization 21

SECTION II:
LEADING OTHERS

Chapter 2: *Leading Others: Creating a Culture of Influence* 23
    Cultivating a Sphere of Influence 25
    Diffusion of Innovation 27

Leveraging Social Capital into Professional Capital 28
Multiply Your Impact: Investing in Your People 30
The Power of Investing in One-on-One Meetings 32
Windows and Mirrors: Coaching and Feedback to
    Empower Growth 34
Empowering and Developing Commitment................. 35

Chapter 3: *Leading Others: Cultivating Commitment* 37
The Committed: The Importance of the Committed 38
Nearly Committed: Prioritizing Commitment for
    Organizational Growth 40
Compliant: Cultivating Commitment 42
Disengaged: Re-engaging the Disengaged 44
Resisters: Managing Resistance 46
Considerations for Cultivating Commitment................ 47
Elevating Organizational Influence 60

Chapter 4: *Leading Others: Dealing with Disengagement and Navigating Resistance* 61
A Comeback Story - Disengaged and Burned Out 61
Re-engaging the Resisters and Disengaged.................. 63
A Leaders Role to Re-engaging the Disengaged 64
Reigniting Engagement 65

Chapter 5: *Leading Others: Navigating Distractors and Mitigating Resisters* 67
Strategies for Navigating Distractors and Mitigating
    Resisters 68
Healing the Dysfunction within a Culture 72

TABLE OF CONTENTS

SECTION III:
LEADING THROUGH CULTURAL MAPPING

Chapter 6: *Leading through Cultural Mapping* 77
    Why Cultural Mapping Matters 77
    Two Roles for Cultural Mapping 78
    Cultural Mapping: What is it? 79
    The Impact of Cultural Mapping 80

Chapter 7: *Creating a Cultural Map* 83
    Phase 1: Creating a Cultural Map – Visualizing
        Professional Networks 83
    Step 1: Map Your People – Categorize Members' Influence ... 85
    Step 2: Categorize Commitment Levels 92
    Step 3: Map the Relational Connectivity and Influence 97
    Emergence of the Cultural Map 100

Chapter 8: *Cultural Mapping Reflections* 103
    Phase 2: Cultural Mapping Reflections – Influence
        and Commitment 103
    Step 1: Map the Community Groups 105
    Step 2: Assess Commitment Levels 106
    Step 3: Evaluate Relational Connectivity and Influence 106
    Cultural Mapping Reflections 110

Chapter 9: *Cultural Mapping Planning* 113
    Phase 3: Cultural Mapping Planning –
        Using the Framework 113
    Step 1: Gain Insights Into Influence 114
    Step 2: Identify Entry Points to Moving Forward 124
    Step 3: Understand Your People – Show What You Know ... 125
    Cultural Mapping for Organizational Improvement 128

Chapter 10: *Moving Forward: 10 Practical Applications of Cultural Mapping* 131
    Understanding Cultural Influence and Connections. 132
    Visualizing Professional Networks 132
    Assessing Communication and the Flow of Influence. 133
    Uncovering the Power of Influencers. 133
    Building a Coalition of the Committed 134
    Multiplying Positive Effects throughout the Organization . . . 134
    Scaling Professional Development and Implementing
        Initiatives. 135
    Addressing Disengagement and Active Resisters. 136
    Amplifying the Unheard: Empowering Voices. 136
    Strategically Investing Your Time and Effort 137

SECTION IV:
LEADING ORGANIZATIONS

Chapter 11: *Leading Teams: Collaborative Cultures of Influence* 141
    Three Rings of Influence 141
    Subcultures: Teams within Organizations 143
    Building Collaborative Cultures of Commitment 144
    Critical Connectors within Teams 145
    People and Subcultures 146

Chapter 12: *Leading Cultural Cascades: Cultivating an Organization of Influence* 149
    Cultural Cascades: Compounding Effect of Commitment. . . . 152
    Leadership Cascades: Leading Others, Teams,
        and Organizations. 153
    The Power of Positive Stories. 156
    Cultivating Intentional Influence 158

TABLE OF CONTENTS

Chapter 13: *Leading Initiative Cascades:*
Organizational Learning 161
    Creating an Ecosystem for Learning 161
    Administrators as Lead Learners 162
    Leveraging Initiative Cascades for Professional Learning..... 164
    Sustainability of the Profession and Initiatives 168
    Leading Organizational Learning 170

Chapter 14: *Ron's Journey of Cultural Transformation* 173
    How Can I Be Ron?.. 173
    Embracing the Joy of the Leadership Journey: Engaging
        in the Right Work 175
    Building the Culture We Want: Transforming
        Organizational Culture................................... 177
    Your Leadership Journey.................................... 179

References 181

About the Authors.. 185

More from ConnectEDD Publishing.............................. 189

Foreword

BY DR. PHIL WARRICK

No person in an organization truly works alone. Each person's actions influence or inform other peoples' actions. It is through relationships, networks, and conversations that organizations are shaped and progress is made. In this insightful work, Dr. Ben Johnson introduces readers to an underexplored aspect of leadership: the power of influence within an organization. Dr. Johnson's research and understanding of human interactions have led him to develop a unique approach—**Cultural Mapping**—that enables leaders to recognize both formal and informal influencers within their organizations.

Traditional leadership models tend to focus on structural hierarchies, assuming authority and influence flow directly from titles and formal roles. Yet, as Dr. Johnson demonstrates, some of the most influential figures in an organization may not be those at the top of the organizational chart. Rather, they are those who, through relationships and trust, inspire, guide, and informally lead others. Dr. Johnson's Cultural Mapping techniques provide a clear, systematic method for identifying these influential individuals, understanding the networks of influence they create, and harnessing their potential to strengthen the organization.

The process of Cultural Mapping, as laid out in this book, is rooted in Dr. Johnson's keen insight into both organizational behavior and individual psychology. His methods empower leaders to strategically engage key influencers to improve an organization's function, efficiency, and morale. Whether applied within a small organization such as a single department in a school or across an entire school staff, Dr. Johnson's influence mapping approach is versatile and scalable, making it relevant for organizations of all sizes and types.

As you embark on this journey through Dr. Johnson's work, prepare to think deeply about how you view influence, leadership, and change. This book is not just about theory; it is a practical guide that will equip you with the tools to understand and navigate the complex web of human influence within your own organization.

SECTION I

Leading Oneself

INTRODUCTION

Intentional Influence: Harnessing Cultural Mapping to Build Commitment

Sitting in his office in the early evening, Ron stared out the window, an internal struggle churning within him. The data on his computer screen filled him with a deep sense of embarrassment, quickly followed by fear and anger. He felt paralyzed, unsure of what to do next. Gazing out at the fading light, his thoughts turned to his father—how much he respected him, and what a remarkable leader, father, and friend he had been. Ron knew that if his dad were still alive, he would be deeply disappointed by these results—and by how Ron's staff perceived his leadership.

As a high school principal, Ron was a well-regarded leader within his extensive network of peers, and from the outside, it appeared he maintained that reputation with his staff and students. Although his school was often seen as a model of positive culture, the reality was more complex—many staff, students, and stakeholders felt unsupported and unheard. This disconnect came to a head when the district began assessing each school's culture through survey data collected from both staff and students.

As the data was collected throughout the fall, it confirmed what Ron hadn't fully seen—staff and students did not feel a strong sense of belonging or perceived care from the administration. Understandably, Ron was devastated by the feedback. It wasn't the individual comments in the open-response section that affected him most; it was the overall perception of his leadership team. His assistant principals were empathetic, compassionate people who didn't deserve the labels reflected in the responses. Ron realized it was he who needed to change. He needed to prioritize building relationships and lead his team in transforming the school's culture.

One thing in particular continued to weigh on Ron, and he couldn't let it go. He had lost his father, Jerry, the previous year, right in the middle of the school year. Jerry was something of a local legend—known and loved by nearly everyone in town. He owned a business where both clients and employees deeply respected him. None of his staff ever left for other opportunities; in fact, some had worked with him for over 40 years. Ron knew this loyalty stemmed from the culture Jerry had built—one grounded in relationships. Jerry led with compassion and empathy, not just in business but in every aspect of his life. Those values weren't just how he managed—they were who he was.

Ron knew, deep down, that he had lost his way. He had forgotten who he was as a leader and lost sight of the importance of helping staff feel they were part of something meaningful—something they were building together. He had overlooked the reality that, in order for staff to meet the needs of all students, they needed a leader who served them by intentionally creating an environment where they felt supported, connected, and empowered to give their best. Ron realized he had a choice to make—a path to choose. He thought to himself, "I can either give up and walk away, or I can do something about this." As he reflected on his dad, a wave of clarity, peace, and renewed excitement came over him. He knew exactly what he had to do next.

The next morning, Ron met with his team and began outlining a plan for how they could work together to improve the school's culture. With more than two hundred staff members, the task felt daunting—but they were determined to face the challenge and make meaningful change. After hours of reviewing the data and dwelling on the negative feedback, they realized they were getting nowhere. Their breakthrough came when they shifted from a deficit mindset to a strengths-based approach—focusing on the positive aspects of the data to leverage existing strengths in addressing areas of need. This perspective allowed them to develop a clear, strategic plan to move forward with purpose and impact.

Despite the sense of defeat, the team recognized that not all staff morale was negative. They knew firsthand that many staff members genuinely felt they worked in a great place. Positive voices were present within the building—and many of those voices belonged to both formal and informal **influencers**. One assistant principal posed a thoughtful question: "How can we get the most out of our top staff members—the ones who are fully **committed** to the vision and direction we've been working toward? How can they help build our culture and influence others?" Ron considered the question for a moment, then responded, "Well, let's start by naming them. Who's on board? Let's get their names up on the whiteboard."

It's amazing how something as simple as writing names on a board can begin to transform an organization. This was the start of what became known as "**Culture Mapping**." The team began by mapping out a network of influence—intentionally naming their culture builders and identifying the colleagues and friends connected to them. From there, they started planning social events and creating opportunities for these culture builders to inspire and develop more culture builders.

As the connections took shape, the team experienced a renewed sense of purpose. They began to see how leveraging professional and social networks could drive meaningful change. This collaborative effort marked a significant step toward transforming the school's culture and aligned with Ron's newfound clarity and determination.

As the year progressed, the team continued collecting data and made quarterly adjustments using the Culture Map as their guide. Ron rediscovered his sense of purpose and reconnected with what leadership is truly about—the joy of serving and leading others. He came to understand that by recognizing the often-invisible culture of influence within the staff and intentionally investing in those who were committed, his team could strategically leverage their leadership and relationships to build capacity among their peers.

Over time, as the data was collected and analyzed, staff began to experience a noticeable shift in how they interacted—with one another, with students, and with leadership. Behind the scenes, the administration's use of Culture Mapping helped lay a strong foundation for this transformation. Ron felt a renewed sense of fulfillment—he had found his way back. By helping create a culture rooted in relationships, he had returned to his core values and rediscovered his purpose as a leader. He found joy in changing the trajectory of individual lives and took pride in seeing others achieve a healthy personal-professional life fit while making a broader impact on the community they served together.

The Joy of the Work: The Power to Influence

The widespread absence of systemic leadership across organizations—particulary in education—highlights a critical gap in the ability to navigate and transform dysfunctional systems. Yet, the essence of true leadership extends beyond formal titles. It lies in the ability of individuals at all levels to enact meaningful change. It is a calling, entrusted to anyone willing to lead with intention and integrity. The practice of Cultural Mapping to "create a culture of intentional influence" is grounded in the belief that while systemic issues may be the source of dysfunction, the power to address them starts within us. By embracing our innate leadership potential and intentionally investing in relationships, we can move systems toward greater functionality through connection and strategic action.

The recent pandemic underscored that educators do far more than deliver academic instruction—they also play a vital role in supporting students' social-emotional and behavioral needs. Addressing the whole child is complex and demanding work, making education a true calling rather than just a job. Educators are passionate and committed individuals who often grapple with finding the right personal-professional life fit. At the heart of authentically leading others is the rediscovery of the joy in one's work—being entrusted to lead—by prioritizing the cultural needs of staff and nurturing a deep sense of purpose in leading the learning.

As leaders, we must continually work to "Cultivate the Culture" and "Lead the Learning" to help our members develop the skills and mindsets needed for our organization. This process is complex and not always linear; at times, it can feel messy and uncertain. Yet, we have the privilege of knowing that transformative change happens when we face challenges together and learn from the fires that test us. These experiences reveal where we need to build capacity in our people and highlight areas where our systems can be improved by providing clarity and structure.

The popularity of social media platforms such as Facebook, X (formerly Twitter), Instagram, TikTok, and LinkedIn highlights the importance of social connections and the powerful influence individuals can have on others' thoughts and behaviors. Yet long before the rise of social media, influential individuals were already shaping our personal and professional lives. Much like a geographic map, Cultural Mapping allows us to visually analyze complex networks of relationships within an organization and identify the key influencers who drive culture and change.

Stanley Milgram's (1960) research on social connections introduced the concept of six degrees of separation, highlighting the interconnectedness of individuals. For leaders, understanding these social dynamics is essential for identifying organizational influencers and assessing commitment to the culture and initiatives. Recognizing the influence these key individuals have within an organization can lead to both obvious and subtle effects in guiding the organization toward its goals. By harnessing their impact, leaders can cultivate the desired culture, drive learning, and effectively scale strategic plans to achieve intended outcomes.

As consultants and coaches in school leadership, we view harnessing Cultural Mapping to serve not only as a diagnostic tool but also as a strategic framework for empowered leadership—one that leverages relational insights to build a more connected and committed culture that aligns all members with the organization's common direction. Cultural Mapping offers an opportunity to create a culture of coherence and structure to what might otherwise be an unrecognized "cultural cascade." Armed with this understanding, leaders can intentionally create a culture of intentional influence that generates momentum for the organization's vision and goals. In doing so, we cultivate an environment that nurtures collective efficacy and fulfillment in the work we do.

Cascades of Leadership

Creating a culture of intentional influence empowers leaders at all levels to practice systemic leadership, transforming challenges into opportunities for growth and meaningful impact. Cultural Mapping not only helps leaders navigate the complexities of their roles but also fosters a culture of influence grounded in relationships and purpose. This framework provides a structured method for any leader—regardless of title—to actively shape and influence organizational culture. At its core, leadership begins with a simple yet powerful truth: be true to

> Cultural Mapping not only helps leaders navigate the complexities of their roles but also fosters a culture of influence grounded in relationships and purpose.

who you are. In that rediscovery lies the joy, purpose, and strength to lead your people well.

Leading Oneself to Lead Others: To lead others well, leaders must first look inward to clearly understanding their core values. As Jimmy Casas (2017) emphasized in *Culturize*, educators must understand and operate from a foundation of their own core values. This approach enables leaders to align their actions with the core values that first drew them into education, helping them reconnect with the deeper motivations behind their commitment to serve. Leaders who embody the values and beliefs of their organization can inspire employees to higher levels of engagement (Maxwell, 2007). Offering guidance and support sends a clear message of investment—giving the time and energy that people often need to be inspired to reach their full potential. Their influence is expressed through words and actions that have both direct and indirect effects, creating a ripple that helps shape organizational culture.

By building relationships with key influencers, leaders can leverage their social capital and convert it into professional capital to gain support for change initiatives and generate momentum for cultural commitment across the organization. Frustration is inevitable in leadership, especially when progress feels slow or it may even feel like an impossible challenge to move everyone. Leaders often ask, "What do I do about those that are disengaged? How do I shield others from the negative influence of active resisters?" The answer: transformation does not require everyone to move at once. Instead, leaders must intentionally invest in the committed members through their "spheres of influence." Leaders move everyone's level of commitment by building capacity in those committed members who have ripple effects that multiply their positive influence across others in the organization.

Leading through Cultural Mapping: *So, how can leaders systemically and systematically scale the professional capital throughout a team or an organization?* Cultural Mapping stands out as a powerful and practical solution. In practice, Cultural Mapping serves as a strategic process for leaders to visualize members' relational connections, commitment levels, influence within groups, and leverage professional capital to build a unified organizational culture of influence and successfully implement initiatives. Through our professional experiences, we have developed and witnessed the transformational power of Cultural Mapping that has empowered leaders to create an environment that fosters a culture where influence and commitment thrive.

Cultural Mapping is a systemic method for cultivating a strong, cohesive culture—especially within large organizations where communication breakdowns are common. This visualization process reveals the underlying networks and communication patterns among staff, while also identifying areas of resistance and gaps in collaboration. This method involves deeply engaging with the organizational landscape to identify both key influencers and those resistant to change, revealing the complex web of power and relational influence that shapes interpersonal connections. It enables leaders to reflect, explore step-by-step processes, and take concrete actions to impact culture and learning across their "spheres of influence." By employing Cultural Mapping, leaders can identify essential personnel, map and understand the hidden flow of influence, and apply a strategic approach to increase commitment to organizational goals and scale initiative implementation.

> **Leaders must understand that Culture Mapping is not just about individual actions, but about the cumulative, cascading effects of those behaviors on the overall culture and the implementation of initiatives.**

Leading Organizations through Teams and Cascades: To truly understand the complex relationship between leadership and the organizational ecosystem, Cultural Mapping serves as a vital tool that enables leaders to uncover and analyze the hidden web of relationships connecting *individuals, teams, and departments*. Leaders must understand that Culture Mapping is not just about individual actions, but about the cumulative, cascading effects of those behaviors on the overall culture and the implementation of initiatives. Organizations are made up of individuals connected through social and professional ties—a form of professional capital that can be intentionally leveraged and harnessed. By recognizing the "rings of influence" within their organization, leaders can focus their impact, build capacity in others, and create teams that nurture a culture of influence. These rings of influence may start small, but they ripple outward, ultimately shaping the entire organization.

Figure- Spheres of Influence

The figure above illustrates the cascading nature of influence. Creating a culture of intentional influence emphasises the importance of beginning with personal alignment at the center in leading oneself.

INTENTIONAL INFLUENCE

Cultural Mapping reveals how one's influence extends outward through other members, teams, and ripple effects throughout the broader organization. A leader's journey in transforming their school's culture reflects the broader work of creating cascades of intentional influence, ultimately leading to positive outcomes for students, educators, and the entire school community. Harnessing Cultural Mapping enables a transformative process that cultivates a committed culture rooted in leadership development at all levels: *leading oneself* to *lead others* by modeling and reinforcing desired behaviors, and systematically *leading teams* and the *organization* by creating cultural and initiative cascades. Drawing parallels to a thriving natural ecosystem, leaders can use Cultural Mapping to nurture interconnected relationships and build a resilient educational environment where your organization can not only adapt but flourish amid change. Leaders must intentionally cultivate a culture of influence grounded in relationships and a strong sense of collective efficacy, the shared belief among a group that through their combined efforts they can positively influence outcomes and achieve meaningful results.

Through three layers of influence, leaders can empower their team by fostering connections and commitment while activating and harnessing cascades of intentional influence.

CHAPTER 1

Leading Oneself: Building a Culture of Influence

The Power of Leadership: Unleashing Cascades of Influence

Ron visited Yellowstone with his young daughter Noelle, whose love of wolves bordered on an obsession for a bright seven-year-old. He patiently indulged her many questions as she eagerly listened, watched, and absorbed everything the National Park rangers had to share.

During their trip, Ron began to understand the profound impact that the reintroduction of wolves in 1995 had on Yellowstone National Park.

After wolves were eradicated in the early 1900s, their absence had disrupted the park's ecological balance. Their return, however, initiated dramatic changes. As a keystone species their mere presence and natural behaviors set off a series of cascading effects throughout the entire ecosystem. Trophic cascades refer to these ripple-like effects, where a single change can lead to widespread ecological transformation. In Yellowstone's case, the reintroduction of wolves curbed overgrazing by elk, which allowed vegetation to regenerate, increased biodiversity, and helped restore ecological balance (Ripple & Beschta, 2012). Other species, such as beavers and songbirds, also began to thrive.

Just as the wolves' resurgence reshaped Yellowstone, Ron realized that effective leadership can serve as a catalyst for transformations that ripple throughout an organization's workplace ecosystem. Leaders' actions, much like the presence of wolves, can unintentionally influence the behavior and outcomes of their teams and colleagues. Inspired by the concept of trophic cascades, Ron recognized the interconnectedness of all team members and how a leader's influence and actions can create ripple effects—triggering cascades of impact across the organization. Understanding these intended and unintended consequences is crucial for building a culture of influence that empowers individuals, fosters collaboration, and drives sustainable results. Conversely, Ron also realized that a lack of systemic leadership can have the opposite effect, breeding dysfunction and toxicity that erode morale and drive employee turnover. Leadership, like wolves in Yellowstone, has the power to either disrupt or heal—and the choice rests with those entrusted to lead.

Presence of Systemic Leadership

Systemic leadership is critical to the success of any organization (Fullan, 2001). Leadership can be viewed as the top of a trophic cascade, where leaders' actions have far-reaching intended and unintended effects across the entire system. The reintroduction of wolves into Yellowstone serves as a powerful metaphor, illustrating trophic cascade principles that apply to school leadership and their role in cultivating a culture of influence and leading learning.

Systemic leaders act as the keystone species essential to maintaining a healthy ecosystem within an organization. Their presence and influence can trigger cascading effects that drive positive change throughout the organizational culture. Without systemic leadership, individuals within an organization may become fragmented, and collaboration diminishes. Conversely, systemic leadership unifies and fosters a culture rooted in collective efficacy. Leaders set the tone for their organizations, articulating a clear vision and adapting to new challenges. During the COVID-19 pandemic, educational leaders at all levels stepped forward to guide their schools through unprecedented times. Teacher leaders played a pivotal role, influencing subcultures and supporting the work of their peers.

The success of a school often depends on the collective strength of its people to meet the needs of students, parents, and the wider community. When leaders function as a keystone species—by inspiring and supporting educators, engaging the community, and nurturing collaborative connections among all stakeholders—they create a cohesive and responsive culture that benefits everyone.

Every day, the relationship between learning and leadership unfolds across classrooms, practice courts, competition fields, stages, department meetings, hallways, boardrooms, and even casual water cooler conversations. While leadership is often perceived through a top-down, authoritative lens, the reality is far more complex. Yet, it is essential to recognize the rich, dynamic interplay behind the scenes. Many individuals—whose influence may not appear on an organizational chart—play vital roles in shaping progress.

Those engaged in the daily operations of an organization understand how certain individuals can significantly impact momentum:

some facilitate the flow of information and ideas, while others may inadvertently create bottlenecks that slow things down. Leaders must skillfully navigate these social and professional networks, acknowledging the power of relationships and individual behaviors to either accelerate or impede organizational progress. By cultivating a shared vision, leaders align the efforts of individuals and groups toward common goals. In doing so, they serve not only as decision-makers but also as facilitators of learning and champions of the organization's future state.

The story of the Yellowstone wolves illustrates how a single systemic change can generate far-reaching effects—a compelling metaphor for the transformative power of leadership. When leadership capacity is built across an organization, these cascading effects multiply, fostering a culture rooted in continuous improvement and collaboration. This kind of leadership not only addresses present-day challenges but also lays the foundation for long-term growth. Whether in classrooms, small groups, athletic teams, or performing arts programs, when subcultures are guided by committed leaders, we find countless opportunities for influence. These micro-leaders—students, teachers, and staff alike—help shape a school's culture in ways that reach far beyond its walls and into the broader community.

Inner Leadership: Becoming the Leader Others Need

Many people are driven by a strong sense of purpose. We believe that all leaders, in some capacity, must serve others and strive to develop leadership within their organizations. To build effective teams, leaders must first focus on their own personal growth by cultivating the mindset and skills necessary to help redefine an organization's collective vision and aspirations. To change the trajectory of an organization—whether a school or broader community—leaders must prioritize trust, connections, and commitment. A key element of shaping a strong culture

LEADING ONESELF: BUILDING A CULTURE OF INFLUENCE

is consistently living and sharing your core values, allowing others to understand the "why" behind your actions (Sinek, 2009). At times, it becomes necessary to return to those core values and establish a clear, simple process to realign everyone with the organization's vision. When trust is established, leaders can begin to build capacity, develop others' skills, and empower individuals to lead from any position. Although culture is shaped by the collective actions of individuals within the system, leadership sets the tone and provides the foundation from which that culture emerges.

Leaders must be intentional about self-care, ensuring we have enough in our own cups to pour into the people and systems we are entrusted to serve. By doing this, we model what it means to live a "rightly ordered life" and create a safe space for others to do the same. Depending on your role, "your people" may include fellow leaders, staff, peers, or students. Regardless of whom you lead, prioritizing their well-being and development is essential. This includes offering the support, resources, and opportunities for their growth. In doing so, we foster a culture that values both personal and professional development—ultimately leading to greater fulfillment and success for everyone involved.

> Leadership is fundamentally about harnessing one's natural strengths to create a cascading impact—producing "ripple effects" that influence the broader environment.

Much like the wolves in Yellowstone, leadership is fundamentally about harnessing one's natural strengths to create a cascading impact—producing "ripple effects" that influence the broader environment. The reintroduction of wolves illustrates the profound effects of systemic leadership and how even small, intentional actions can transform an entire ecosystem. This metaphor applies directly to schools, where seemingly minor, values-driven actions by leaders can spark significant positive change. When leaders operate from their core values and invest in relationships, they expand the leadership capacity of others through authentic, influential leadership. These efforts can drive incremental shifts in behavior and guide meaningful pedagogical changes that, over time, strengthen a cohesive school culture and support improved student outcomes.

Leadership shapes an organization's culture, and the ability to navigate both visible and invisible influences is crucial to its success. Visible influences—such as organizational structures, policies, and the physical environment—are easy to observe. In contrast, invisible influences like values, beliefs, and norms are less tangible but equally powerful. Leaders must engage with these underlying values and align them with organizational objectives to effectively address invisible influences. Tools such as surveys, interviews, and focus groups help reveal employees' perceptions, aspirations, and motivations, guiding leaders in making necessary cultural adjustments. Aligning visible elements with these goals then reinforces a healthy cultural shift. Leaders skilled at leveraging both visible and invisible influences can foster a sense of belonging and commitment, driving the organization toward a positive culture.

The Yellowstone example illustrates the power of interdependent influence to drive meaningful change. Just as the wolves helped restore the health of rivers, leaders must adopt a long-term vision rooted in patience, adaptability, and strategic action. Leaders must encourage staff and students to share ideas, take thoughtful risks, and actively participate in shaping a vibrant school culture. Transformative change requires leaders to not only guide but also inspire ongoing dedication to improvement and empower the school community to take ownership of their learning and cultural development.

LEADING ONESELF: BUILDING A CULTURE OF INFLUENCE

Leading a Culture of Influence

Leading by influence is a vital skill for cultivating a collaborative and innovative organizational culture. As leaders build relationships, trust, and open communication, they can leverage their personal influence and expertise to guide others toward shared goals. In less hierarchical, more autonomous organizations, the ability to lead by influence is more relevant than ever (Wheatley, 2006). This approach creates a workspace where ideas flow naturally and teamwork thrives. Effective leaders model the desired behaviors and personalize their communication to resonate with diverse team members through one-on-one or small group conversations. They create conditions that support learning and growth while understanding the unique motivations driving each individual. Such investments in building relationships require intentional time and energy to cultivate a culture where people are truly committed—not just compliant.

Reflecting on the leader's role in this process underscores their critical responsibility in shaping and analyzing organizational culture networks to ensure the success of the cultural cascade. In today's fast-paced world, where technology, stress, and professional challenges can create divisions, it is the leader's privilege and duty to nurture a highly effective system where individuals feel connected, experience belonging, and thrive in a culture of empowerment.

As leaders engage in Cultural Mapping, they must be intentional in cultivating a positive cultural influence. This involves deeply understanding the organization's strengths and areas needing attention, while applying techniques that systematically embed a culture of influence aimed at continuous improvement (Collins, 2001). By building capacity and empowering faculty, leaders can inspire individuals and small groups to lead learning and influence culture, ultimately driving improvement across the entire organization.

Cultivating the Culture and Leading the Learning

In education, the pendulum often swings from one extreme to the other, overlooking the need for perspective and balance. School administrators must understand that management and leadership are deeply intertwined and cannot be separated. Effective administrators are actively involved in a wide range of leadership responsibilities—such as handling discipline, conducting walk-throughs, being a welcoming and accessible presence, attending Professional Learning Communities, and participating in after-school events. Through these daily interactions, leaders maintain visibility and supervision while also gathering valuable input and insights about the social networks and relationships within their organization.

At the heart of sustained school reform is leadership that embeds improvement efforts into the fabric of the organization. It is essential for leaders to intentionally reframe the work to ensure everyone is connected to the organization's mission and vision. To sustain progress and maintain a systematic approach, leaders must be deliberate in investing in people and strengthening systems. Marzano and colleagues (2005) emphasized that merging managerial roles with instructional leadership responsibilities is key to achieving this goal. By doing so, the principal not only initiates the work but also serves as a lead learner to ensure proper implementation that becomes embedded in the school's culture. Leading with influence across professional networks is essential for driving positive change. By balancing managerial tasks with instructional leadership, administrators can foster a culture of continuous improvement and ensure the successful implementation of initiatives. School leaders, acting as catalysts for improving both culture and student achievement, must adopt a systemic approach to building a collaborative culture, becoming both "Cultivators of Culture" and "Leaders of Learning."

LEADING ONESELF: BUILDING A CULTURE OF INFLUENCE

Leading Change Across an Organization

Organizational culture is rooted in the shared beliefs, values, and behaviors that shape how people work and interact. Over time, certain practices become so ingrained in the organization's identity that changing them can be difficult. These embedded norms—often described as "the way things have always been done"—can create barriers to innovation and progress. Yet, cultural change is essential as culture influences attitudes and behaviors, ultimately determining the success or failure of any initiative.

The metaphor of a trophic cascade provides valuable insights into effective school leadership, emphasizing the complex nature of schools as systems with many interconnected parts. School leaders play a central role in setting the school's direction and tone, much like a keystone species in an ecosystem. Schools are constantly evolving, and change is a necessary part of that evolution. Whether it's adopting new teaching methods or integrating new technology, change is essential to meet students' needs. Adopting a leadership approach rooted in streams of intentional influence enables leaders to navigate the school's complex interactions effectively through times of change and uncertainty.

However, leading change in schools is not an easy task. It requires a deep understanding of the organization's culture and dynamics. Like ecosystems, organizations rely on systemic leadership. A toxic or dysfunctional culture can lead to disengagement and high employee turnover. When dysfunction arises, it is up to leaders to step forward and guide the transformation toward a healthier professional ecosystem. School leaders must identify key players and influencers within their community and actively engage them in the change process. Embracing the principles of leading through a culture of intentional influence enables leaders to ignite and unleash powerful cultural cascades, where small, intentional actions produce far-reaching, positive change.

Through the strategic use of Cultural Mapping, school leaders can create an environment that reflects the beneficial effects of trophic cascades—fostering a culture where influence and commitment thrive. This systematic method provides leaders an avenue to visualize and examine the relationships within their organization, much like how trophic cascades reveal the interconnectedness and impact of species in an ecosystem. Echoing the influence of Yellowstone's wolves, effective leaders can leverage their influence to identify concrete, actionable steps toward cultivating a thriving organizational ecosystem built on commitment and interconnected relationships.

> Embracing the principles of leading through a culture of intentional influence enables leaders to ignite and unleash powerful cultural cascades, where small, intentional actions produce far-reaching, positive change.

SECTION II

Leading Others

CHAPTER 2

Leading Others: Creating a Culture of Influence

Cultivating a Sphere of Influence

True leadership is not solely about making decisions—it's about cultivating a "Sphere of Influence" that radiates outward to shape the culture of an organization. An individual's initial "circle of influence" includes those in close proximity—colleagues, subordinates, and stakeholders—with whom they have strong relational ties and whose actions, decisions, and behavior they directly impact.

However, an individual's influence extends beyond this immediate circle. A sphere of influence originates within this core group and expands outward through the relational ties of those connected to them, reaching additional rings of influence across the organization (See Figure). A leader grows their sphere of influence by intentionally strengthening their own relationships and fostering connections among others—thereby diffusing influence throughout the organization and amplifying cultural impact.

Great leaders understand the importance of intentionally building strong relationships by investing time and showing vulnerability with colleagues and those they are responsible for leading. A powerful "sphere of influence" is not created through giving orders or micromanaging, but through intentional connection—recognizing and celebrating team members' accomplishments and fostering an environment where everyone feels valued, respected, and encouraged to collaborate. This, in turn, builds trust and commitment.

As a result, leaders both directly and indirectly extend their influence by empowering others to impact their own circles of influence. Over time, this creates "ripple effects" that stretch beyond the leader's initial circle, gradually expanding their sphere of influence and contributing to the broader success and well-being of the organization.

Figure- Spheres of Influence

Diffusion of Innovation

Rogers' (1962) *Diffusion of Innovation Theory* explains how new ideas and initiatives spread within an organization. The process follows a classic normal distribution curve and includes five categories: innovators, early adopters, early majority, late majority, and laggards.

Categories of Adoption

1. **Innovators (2.5%)**
   At the leading edge of the curve are the innovators. These individuals eagerly embrace new ideas and are willing to take risks. They are often the first to try out new initiatives and can help pave the way for broader adoption.
   Example: A teacher who immediately integrates a new technology tool into their classroom without hesitation.
2. **Early Adopters (13.5%)**
   Following the innovators are the early adopters. These individuals are open to change but tend to be more thoughtful and deliberate before fully committing. Often seen as opinion leaders, they hold considerable influence within their peer groups.
   Example: A respected department head who carefully evaluates a new educational program before advocating for its use among colleagues.
3. **Early Majority (34%)**
   The early majority are more cautious. They prefer to see evidence of success before adopting new ideas and are influenced by the experiences of early adopters. Their engagement is essential for broader cultural shifts because it signals wider acceptance.
   Example: Teachers who observe the success of a new teaching method in other classrooms before deciding to try it themselves.

4. **Late Majority (34%)**
   The late majority's adoption often hinges on the sway of the majority and they tend to be more skeptical and resistant to change. They usually adopt new practices only after they have been widely accepted and peer pressure increases.
   Example: Staff who only start using a new grading system once it is mandated by the administration *and* widely used by their peers.
5. **Laggards (16%)**
   Laggards are the most resistant to change. They typically maintain traditional practices and adopt innovations only when absolutely necessary.
   Example: Educators who continue using outdated methods and only shift when no alternatives remain.

Recognizing this distribution is essential for leaders aiming to implement change effectively. By first engaging innovators and early adopters, leaders can leverage their influence as opinion leaders to generate early momentum. This strategic approach builds a strong foundation of support, which can help persuade the early majority, late majority, and eventually even the laggards. Over time, this progression fosters broader acceptance and paves the way for lasting, sustainable change throughout the organization's transformative journey.

Leveraging Social Capital into Professional Capital

The concept of professional capital consists of three essential components: human, social, and decisional capital (Fullan & Hargreaves, 2012). Notably, relying solely on human capital—the individual talents and qualities people bring—is not enough. It must be supported and amplified by social capital, which emerges when committed groups

LEADING OTHERS: CREATING A CULTURE OF INFLUENCE

work collaboratively to drive systemic improvement. Social capital has the power to elevate individual capabilities, ultimately benefiting the broader team, school, or system. As in sports, the presence of a few exceptionally talented individuals doesn't necessarily guarantee overall team success. Similarly, in education, the concept of professional capital encompasses not only the skills, knowledge, and understanding of individuals but also the essential elements of social and relational trust within a professional community. Individuals who possess decisional capital—strong decision-making capabilities—can strengthen professional relationships and expand their influence by actively cultivating and applying their professional capital within their organizations and communities.

As any leader knows, achieving 100% consensus is nearly impossible. That's why leveraging social capital to strengthen professional capital is essential for embedding desired practices and beliefs within an organization's culture. Reaching a tipping point—often around 35% alignment on shared values and goals—is critical for driving cultural or innovation-focused initiatives forward. To support this shift, leaders must proactively apply strategies to help bridge the gap between current reality and the desired future state. This requires embracing steady progress and fostering a sense of patient urgency—working through those who are willing and ready to lead change.

Whether a leader is working to scale cultural connections or implement an initiative, the strength of the idea alone is not enough—it's essential to harness existing professional capital. Cultural Mapping supports leaders in understanding the social dynamics of the workplace, enabling initiatives to spread through grassroots influence rather than relying solely on hierarchical authority. Effective leadership depends on leveraging these professional and social relationships to build a culture rooted in trust, influence, and collaboration. Ideas tend to spread more rapidly when they come from trusted individuals—those with both formal and informal influence. It is through these bonds that individuals can effectively spread and diffuse their influence within the organization's culture and learning environment. By accurately identifying interconnected clusters and key influencers, leaders can accelerate the diffusion of ideas and initiatives, acknowledging the critical role that personal relationships play in moving others from compliance to commitment.

The Cultural Mapping process supports understanding an organization's professional capital, social networks, and the analysis of relational influence. This enables reflective conversations and targeted coaching aimed at engaging key influencers who can lead with commitment toward the organization's desired culture. This approach to leading through influence highlights the importance of collaboration and continuous improvement in fostering a supportive environment that benefits both educators and students. Leaders who build trust, establish credibility, and effectively tap into social networks are more likely to drive lasting change and cultivate a positive, thriving workplace culture.

Multiplying Your Impact: Investing in Your People

Our role is to create the conditions that allow meaningful conversations to take place. This involves intentionally investing time in getting to know our team members and consistently modeling the behaviors we hope to see in others. Leaders must be attuned not only to moments of joy and success but also to the daily challenges their team members face. A true commitment to continuous improvement depends on effective capacity building—grounded in an understanding of each individual's needs, strengths, and challenges, as well as the collective needs of the group.

We all wish we had more *time* to invest in our people. Yet, it's important to recognize that while time is a finite resource, Covey's

(1989) principle of proactive leadership reminds us that leaders must strategically prioritize and allocate their time to maximize impact. By building the capacity of others, we expand our sphere of influence empowering committed members to influence those they lead, which in turn creates a ripple effect that extends throughout the organization.

> By building the capacity of others, we expand our sphere of influence

The role and emphasis placed on administrative attributes have evolved significantly over the past few decades. There has been a shift from prioritizing managerial skills to focusing on attributes that enhance organizational culture and support instructional practices. As part of creating a culture of influence, leaders must engage in frequent formal and informal conversations to influence the thinking and perspectives of their people. The professional dialogue that emerges from intentional leadership practices—such as one-on-one meetings—serves as a valuable framework for providing feedback and identifying themes that both leaders and sub-leaders can address. When leaders engage in on-going conversations it becomes clear where to invest time and influence in order to shift individual and group commitment levels toward the desired culture or initiative.

One effective way to cultivate commitment among individuals, teams, and the broader organization is by fostering a culture of influence. This requires leaders to intentionally identify and invest in individuals, building their capacity to extend cultural influence (Kegan & Lahey, 2016). By doing so, we empower individuals to impact not only those within their immediate circle of influence but also those within their broader network—their sphere of influence. A practical strategy for building this capacity is to provide targeted support and professional learning opportunities that develop the skills and knowledge needed to become effective agents of change.

At the heart of both our work and personal lives is the joy found in the connections we build and the impact we have on those we encounter each day. When building relationships with those you aim to lead, authenticity and feedback are essential. Every leader brings inherent strengths that, when expressed authentically, can inspire and support the growth of others. This approach creates a "ripple effect" across the organization, as individuals become more invested and equipped to influence those they are connected to—ultimately leading to cultural cascades.

The Power of Investing in One-on-One Meetings

The core work of educators is the training and development of others. Whether serving as classroom leaders, peer leaders among colleagues, building administrators, or district-level administrators, embracing this responsibility gives us permission to once again prioritize our time and effort toward creating a culture of influence. As leaders commit to developing others, their role should extend beyond building knowledge and skills to also nurturing and empowering those they lead. As leaders, our role is to foster individual growth—one conversation and one investment at a time—to positively impact the collective skill set.

LEADING OTHERS: CREATING A CULTURE OF INFLUENCE

As leaders, we are in the "people business," and therefore, we must actively lead our people. We believe the most effective way to engage and move people forward is by establishing a regular schedule for one-on-one meetings. Depending on workload, the ideal frequency for leaders is to meet with team members weekly or biweekly. Consistency is key. Once a schedule is set, it's important to communicate to team members the purpose and agenda of each meeting. This helps them prepare and ensures both the leader and team members are aligned on the meeting's goals and important topics.

One-on-one meetings are an avenue for leaders to build a culture of influence not simply opportunities to offer solutions; rather, they should be approached as coaching conversations that encourage reflection, invite the expression of concerns, and actively guide team members toward their personal and professional goals. By adopting a coaching mindset, leaders create a supportive space where they can mentor and help team members develop and refine their skills.

When used effectively, one-on-one meetings become the foundation where a culture of influence takes root, empowering team members with the confidence to lead. These two-way conversations are essential for leaders to connect deeply with those they serve, building capacity and fostering a culture of influence and empowerment that enables team members to thrive. Leaders support others in becoming their best selves by understanding their perspectives, strengths, and the challenges they face both personally and professionally. The goal of these meetings is to build capacity and self-awareness—not to solve every problem. Over time, team members grow more reflective and empowered to tackle their own challenges, contributing to a stronger sense of collective efficacy.

Windows and Mirrors: Coaching and Feedback to Empower Growth

Top athletes and musicians, at every level, understand the power of coaching and feedback. The same is true for leaders, who benefit from mentors, colleagues, or critical friends offering insights into our blind spots to foster professional growth. When we act as a critical friend, our constructive feedback should always be delivered with positive intent. Once someone becomes aware of their blind spots, they gain the power to address them. This raises an important question: *Are people unaware of their blind spots, or do they need collaboration and coaching to improve?* As leaders, it is our responsibility to find the answer and provide support by wearing the hats of coach, collaborator, and consultant. This often means intentionally engaging in conversations that empower team members to share solutions, overcome barriers, and receive essential support along their journey.

One-on-one meetings, enriched with reflective questions and conversations, provide powerful opportunities to help others uncover their potential which nurtures a self-sustaining culture of learning and growth. When used intentionally, these conversations support an individual's journey through the perspectives of "windows and mirrors." Thought-provoking questions act like a mirror, prompting self-reflection and enabling individuals to generate their own solutions or envision an ideal version of themselves. Leaders empower individuals to see themselves objectively and discover their capacity for growth by clearing away distractions and offering gentle guidance.

In coaching, leaders stand alongside their people as they look through a metaphorical window, helping them gain a broader perspective beyond their current circumstances. Sharing stories of individuals, teams, or organizations who have faced similar challenges offers inspiration and allows people to explore different strategies for navigating their own path forward.

These reflective conversations foster a culture of influence that values growth and builds self-trust, enabling individuals to achieve their personal and professional goals. Leaders who engage in this way often rediscover the joy of working with others and contributing to a community thriving on continuous growth.

Empowering and Developing Commitment

Cultural Mapping systemically creates a collaborative culture across an organization. When leaders intentionally expand their "sphere of influence" they shape a positive and productive culture by nurturing connections and commitment. For focused leadership development, leaders must identify high-potential individuals. Leaders can grow sub-leaders and improve their confidence to subsequently lead others by providing mentorship, coaching, feedback, and opportunities for skill development. Developing skillsets in those committed leaders empowers them to have a multiplying effect throughout the organization. Leaders can set up strategic partnerships and harness collaborative structures to maximize the power of teamwork and counteract negative influences. This creates a cascading effect of influence that enhances the implementation of learning initiatives and aligns individuals with the organization's vision.

CHAPTER 3

Leading Others: Cultivating Commitment

Remember coach Bill Belichick's famous mantra for the New England Patriots' success? "Do your job." It's a simple yet powerful idea that applies to any organization. Every species thrives by operating from its natural strengths and playing a specific role within its ecosystem. The same holds true for individuals within an organization—everyone has a part to play for the organization to succeed. Regardless of one's role, we strengthen our "spheres of influence" by recognizing each person's contributions, ensuring they work to the best of their abilities, and embracing their responsibilities while striving to positively impact those within their "circle of influence." When everyone takes care of their own corner and operates from their natural strengths, a natural flow of influence emerges throughout the organization. When leaders understand members of their organization, they can work to operate from their natural strengths and proceed with moving members across a continuum of commitment. The following five levels of commitment align closely with Rogers' categories of adoption—for example, committed individuals are similar to innovators and early adopters.

The Committed: The Importance of the Committed

In the realm of organizational change, leaders must focus on harnessing the potential of influential individuals who can spark a "ripple effect" toward building a culture of collaboration and influence. The synergy between individual efforts and collective capacity building is crucial for generating momentum and supporting committed members. However, even high performers need like-minded collaborators to avoid isolation and burnout. In education, fostering collaborative environments—where team members can freely "ping" ideas off one another—encourages the exchange of ideas vital to a supportive workplace. The notion of rallying around the organization's "best people" underscores the essential role of collaboration in preventing isolation and amplifying positive influence. Creating spaces that promote idea exchange is key, as isolation can significantly hinder leadership effectiveness and stall the momentum for positive change.

Leaders bear the responsibility to create the conditions that foster collaboration between highly committed individuals and those nearing full engagement. By nurturing a collaborative community, individuals are empowered to lead both within their current roles and across the broader organization, enhancing their sense of belonging and purpose. A critical aspect of leadership is understanding how many members are fully committed and identifying those who are open to deepening their commitment to the organization's vision.

The focus often falls on the "willing" — individuals eager to embrace challenges and contribute to meaningful change. Leaders naturally gravitate toward these enthusiastic staff members, recognizing the immense value of partnering with those ready to advance progress. This approach is not about favoritism, rather about appreciating the importance of aligning with individuals determined to drive positive change. By strategically engaging these committed members, leaders can effectively propel the organization forward and build momentum toward a collaborative environment aligned with the organization's goals and vision.

Stories From the Field: Committed

Ron had a knack for spotting untapped potential and talent among his staff. Ms. Amelia Riviera was a young, promising teacher he had hired and watched as she quickly became a favorite among students and earned the respect of veteran staff. Amelia was dedicated, always going the extra mile preparing lessons and offering constructive feedback to all students—from high flyers to those struggling to learn. She never saw herself as a leader among her peers, focusing instead on what was best for her students.

Ron knew Amelia had more to offer the larger school community. One afternoon, he stopped by her classroom to have the conversation he had been planning for a month. He told her she was doing great with her students and added, "I think you have the capacity to influence your peers." Amelia was a bit taken aback and replied, "I'm just a teacher. Honestly, I didn't go into education to move to the 'dark side' of administration." Ron laughed and said, "I didn't expect to move into formal leadership either when I started. Remember, leadership isn't just a title — it's about influence, and you've already earned the respect of other staff members, including many veterans.

I want to give you an opportunity to share your ideas and practices as a teacher-leader. In time, we will see where life takes you."

Ron explained he was launching a new "Project-Based Learning" initiative and wanted Amelia to be one of the lead teachers to receive professional development and training. The goal was for her to become a model teacher who would share lessons learned and build capacity to help others integrate more student-centered practices. "You're a natural and doing exactly what we need —others can learn a lot from you!" Ron exclaimed. Sensing her hesitation about leading colleagues, he reassured her, "You won't be alone. I'll be learning alongside you and a small group of other teachers. I also plan to engage in monthly mentoring conversations to help you feel empowered in leading others through your natural influence—not positional authority."

Throughout the year, Ron worked closely with each teacher to build confidence in the new learning and offered feedback on how to guide and lead others. Amelia excelled, not only developing and implementing student-centered learning through PBL but also breaking down the process into manageable steps, showing how simple shifts could empower students to own their learning.

Ms. Riviera continued to grow as a leader—a teacher-leader without a formal title or authority—but she embraced the opportunity to develop her skills and influence other staff members. It all began with a simple conversation and a gentle nudge from someone who saw her untapped leadership potential. Ron saw that his investment in building Amelia's capacity had planted seeds that empowered her to create positive ripple effects throughout the organization.

Nearly Committed: Prioritizing Commitment for Organizational Growth

Nearly committed staff are on the "cusp" of full engagement. Identifying individuals with potential for greater commitment energizes leaders to focus and optimize their efforts. Our understanding of professional capital highlights the inherently social nature of humans—we seek collaboration with those who share our values and influence our actions. By "leveling up" nearly committed individuals, leaders can significantly impact an organization's culture when they intentionally invest in their development. To do this, leaders must get to know their team members, identify barriers preventing the shift from near commitment to full commitment, and provide growth opportunities to unlock their potential.

While it's important not to neglect anyone in the organization, as cultivators of culture, we must strategically focus our time and energy on those with immediate potential to advance. By investing in individuals on the cusp of full commitment, leaders can accelerate their progress and build positive momentum. Instead of concentrating efforts on "flipping resisters," transforming nearly committed staff into fully committed members offers a quicker return that strengthens the culture. It's essential to assess their presence within the organization and develop strategies that leverage a culture of influence and investment to support their full commitment by year-end. Once fully committed, these individuals become additional positive voices—serving as influencers and champions for the culture, initiatives, or best practices leaders want to scale across teams and the broader organization.

Stories From the Field: Nearly Committed

Ron once collaborated with Steve, a math teacher who also developed iPhone apps. One day, Steve came to Ron's office and mentioned his plans to attend an iPhone application developers conference. During their conversation, Ron brought up a course the school had previously offered called "Math for Computer Sciences," which hadn't been taught recently due to low interest. He suggested Steve rework the syllabus and teach the course, using iPhone apps as a hook to engage students in coding and the math behind computer science. Steve was initially puzzled but returned two weeks later with a comprehensive course plan and a request for the necessary resources.

The revamped iPhone Apps course, teaching coding and app development, attracted fifteen students in its first year. Enrollment surged to nearly 50 students the following year and continued to grow. Remarkably, one student applying to an engineering program submitted their app's download metrics as part of their application essay, which earned them a full scholarship. This story highlights the value of recognizing and tapping into the unique skills and passions within staff to enrich students' educational experiences.

We all have similar stories showing how educators can create meaningful experiences when leaders remove barriers or encourage innovation. For example, Brian, a PE teacher, shared with Ron his transformational journey of completing a marathon. Inspired by the determination and grit he developed during training, Brian wanted to instill those lessons in his students. Ron suggested he might teach a class where students run a marathon. Brian laughed and asked if Ron really thought they could do it. Ron admitted that training for a 5k might be more realistic, but Brian surprised him by saying he believed the students could run a half marathon. To this day, Brian's students from all walks of life train and run a half marathon in both fall and spring semesters. The mental and physical preparation required instills important values—showing how these lessons are often "caught" through experience rather than simply "taught."

Compliant: Cultivating Commitment

Leadership requires truly understanding everyone in your organization—including your "compliant" staff. Taking the time to learn their stories helps identify the obstacles holding them back and provides insight into how to support and engage them. Imagine if investing just 15 minutes in a conversation to address a staff member's concerns could change the trajectory of their commitment. It is the leader's responsibility to make time to listen and offer the right support. This small action has the potential to become a pivotal moment in shifting your organization's culture.

> Our ultimate objective as leaders is to nurture a culture of commitment rather than mere compliance.

Our ultimate objective as leaders is to nurture a culture of commitment rather than mere compliance. Approaching leadership with the right mindset and intentions can help achieve these desired outcomes. For those "stuck in the middle," fully committing to a new initiative or cultural shift can be challenging. They may hesitate, taking a wait-and-see approach, evaluating the initiative's longevity based on peer support and the leader's sustained dedication. In such cases, it's essential to plant the seeds of change and build trusting relationships with these individuals. While the benefits may not appear immediately, these investments lay the foundation for future progress. Patience and consistency are key, as it can take time for these individuals to trust their leaders and fully embrace the culture of commitment we seek to cultivate.

Stories From the Field: Compliant

Keith Daniels had taught history at Ron's school for nearly a decade. He was organized and reliable, but it was clear he had lost the passion that initially drew him to the profession. Keith arrived on time, taught his lessons, and left like clockwork most days. He wasn't seen as resistant to change, but neither was he the teacher to volunteer or eagerly embrace new ideas. Administration viewed Keith as dependable and consistent, yet his name rarely came up for leadership roles or committee nominations. Likewise, parents and students seldom complained about him, but he wasn't often mentioned when students shared the highlights of their day. To most of his peers, he seemed indifferent—compliant but uninspired. Still, Ron had a gut feeling that Keith's story wasn't finished and that another chapter awaited.

Disengaged: Re-engaging the Disengaged

While it may be tempting to focus solely on highly committed individuals, leaders should also recognize the potential impact of investing in disengaged members. It's important to distinguish between those who are resistant and those who are disengaged, burned out, or disenchanted with their commitment to the work or the organization's vision. With disengaged individuals, leaders need to step back and reflect on missed opportunities for intentional connections within the culture. Taking responsibility for these oversights and considering what could have been done differently is essential for growth. These moments offer a valuable chance to recalibrate with the individual and help them return to the enthusiasm they had when first hired. Finding joy in leading others back to a better place is a powerful leadership experience. By reflecting on strategies to re-engage disengaged staff—learning their stories, supporting relational connections, providing targeted encouragement, and creating meaningful opportunities—leaders can spark transformative outcomes and unlock new potential for influence.

Adopting a "windshield looking forward" approach, while occasionally glancing in the rearview mirror to understand where individuals are coming from, helps leaders focus on investing in those who are disengaged. Learning the stories behind disengaged staff offers valuable insights into how they arrived at their current state. It's important to

> Learning the stories behind disengaged staff offers valuable insights into how they arrived at their current state.

recognize that many disengaged individuals were once passionate and driven. Although burnout may have dimmed their fire, remembering their past enthusiasm is vital. Leaders should concentrate their efforts on finding ways to rekindle and reconnect disengaged staff with positive influences within the organization, helping them rediscover their motivation and passion.

Stories From the Field: Disengaged

Ron had a teacher, Larry, who had been quietly observing how Ron was working with several committed teachers retooling the Humanities curriculum. This small group was eager to take on new challenges and make a meaningful impact. Ron invited Larry, a seasoned drama teacher, to join the effort to reimagine the Humanities curriculum by integrating history, English language arts, art, drama, and music. One day, after watching these interactions for some time, Larry came into Ron's office carrying a stack of old course proposals.

Larry shared ideas he had developed back in the late '80s, a time when he was passionate about making a difference in students' lives. Over the years, his proposals had faced a series of rejections, which eventually led him to stop trying to influence change on a larger scale. That day, he showed Ron proposals for a "Film to Lit" class and a "Science Fiction Lit" course aimed at 10th to 12th graders. Larry believed that by tapping into students' interests through different approaches, he could better engage and "hook" them to learn the same essential skills and knowledge. Since the late 1980s, he had hoped to finally hear a "yes" to his ideas, eager once again to make a positive difference. He also joked that he didn't want to "waste his excitement" again, believing that they could do better for students.

Ron felt a lump in his throat that day. He saw Larry's passion and commitment rekindled and gave him a resounding "Yes!" along with an enthusiastic offer of support to make his dream a reality.

This story—and many like it—shows that when we learn a person's history, we understand their journey. Larry had once been fired up with passion, but over time, setbacks and rejections caused him to become disengaged. With the right support and encouragement from leaders and colleagues, disengaged staff can rediscover their purpose and find their way back to a meaningful, purpose-filled life.

Resisters: Managing Resistance

On the other hand, resisters are the laggards who actively block the progress and changes necessary to achieve a desired cultural shift or implement an initiative. Leaders can sometimes fall into the trap of investing an excessive amount of time and energy trying to "flip" these individuals. This impulse may stem from ego or a kind of "savior complex"—the belief that they alone can reach and transform even the most resistant personalities.

While we should never completely give up on anyone, leaders must carefully weigh the considerable time and energy required to engage resisters. Since both are finite resources, it's essential to make strategic decisions about where to invest them. Overcommitting to resisters can come at the cost of supporting those who are more open and ready to grow into committed staff.

Rather than forcing change on resisters, leaders should aim to limit their negative influence. One effective strategy is to invest in those around the resister—especially individuals within the same group or social circle. Moving the needle with these individuals can produce a greater positive ripple effect across the organization. Later we will explore strategies for mitigating the influence of resisters in more depth.

Stories From the Field: Resisters

We have all been in meetings where one staff member consistently raises objections or questions—regardless of the topic. Rusty was that person. He took pride in wearing the "black hat," often serving as a vocal critic of Ron and the administrative team. In nearly every staff meeting, he would raise his hand and begin with, "Maybe it's just me, but…"

Ken, the previous principal, was a seasoned leader who once set an ambitious one-year goal: to bring Rusty around and "flip" him into a champion of the culture. By the end of the year, Ken had made some progress, but the outcome was far from a "Hollywood ending."

Leaders must reflect and ask themselves whether the significant time and energy required to engage resisters like Rusty might be better invested in empowering and elevating the nearly committed or compliant. These individuals often hold far greater potential to help move the culture forward.

Considerations for Cultivating Commitment

Leaders can cultivate a thriving culture of commitment by investing in their spheres of influence, nurturing relational connections, and empowering staff through professional development, mentoring, and one-on-one coaching. Nurturing these individuals is crucial for fostering a culture that drives change from within. By intentionally investing time in one-on-one meetings, leaders can better understand the aspirations and challenges of members. Through coaching and professional development support, leaders equip them with the awareness, knowledge, skills, and self-confidence needed to become fully committed and effective contributors. Additionally, leaders should encourage connections between members and fully committed individuals, as these relationships can be transformative—opening doors to collaborative learning, mutual growth, and the development of active champions. Across the continuum of commitment, leaders can adapt their approach – ranging from intentional investments through collaboration, capacity building, and empowerment of members to placing concrete expectations with guardrails for those who need it.

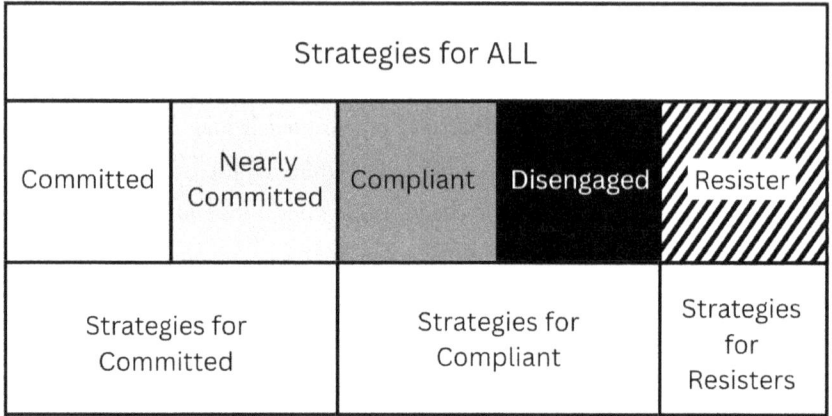

Figure - Continuum of Commitment

1. Steps Leaders Can Take to Build Commitment in Team Members

a. **Build Relationships**

Leaders create opportunities to build trust through open communication and intentional relationship-building with individuals and small groups. Commitment and connection are strengthened through each interaction—whether during one-on-one meetings, social gatherings, or team-building activities. At its core, leadership is rooted in the joy of building relationships and engaging in meaningful daily interactions with the people we are entrusted to lead. When strong, trusting relationships exist, we can inspire and re-engage those who may have become disconnected from the larger organization. By demonstrating genuine care for their well-being and investing in the success of these small groups, leaders help strengthen commitment towards a shared purpose.

b. **Invest Your Time**

Cultural Mapping helps leaders identify individuals who may be disengaged from their work or the broader goals of the organization.

To rekindle their commitment and realign them with the organizational vision, leaders—or those they empower—must intentionally connect with these individuals and invest time in building meaningful relationships. By doing so, leaders demonstrate a genuine commitment to re-engaging disengaged members and affirm the value each person brings to the organization.

c. **Understand Their Perspective**

Leaders should make it a priority to listen to the concerns and feedback of individuals or small groups to better understand their perspectives. Scheduling one-on-one meetings can create a safe space for open dialogue. During these conversations, it is important to avoid interrupting or dismissing their concerns, as doing so demonstrates respect and helps uncover valuable insights into the root causes of disengagement. Effective leadership relies on being fully present—listening with the intent to understand—which requires patience and thoughtful questioning to reveal deeper understanding.

d. **Provide Clarity**

To ensure everyone is aligned, leaders should communicate the organization's goals and expectations with clarity. As social beings, we crave connection and the assurance that we are part of something larger. When individuals understand how their roles and contributions align with the broader mission, it provides a strong sense of purpose. Leaders should begin with the end in mind, clearly articulating the benefits and rationale behind any change or initiative—both for the organization and for the individuals involved.

Brené Brown popularized the phrase, "Clear is kind," and this principle holds especially true in leadership. Transparency is essential—leaders must be clear about the level of involvement and input expected during any decision-making process. By addressing misunderstandings and providing accurate information, leaders can "clear the air" and build trust around the cultural vision and direction.

e. **Identify Common Ground**

   Look for areas of common ground or shared goals between the staff member and the organization. Identify ways the change or cultural alignment can support and enhance their work. Leaders can offer opportunities for these individuals or small groups to engage in projects or initiatives that align with their interests and strengths. When disengaged staff members begin to see how their passions connect to the organization's mission and direction, they are more likely to feel valued and re-engaged. This renewed alignment can reignite their sense of purpose and contribution within the organization.

2. Nurturing Committed Leaders: Building Influence by Empowering Leaders

Understanding the value and necessity of nurturing individuals committed to the organization's vision is essential for sustaining dedication and building a culture of influence within an organization. Leaders should prioritize capacity building, skill development, and mentorship to empower these individuals to maximize their impact on others. To move individuals and teams forward, leaders must leverage the natural strengths and abilities of these committed influencers throughout the organization. While compliance and alignment with the vision are important, the greater focus lies in embracing the collective mission and working collaboratively to inspire others to bring it to life. Committed individuals act as catalysts for change, and their ongoing growth and empowerment are vital to amplifying their positive impact—creating cultural cascades and driving the scaling of initiatives.

LEADING OTHERS: CULTIVATING COMMITMENT

3. Nearly Committed: The First Followers

When we think about leadership, many of us picture a charismatic person out front with big ideas and a compelling vision. The simple truth is that real leadership is not a solo act—achieving a common goal requires assembling a team with complementary skills who are willing to work together. To create a movement, a leader must recognize that the power of the "first follower" is just as important, if not more so, than the leader in transforming an idea into a movement.

This concept is vividly illustrated in the YouTube video, *"The First Follower: Leadership Lessons from Dancing Guy."* The video shows a lone man dancing wildly at a music festival. At first, people ignore him—his dance moves seem awkward, some appear embarrassed, and a few even laugh. Then, a "first follower" steps in and starts dancing alongside him. Soon, another joins, then another, until a crowd enthusiastically gathers to dance together. The message is clear: the "first follower" is essential to creating any movement. Without that first follower, the lone dancer would be seen as a "weirdo." With the first follower, a new social norm takes shape, making it easier and more inviting for others to join.

The magic of the first follower lies in their power to shape others' perceptions. By joining in, the first follower validates the lone dancer's actions and creates a safe space, signaling that it's okay to join the fun. They establish a new norm and activate the threshold effect, making it acceptable for others to follow. As more people join the movement, momentum grows, turning those who were once hesitant into fully committed participants—and inspiring even more to join.

This idea holds important implications for leaders in any setting. It suggests that the focus shouldn't only be to convince those who are already fully committed but also on engaging those who are nearly there. Getting even one person to join can create a ripple effect. Similarly, building a movement and expanding your circle of influence isn't about winning over critics; it's about finding that "first follower" who helps spark a new social norm, making it easier and more acceptable for others to join. Since individuals have different thresholds before they're willing to join, this highlights the power of the "first follower" and the momentum their involvement can create.

The video illustrates that leadership is not solely about personal charisma or a grand vision. At its core, leadership is about understanding that we are in the people-building business—it's the ability to connect with others and foster a sense of community. The first follower is not just someone who recognizes the leader's vision but someone who becomes genuinely connected to the leader. This requires a leader who can create a safe environment where others feel comfortable taking the risk to join, rooted in strong personal relationships and a culture of inclusion and belonging.

4. Cultivating Collaboration and Facilitating Feedback

Building a culture of influence requires intentional collaboration and dialogue among committed individuals. Leaders should actively seek input from these individuals, as they bring valuable insights and expertise on key organizational matters. By leveraging their expertise, valuing their input, and involving them in shaping the culture, leaders ensure their perspectives contribute meaningfully to organizational growth. Facilitating formal feedback sessions creates a supportive environment grounded in collaboration, trust, and transparency. Engaging committed members in decision-making and involving them in the rollout and scaling of initiatives amplifies their influence and fosters a sense of ownership and collective responsibility in shaping the cultural landscape. This collaboration enables committed leaders to support and learn from one another, further strengthening their collective influence throughout the cultural cascade.

5. Fostering Connections among Highly Committed Individuals

Leaders may also intentionally foster connections between committed individuals and others. By creating opportunities for connection and collaboration, leaders can empower these individuals to contribute meaningfully to the culture and help scale key initiatives. Strategic actions—such as thoughtful team placements, team-building activities, collaborative projects, inclusive social events, and mentorship programs—can amplify their impact. This approach not only strengthens the influence of committed individuals but also cultivates a more connected, collaborative, and supportive organizational culture where all members can thrive.

Strategies to Influence Connections

Strategically influencing the connections between individuals within a network can encourage interaction across subgroups, promote inclusivity, and help prevent the formation of echo chambers. Practical steps include:

Team-Building Activities

Design workshops emphasizing empathetic communication and encourage collaboration among staff.

Purpose: Facilitate events that bring together members from different subgroups to foster new connections.

Examples: Host workshops, retreats, or problem-solving exercises that require collaboration among individuals who don't typically work together.

Cross-Departmental Collaboration

Promote collaborative projects designed to break down interdepartmental barriers while fostering a shared sense of purpose.

Purpose: Develop projects that encourage cooperation across departments or teams.

Examples: Form task forces or committees with members from various departments to work on key initiatives, encouraging diverse perspectives and input.

Informal Social Interactions

Orchestrate strategic events to strengthen relationships by developing activities that actively engage team members. Your social committee may create additional opportunities to bring together individuals from different departments, sparking new or deeper social connections that often lead to increased professional collaboration and interdisciplinary work.

Purpose: Social events create opportunities for casual connections that build relationships beyond formal work settings.

Examples: Organize social events, "lunch and learn" sessions, or after-work gatherings to promote informal conversations and deepen relational ties. Staff members may organize themed potluck events such as a Chili Cook-Off, Souper Bowl, and Let's Salsa Get Together—each featuring a Traveling Trophy.

Mentorship Programs

Introduce or enhance mentorship programs, pairing experienced teachers with newcomers.

Purpose: To build relationships and promote a culture of guidance and support.

Examples: New teacher Mentor-Mentee program, Technology Leads, New Teacher Seminars

These strategic efforts not only help new teachers acclimate to the school's culture but also reinvigorate veteran staff by providing a renewed sense of belonging, fresh connections, and cross-pollination of ideas.

6. Empowering the Committed to Move Others

Leaders can strategically leverage the commitment and relational connections of those aligned with the cultural vision to influence and engage others across the organization. Cultural Mapping enables leaders to identify influencers, cultivate commitment, and build capacity to empower a culture of influence among committed members within their organization. Leaders should embrace Dweck's (2006) concept of a "growth mindset" when applying strategies to increase the capacity of both nearly and fully committed individuals who can, in turn, influence the compliant members within their subculture groups. By intentionally focusing on building the capacity of committed leaders, facilitating open dialogue, and investing in professional development, leaders equip and empower these individuals to use their influence to engage compliant members through their network connections. Encouraging open dialogue and collaboration fosters a sense of belonging and helps secure buy-in from the compliant group for organizational initiatives. This approach can unlock the potential of the compliant group, bringing them into the fold and fostering a more connected and influential organizational culture.

The real magic happens when leaders intentionally nurture relationships and leverage the influence of committed team members on those surrounding disengaged or resistant individuals. These committed members can help reignite others' potential and realign them with the organization's vision and initiatives. Encouraging both professional and social connections is vital in re-engaging disengaged individuals. By creating opportunities for meaningful interaction and collaboration with engaged colleagues, leaders can help spark a renewed sense of belonging, purpose, and support. These relationships play a key role in restoring passion and commitment. Harnessing the power of fully committed individuals helps bridge the gap between disengagement and re-engagement.

As previously emphasized, Cultural Mapping is a valuable method for identifying key social influencers—particularly informal leaders who bridge different subcultures within the organization. To influence change, leaders can either build the capacity of an individual or strengthen those around them, cultivating peer influence. This can be a deliberate short-term effort or a long-term strategy that leverages leadership influence within subgroups. Ultimately, facilitating connections with committed individuals is a powerful way to reignite engagement and foster meaningful relationships that support a thriving, aligned culture.

> To influence change, leaders can either build the capacity of an individual or strengthen those around them, cultivating peer influence.

Stories From the Field

Over the years, Ron invested time and effort in building Ms. Amelia Rivera's capacity to take on the role of head of the Social Studies department. Amelia was a passionate teacher-leader, full of energy and vision—not only to impact the students in her classroom but to transform the school's teaching culture. Her enthusiastic attitude and openness to having her classroom observed and receiving feedback put others at ease. During PLC meetings,

LEADING OTHERS: CULTIVATING COMMITMENT

Amelia often shared her student-centered teaching methods with department members.

Keith Daniels, on the other hand, was polite but non-committal, often saying, "What I'm doing works fine." Yet over time, Amelia continued to share and invite others to collaborate and observe one another. Keith grew curious as he noticed how engaged students were in Amelia's classroom across the hall. During his prep periods, he began watching for five, then ten minutes, seeing students collaborating in groups, debating historical scenarios, and discussing current events within their historical context. The energy in her room was palpable—a productive buzz signaling engagement and ownership of learning. Keith realized this was very different from his lecture-based approach, and something about it sparked a deeply buried excitement within him.

Amelia stopped in Keith's room one afternoon to check in and asked, "What did you think?" Keith replied that "It was interesting... though I'm not sure it would work with my students." Ms. Riviera smiled and replied, "Maybe not all at once - but what if we start small? I'll help you plan, and we can try a little shift with something new and see how they respond. What do you think?" With a little hesitation in Keith's voice, he agreed to give it a shot. They planned for him to introduce a mock trial in one of his history classes and see how it compared to student engagement with the same topic in previous years.

As students took on roles and researched historical figures, Keith was surprised to see even the most disengaged students light up. They argued nuances of the case, challenged one another, and showed ownership of their learning and a deeper understanding of the material—things he had not witnessed before in his classroom. Seeing this spark of engagement ignited something within Keith. He began reading more about different teaching methods and accepted Amelia's invitation to join her at a professional development training Ron was supporting. Over time, Amelia and Keith formed a collaborative team that helped spread student-centered learning methods throughout the Social Studies department. Ron invited them to share their approaches at a staff meeting. Keith began mentoring younger teachers interested in these strategies and openly invited others to observe his classes. The once stoic Mr. Daniels was no longer the quiet teacher "just getting by"—he became a catalyst for change among the staff.

One day, Ron asked Keith about his transformation: "What was the 'it' that caused the shift?" Keith explained that it wasn't about completely reinventing himself but reigniting the passion he had when he first started teaching. He credited Amelia's care and gentle encouragement for helping him "rediscover why I got into this profession in the first place and find joy in my work." Smiling as he looked around his classroom, he added, "Now I get to help others find that spark, too."

7. Understanding Origin Stories: Learn Their Story

When we encounter employees who seem disengaged or uninterested in their work, it's natural to feel frustrated. Often, we may assume they are beyond help and feel tempted to mentally "write them off." The same tendency occurs in education—when teachers struggle to connect with certain students, it's easy to believe, "I've done all I can; there's no hope for change." This mindset, however, can cause more harm than good and closes the door to meaningful connection.

The truth is, everyone has a story. Do we truly know their personal and professional journeys? Disengagement often has deeper roots, and it's essential to determine whether it stems from personal or professional factors. If it's personal, perhaps an outside issue is impacting their performance. If it's professional, we need to understand what is causing the disconnect from the organizational goals. As leaders, it's our responsibility to have thoughtful conversations that uncover these stories, helping us understand the function of their behavior and discover ways to re-engage them.

To genuinely support all members across the continuum of commitment, we must explore these "origin stories." When we take time to learn someone's background—their motivations, challenges, and aspirations—we gain insight into how to reconnect them with purpose. Many disengaged individuals lack a sense of meaning in their work. By identifying opportunities that align with their passions and strengths, leaders can offer meaningful "on-ramps" back into a culture of purpose. These tailored opportunities can reignite their drive and help them reconnect with others and the broader mission of the organization.

Stories From the Field: Disengaged and Burnt-out

"If you say someone is burned out, you better show me when they were ever on fire!" This implies that individuals experiencing burnout may never have truly been passionate or driven from the beginning. However, this sentiment is flawed. We have seen burnout affect even some of the most motivated and dedicated people we know. Factors like prolonged stress, overwhelming workloads, lack of recognition, or toxic work environments can cause anyone to lose their way. Even the most committed individuals can struggle. When team members are struggling, it is our responsibility—regardless of title—to recognize the signs and help them find their way back to meaningful contribution and the satisfaction that comes from purposeful work.

Consider Larry's story. He began his career on fire, full of passion and drive. But over time, repeated rejection and setbacks wore him down, and he eventually fell into a routine, losing that initial spark. Fortunately, Larry's colleagues and leaders saw his potential and helped him re-engage by giving him opportunities to create courses like US Humanities and Film to Literature. This reignited his passion, and he ended his career as the best version of himself—just as he had begun over three decades earlier. Larry's story shows that burnout doesn't have to be the end of the road. Progress over perfection is key. With commitment, the right support, and guidance, we can all help our team members find their way back—not just to survive, but to thrive.

Elevating Organizational Influence

Cultural Mapping is a powerful tool for creating a culture of influence, helping leaders examine their cultural networks, cultivate influencers, and build capacity among emerging leaders on staff. Leaders can foster higher levels of commitment within the organization by strategically identifying individuals with untapped potential and providing them with growth and development opportunities. Since we are in the "training and development business," leadership development should be approached as an ongoing process of identifying, nurturing, and enhancing the skills of potential leaders who, in turn, have an expanding effect. Leadership development involves creating influence through a blend of experiences—formal training, coaching, mentoring, and on-the-job learning. Developing others requires a commitment to their continuous growth, helping them become reflective practitioners who can lead themselves and others. When leaders intentionally invest in building others' capacity, they truly get to know those they aspire to lead. Empowering others creates cascades of influence where commitment thrives through "ripple effects" that multiply as they spread through their "spheres of influence."

CHAPTER 4

Leading Others: Dealing with Disengagement and Navigating Resistance

A Comeback Story: Disengaged and Burnt Out

*I*n a moment of vulnerability, Larry admitted to Ron that he did "not want to waste his excitement again." He had previously burned out and lost his passion, but the important thing is that he once had that fire within him. Even when we feel burnt out and drained, we can always work toward reigniting that flame. As leaders, we may not have caused the disengagement and dysfunction, yet it is our responsibility to lead the healing of the organization. There is always room for improvement and growth, and we all have a comeback story still to be written.

> As leaders, we may not have caused the disengagement and dysfunction, yet it is our responsibility to lead the healing of the organization.

During a classroom observation, Ron encountered the concept of "non-assimilation," a medical term describing the body's failure to absorb nutrients despite consuming food. He reflected on how this idea could apply to cultural assimilation. Just as the body can fail to absorb nutrients, individuals exposed to a positive culture may fail to adopt the desired attributes. However, we firmly believe that those who have not yet experienced a positive culture still crave systemic leadership to guide them. If there remains a small desire to be receptive, even when someone seems disengaged, we can create the right conditions within our culture to encourage movement, helping them eventually absorb and integrate the desired beliefs and mindsets.

Of course, we all strive to create a workplace culture where individuals feel a deep sense of purpose and connection to their work. Yet, it is not uncommon for employees to feel disconnected within the organization. Rather than seeing themselves as part of a team or community, people often view themselves as independent agents. There is no "magic pixie dust" to fix this; instead, it requires the hard work of both head and heart to help build connections and foster a shared investment in the vision. We need to help individuals understand and recognize how their work contributes to the broader goals of the organization.

Unfortunately, as in many professions, there are times when individuals lose their sense of purpose or become stuck in survival mode—leading to stagnation and continuing to operate the same way for years rather than evolving. When educators find themselves in this state, it becomes the responsibility of leaders—whether fellow teachers next door, department heads, administrators, or coaches—to step in and offer support. It's essential for leaders to show empathy, stepping into the "foxhole" alongside them to help forge a way forward. Through encouragement, guidance, and a supportive environment, leaders can help struggling educators rediscover their passion and reengage with their professional purpose.

Re-engaging the Resisters and Disengaged

Leadership is not solely about achieving results or working only with the willing—it also involves addressing distractions and dysfunction within an organization. Experienced leaders are well aware of the challenges posed by resistance to change. An employee may become a resister, actively opposing new directions or initiatives, or they may be disengaged, feeling disconnected from the broader organization. Resistance can stem from various factors, including a lack of connection and belonging, uncertainty about change initiatives, fear of the unknown, or concerns over trust, autonomy, and professional control (Lencioni, 2002). Identifying the root causes of resistance is essential to helping staff move toward support and engagement. School leaders must understand these dynamics in order to effectively address concerns and build the cultural commitment necessary for successful implementation of change.

When we shift our perspective from viewing individuals as resisters to recognizing that they may simply be disengaged, our actions toward them begin to change. Reframing our mindset to focus on the joy of working with the people we lead allows us to see them for who they truly are, who they were, and who they have the potential to become. As leaders, we must approach our role through a lens of care and service to our employees. Genuine empowerment can only take root when individuals feel a sense of connection, belonging, trust, and support from their leadership.

In the pursuit of creating a culture of influence, leaders often encounter disengaged individuals whose potential remains untapped. To reconnect with these individuals and influence their thinking and perspectives, leaders must intentionally apply the previously suggested considerations for cultivating commitment.

Several additional proven approaches can help address resistance to change. Effective communication is essential to build trust, clarify the purpose of change, and dispel uncertainty. Education and training provide staff with the knowledge and skills needed to better understand and embrace the change. Involving staff in shaping the culture or initiative offers a sense of control and ownership, increasing commitment. Lastly, providing support and recognition helps individuals feel seen, valued, and encouraged, ultimately generating momentum and sustaining progress.

A Leaders Role in Re-engaging the Disengaged

Understanding that the responsibility for creating and maintaining a positive culture ultimately rests on the shoulders of leaders—they need you. However, the reality is that in every organization, there are individuals who have lost their way and become disengaged from the culture. Let's be clear: at a minimum, this disengagement can negatively impact the individual or the team—and if left unaddressed, it can become detrimental to the organization as a whole. That's why it's essential for leaders to recognize disengaged individuals early and take intentional steps to re-engage them.

We must remember that successful transformation—whether cultural or operational—requires a systemic, ongoing process. This means proactively managing resistance, engaging stakeholders, and embedding new beliefs and practices throughout the organization. As we work to shape a desired culture or implement a new initiative, we should resist the temptation to view disengaged or resistant individuals merely as barriers. Instead, we must see them as opportunities for reconnection and growth within the team.

As the saying goes, "Insanity is doing the same thing over and over again and expecting different results." Likewise, we cannot expect different outcomes unless we create the conditions for influence and invest intentionally in those who need re-engagement.

Reigniting Engagement

Reconnecting disengaged individuals with their passions and deeper purpose is essential to creating a culture of influence where every member's potential is fully harnessed. We can recognize the signs and identify those who feel disconnected from the culture and their work. Understanding existing relationships and power dynamics helps leaders anticipate resistance and address it proactively. Leveraging fully committed individuals as catalysts for cultural change enables leaders to inspire disengaged members to reconnect with the organization's vision and goals.

Understanding the personal and professional origin stories of disengaged individuals provides valuable insights for leaders to identify points of leverage and tailor engagement strategies. When leaders take a personal approach to building professional relationships, they help disengaged individuals re-engage in a supportive environment where they feel valued and connected. This sense of belonging leads to more inspired staff who can reintegrate and become productive contributors to the organization.

By reigniting engagement, leaders unlock the potential of disengaged individuals and contribute to the overall success of building a culture of influence. Ultimately, through steady, incremental progress, leaders can cultivate more positive staff members, driving cultural cascades throughout the organization and fostering a culture of excellence.

CHAPTER 5

Leading Others: Navigating Distractors and Mitigating Resisters

When leaders understand the intricate web of relationships and interconnections within their organization, they can not only identify positive channels of influence but also uncover sources of disengagement and active resistance. Creating a culture of influence requires leaders to navigate and address the challenges posed by distractors and active resisters. To do this effectively, they must proactively detect and manage toxic behavior—especially when these individuals hold significant relational or professional influence within the organization. The focus should be on identifying those who have become disengaged or actively resist change and who may pose a risk to creating productive cultural cascades—even when they don't display obvious "warning signs."

Recognizing the roles and positioning of active resisters is essential for mitigating negative influence. Managing these individuals, whether they have formal or informal influence, is a critical part of building a culture of influence, as they can strongly sway outcomes by either inciting resistance or fostering support. This may involve intentionally reducing their reach or impact that contributes to a negative culture—whether across the organization or within specific groups—while simultaneously reinforcing positive connections.

While some resistance can be mitigated, it is crucial for leaders to build capacity within their networks and identify connected members who can influence resisters, providing a buffer or even fostering positive commitment. Leaders can cultivate a thriving culture by investing in positive spheres of influence, nurturing relational connections, and guarding against negative influences that hinder organizational progress. Additionally, employing various strategies to dismantle resistance and empower committed individuals to become agents of change is key to ensuring positive cultural cascades flourish within the organization.

Strategies for Navigating Distractors and Mitigating Resisters

1. Understanding the Influence and Mitigation of Active Resisters

It is crucial for leaders to recognize the power of active resisters within an organization, as these individuals often hold significant influence over others' opinions and actions. Conducting comprehensive Cultural Mapping helps leaders identify resisters, understand the extent of their influence, and uncover the interconnected relationships at play. These insights enable leaders to assess the impact resisters have on organizational outcomes and the level of vocal support they command. With this understanding, leaders can strategically focus efforts on building positive influence within these networks and mitigate the negative effects of resistance.

Toxic behavior among resisters can be insidious, as individuals with such traits may initially appear charming and well-integrated, while not openly expressing their true opinions or actions. Leaders must develop the skill to detect these individuals early—before they gain power and sway others within teams or the organization. Reflective practices encourage leaders to explore organizational dynamics more deeply, identify those connected to resisters, and gauge the degree of their vocal support. By grasping the full scope of their influence, leaders can take deliberate steps to address toxic behavior and proactively prevent its harmful effects from spreading. When leaders remain vigilant and proactive, they can effectively mitigate the damage of toxic resistance and safeguard the well-being of the entire organization.

2. The Containment Strategy: Surrounding and Cutting Off Influence

Direct confrontation is not always the best approach. Leaders must carefully balance engaging with active resisters while containing their potential negative influence. A "Containment Strategy" involves systematically limiting resisters' ability to sway others connected to them. This strategy is valuable because it allows leaders to redirect their time and energy toward strengthening other members who already have relationships within the resister's circle of influence.

Leaders can indirectly reduce the impact of active resisters by upskilling and building the capacity of other influential team members, thereby insulating the group against the resister's influence. Providing support to those around resisters helps prevent the spread of dissenting views. This approach encourages a more natural shift toward the organization's desired direction and fosters a culture of influence aligned with its goals.

3. **Buffering Connections and Influence**

Rather than focusing solely on converting resisters into champions, leaders must prioritize their time and energy to empower and foster positive commitment among other individuals connected to active resisters. Empowering these members can amplify positive influence and gradually shift the perspectives of resisters. Leveraging relational influence is a powerful way to address active resisters by identifying members who can organically influence them and collaborate to shift the narrative. Additionally, leaders can buffer the negative impact of resisters by strengthening the commitment of staff members who are directly influenced by them. This dual approach—through peer interactions and one-on-one coaching—helps counteract resistance while fostering deeper commitment that spreads through their networks, multiplying the overall positive influence. This cascading impact fosters a culture of influence and yields a greater return on investment.

4. **Engaging Distractors and Active Resisters: Nudging and Shifting Perspectives**

Leaders can selectively dedicate some time to empathetically address disengagement and resistance—through one-on-one meetings—to gain deeper insights into individual personal and professional challenges. This understanding enables tailored, ongoing support that can gently foster perspective shifts and potentially re-engage these individuals in contributing to the organization's goals. Leaders need to be mindful of how they engage with resisters, as cultural undercurrents often form based on perceptions of these interactions.

5. Shielding Against Energy Vampires: Addressing Toxic Individuals

Leaders must remain vigilant in protecting themselves and their teams from the harmful effects of "energy vampires"—those toxic individuals who drain emotional and psychological energy (Gordon, 2007). Signs to watch for include constant complaining, consistent negativity, and persistent criticism. These individuals sap the energy and morale of others, making it difficult for colleagues to stay productive or engaged, especially during meetings.

No workplace is immune to the impact of energy vampires, as they can appear in any environment. Leaders have a responsibility to address toxic behaviors directly, as such individuals can create a negative, unproductive atmosphere that demoralizes employees and damages the organization. Toxic behaviors may manifest as disengagement, resistance, or even active sabotage, and can include harmful actions like bullying, harassment, or discrimination. It is crucial for leaders not only to identify these individuals but also to take deliberate steps to mitigate their influence and protect their teams from their damaging effects.

Leaders can protect their teams by setting clear behavior expectations and fostering a workplace where negativity is not tolerated and is promptly addressed. At times, this may require holding individuals accountable or facilitating conflict resolution. It's important to approach these situations with an empathetic ear and genuinely listen to their concerns. However, leaders must intentionally strike a balance—asking questions that show compassion while clearly communicating firm expectations when addressing toxic behavior. Above all, we have a responsibility to protect others in the organization from negative influences.

We want to help these individuals rediscover their deeper purpose and build positive connections by rekindling the passion that initially drew them to their profession. While disengaged individuals can often be realigned through meaningful relationships, there are resisters who operate from a "won't" mindset. These individuals resist change, fuel discontent, and thrive on drama. It's important not to dismiss them outright, as doing so can create harmful cultural undercurrents.

Managing resistance effectively is challenging, but addressing toxic behaviors is crucial for creating a safe and productive work environment for all. The more we invest in a positive, thriving culture—one built on transparent communication, mutual respect, and celebrating successes—the more we diminish the influence of negative voices within our organization.

Healing the Dysfunction within a Culture

Understanding and addressing the influence of active resisters is essential for maintaining a healthy organizational culture. By using Cultural Mapping to proactively detect and mitigate toxic behavior, leaders can protect the well-being of their team members and foster a positive, productive work environment. Resistance to change is a common challenge many leaders face when implementing new initiatives. Recognizing the sources of resistance and developing effective strategies to address them is crucial for successfully driving change and cultivating a positive culture throughout the organization.

Leaders must acknowledge that resisters and disengaged members exist within the organization and take ownership for bringing them back by initiating the process to heal cultural dysfunction. This involves influencing the behaviors and perspectives of members while containing potentially harmful dynamics. It's essential to see the person, not just the problem—by reframing our thoughts and language about disengaged individuals, we can adopt more effective approaches to reengage them. Identifying where and with whom these opportunities exist is key.

Let's strive to build healthier organizations by minimizing toxic behavior through a focus on relationships, reframing resistance, and harnessing the power of positive influence. Supporting individuals in ways that help us truly understand their thoughts and needs is critical. Returning to the joy of the work—working with the people we are entrusted to lead—allows us to see each person for who they truly are and uncover the best version of every staff member.

SECTION III

Leading through Cultural Mapping

CHAPTER 6

Leading through Cultural Mapping

Why Cultural Mapping Matters

Social networks consist of groups of people connected through relationships such as friendships, family ties, or professional affiliations. These networks evolve over time and are built on trust and shared social norms. Social networks play a significant role in our lives, both personally and professionally, shaping how we think, behave, form attitudes, and influence our decision-making (Barabasi, 2003). For leaders, understanding the impact of social networks is essential when leading change within their organizations.

Cultural Mapping is an invaluable approach for school leaders seeking to cultivate a culture of influence and lead learning initiatives within their organizations. This method allows leaders to understand the social forces within their network and identify informal

> For leaders, understanding the impact of social networks is essential when leading change within their organizations.

leaders and key influencers who shape staff culture and advocate for change (Cross & Parker, 2004). Cultural Mapping also helps overcome resistance and monitor commitment to initiatives. By using this approach, leaders can recognize individuals with the professional capital to drive positive change, leverage their networks and skills to build relationships, foster commitment, and promote initiatives throughout the organization (Fullan & Hargreaves, 2012).

Cultural Mapping is a process that not only strengthens overall culture but also reveals gaps in commitment and collaboration within an organization. Through reflection, leadership teams can develop strategies to bridge these divides and foster a more connected, unified environment. This approach empowers leaders to enhance collective commitment, scale initiatives more effectively, and foster a culture of shared ownership and empowerment.

Unlike the traditional, hierarchical "Christmas tree" model of organizational structure, Cultural Mapping acknowledges the complexity of schools as systems composed of overlapping groups and coalitions that extend beyond simple categories like departments or grade levels. It highlights the influence of roles such as department chairs, team leads, and other informal leaders, emphasizing the need to understand the nuanced professional and social networks that shape organizational culture. These strategic relational insights are essential for leaders aiming to drive change and nurture a supportive, innovative environment among their staff.

Two Roles for Cultural Mapping

When used with intentionality, Cultural Mapping serves two primary purposes: to systemically support the cultivation of culture <u>and</u> to lead learning among individuals, groups, and the organization as a whole. Cultural Mapping can be used as a strategic approach to strengthen instructional leadership practices by prioritizing improvements in teaching and learning while also deepening understanding of the cultural influences within an organization. This holds true whether a leader is working within a school to scale an initiative or in the corporate sector seeking to systematize and replicate best practices.

By examining the social connections among members, leaders can gain valuable insight into how information flows and how collaboration occurs among teachers. This analysis can uncover opportunities to foster meaningful connections, enhance communication, and support deeper collaboration. When leaders intentionally promote collegial relationships and consistent communication, they help cultivate a sense of belonging and elevate levels of commitment across the organization.

When a leader invests the time and energy to construct a Cultural Map of the people within their organization and engages in the reflective process, they gain valuable insights into how to leverage professional capital to strengthen the culture of teams or the organization as a whole. Similarly, the insights gathered through Cultural Mapping can inform leadership decisions and processes, allowing for the thoughtful reconfiguration of initiative implementation and the strategic scaling of desired practices across individuals, groups, and the broader organization.

Cultural Mapping: What is it?

Cultural Mapping is a process of creating a visual diagram that illustrates the relationships and connections among individuals and groups within an organization. These maps highlight levels of commitment, formal and informal influence, and the strength of relationships (e.g., who seeks advice from whom and the degree of impact). Unlike traditional methods that rely heavily on formal structures, Cultural Mapping emphasizes informal interactions and relational patterns that reveal the social networks driving influence within organizations (Scott, 2013). Rather than depending solely on formal surveys, Cultural Mapping invites leaders to reflect on informal conversations and observations with staff. By analyzing these connections, leaders can identify patterns of interaction and uncover areas where connectivity and commitment can be strengthened. This process reveals informal power dynamics and influence pathways, allowing leaders to gather qualitative insights and translate them into a visual representation that deepens understanding of the cultural forces shaping the organization.

Cultural Mapping provides leaders with valuable insights into how influence and ideas circulate by visualizing the professional and social networks within an organization. It reveals relational connections and varying levels of commitment among staff. This process enables administrators to identify key influencers and pivotal figures, offering a strategic approach to fostering cultural cohesion and promoting professional learning. By charting relational dynamics and behaviors across individuals, teams, and organizational levels, leaders gain a deeper understanding of the cultural forces at play and opportunities for meaningful change. Cultural Mapping supports the strengthening of relationships and the bridging of gaps, ultimately enhancing both organizational culture and professional practice. Through this visual representation of cultural networks, leaders can strategically cultivate a more unified culture and foster a learning environment grounded in purposeful, relational influence.

The Impact of Cultural Mapping

Cultural Mapping is more than just a tool—it is a strategic approach to educational leadership and management. This process provides leaders with valuable insights into often-overlooked influences within schools, while also offering a structured method to build capacity across the organization. By equipping administrators with training for Cultural Mapping, analysis, and action planning, leaders can better understand the underlying dynamics driving meaningful change within groups, departments, and the broader school or district.

This methodology enables leaders to swiftly collect and analyze data on professional capital, encouraging a critical examination of visual data to influence professional learning practices and drive cultural shifts. By visually mapping commitment levels, connections, and relational influence, Cultural Mapping helps identify key influencers, recognize behavioral patterns, and pinpoint strategic leverage points to intentionally direct influence across subcultures within the organization. These visual representations reveal the "invisible energy" of influence and organizational dynamics, offering a clear path for targeted leadership interventions. Cultural Mapping equips leaders with the insights needed to effect change at both individual and systemic levels, guiding strategic actions that enhance organizational culture and support initiatives aimed at improving student outcomes. Through this process, leaders are empowered to transform their organizations into more cohesive and committed communities. Ultimately, Cultural Mapping underscores the transformative power of understanding and leveraging professional and social networks to create thriving environments where every member feels connected, valued, and empowered.

Process for Cultural Mapping

	Creating a Cultural Map	Cultural Mapping Reflections	Cultural Mapping Planning
Step 1:	Map Your People - Categorize Members' Influence	Map the Community Groups	Gain Insights Into Influence
Step 2:	Categorize Commitment Levels	Assess Commitment Levels	Identify Entry Points to Moving Forward
Step 3:	Map the Relational Connectivity and Influence	Evaluate Relational Connectivity and Influence	Understand Your People – Show What You Know

CHAPTER 7

Creating a Cultural Map

Phase 1: Creating a Cultural Map – Visualizing Professional Networks

Cultural Mapping is a dynamic tool for school leaders, enabling them to chart and influence the network of interactions that shape their institution's culture. More than a simple observation technique, it is a strategic, non-intrusive process that helps organize and analyze the nature and frequency of relationships within the organization to strengthen commitment and shape the educational environment. This method not only visualizes a school's relational networks but also lays the foundation for targeted influence that drives meaningful cultural transformation. By examining patterns of communication and connection, leaders can identify key influencers and uncover the underlying forces that support or hinder progress. Through this process, administrators gain deeper insight into the social fabric of their school and learn to foster a collaborative, committed culture grounded through intentional influence. Cultural Mapping harnesses the power of social networks, enabling leaders to strategically align schoolwide efforts and lead impactful, transformative change, ultimately cultivating the desired culture and strengthening professional practice.

Cultural Mapping can be an essential part of a leadership strategy that goes beyond simply implementing initiatives; it empowers leaders to actively shape school culture and guide the pedagogical efforts of individuals and faculty groups. This chapter explores how Cultural Mapping offers a framework to visualize and understand the complex relationships within a school—revealing the flow of influence, identifying where power resides, and uncovering areas of potential resistance to change.

When initiating Cultural Mapping, leaders begin by defining the boundaries of the area to be explored—much like setting borders on a geographical map. This step is essential to determine whether the focus will be on a specific department, grade level, team, or the entire organizational network, thereby establishing the parameters for the mapping process. Once the scope is set, the next step is to visually organize this defined space by identifying key players and influencers within the network. Leaders should then select a key influencer known for their strong relational ties and broad influence across the group and organization.

A critical aspect of Cultural Mapping is recognizing that its true value lies in the reflective process of creating the map and analyzing the patterns of influence. The map serves as a temporal snapshot, offering insight into the leader's perspective on social relationships and cultural dynamics at a specific point in time. Regularly revisiting and updating the Cultural Map is important, as it provides a lens into evolving cultural shifts, relational dynamics, influence patterns, and levels of commitment. This ongoing engagement deepens leaders' understanding of their organization's culture and equips them to guide intentional, meaningful change.

Step 1: Map Your People – Categorize Members' Influence

Step one in creating a Cultural Map is to begin by mapping the individuals within the targeted scope. The qualitative data a leader uses to inform this process is derived from both objective and subjective sources.

Data Collection

- **Subjective Information:** This includes personal observations, informal conversations, and patterns of behavior. For example, when assessing an individual's commitment to the school culture, a leader might consider observable traits such as engagement, tone in feedback, and participation in various settings (large groups, small teams, or one-on-one interactions).
- **Objective Information:** This consists of quantifiable data, such as survey responses or performance metrics. For instance, when mapping support for an initiative like Standards-Based Grading (SBG), Positive Behavior Interventions and Supports (PBIS), or Project-Based Learning (PBL), leaders might use formal assessments or structured surveys to objectively measure individual levels of commitment.
- **Converging Information:** The combination of objective and subjective data—such as behavioral observations, conversations, surveys, and assessments—allows leaders to draw more accurate conclusions about individuals' connections and commitment levels within the organization.

Categorize Members' Influence through Visual Representation

When constructing a Cultural Map, all members of the organization are initially represented as circles with their initials inside. *(See Figure)* To support effective reflective conversations, use the information gathered to categorize each individual's level of influence. If unsure about a person's influence, it's best to default to the lower level and classify them as a typical member of the organization (circle).

Symbols:

To visually organize members by their type of influence within the map, each individual is assigned a shape—circle, triangle, or square—based on their formal or informal influence:

- **Circle**: Represents a member with no perceived formal or informal influence.
- **Triangle**: Denotes an informal leader—someone without a formal title but recognized for their relational influence.
- **Square**: Identifies a member holding a formal leadership role within the organization.

To accurately assign these shapes, leaders should observe behaviors and relational patterns that signal influence, such as who others turn to for advice, who initiates collaboration, or whose opinions visibly shape group decisions. The goal is to develop a comprehensive Cultural Map that clearly reflects the types and levels of influence each member holds within the organization.

Formal Leaders (Square)

Formal leaders are represented by a **square**. These individuals hold official titles or roles—such as department chairs, building leadership team members, team leaders, grade-level leads, or administrators. While they are essential to the organizational structure and possess positional authority, they may not always have strong relational influence within the school community.

Definition: Formal leaders are those who hold recognized positions of authority and influence others through established organizational channels, including structures, policies, and procedures.

Look-Fors – Formal Leaders

- **Official Titles and Roles:** Holds positions such as department chair, team leader, grade-level leader, or administrator.
- **Goal Setting and Task Assignment:** Frequently sets goals, delegates tasks, and provides structured feedback.
- **Formal Communication:** Relies on established channels (e.g., email, meetings) to communicate information.
- **Decision-Making Authority:** Has the authority to make decisions impacting their team or department.
- **Policy Implementation:** Responsible for enforcing and supporting organizational policies and procedures.
- **Visible Leadership:** Often facilitates meetings, leads projects, and drives formal initiatives.
- **Performance Management:** May be involved in performance evaluations and staff development.

Representation: Depicted as a **square** with initials inside.

Informal Leaders (Triangle)

Informal influencers, or key opinion leaders, are signified by a **triangle**. Key Opinion Leaders (KOLs) are influencers who are central figures within an organization whose respect and trust grant them a significant sway over their peers' attitudes and behaviors (Gladwell, 2000). They are the well-connected folks often seen as respected and trusted "thought leaders" in their professional network. The power of informal leaders should not be underestimated. These are the people everyone turns to with their problems or news. They might be the "popular" figures everyone gravitates toward, the quiet individuals others confide in, or the ones whose rooms often become gathering places at lunch. They are respected and often the "go-to" people for others. We have seen this happen before when announcements are made that an administrator has accepted a new position or an assistant principal will be moving on. Notice who staff gather around when the faculty meeting ends. Whose room do individuals go to during breaks or at the end of the day in the parking lot? Informal leaders often hold significant influence with staff, even without the formal titles. Spotting these influencers is important for school leaders when driving change because they can be powerful advocates for new initiatives and cultural shifts.

Definition: Informal leaders influence others through personal and professional relationships, social networks, and informal communication channels. They are often respected and trusted by their peers.

Look-fors:

- **Social Networks:** Maintains strong personal and professional relationships with many colleagues across the organization.
- **Trusted Advisor:** Frequently sought out for advice, support, or guidance on both professional and personal matters.

- **Influential Presence:** Has a noticeable impact on team morale and the overall workplace culture.
- **Informal Gatherings:** Often seen engaging with peers during lunch breaks or social events.
- **Problem Solver:** Colleagues regularly approach them with problems or important news.
- **Respected Opinions:** Their views are valued and respected by peers, even without formal authority.
- **Community Builder:** Actively fosters a sense of community and collaboration among colleagues.

Representation: Triangle with initials inside.

Dual Roles both Formal and Informal Leader (Shapes Overlap)

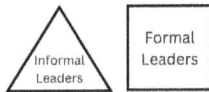

It's important to recognize that some individuals serve as both formal and informal leaders. When you identify these dual-role leaders, represent them with a **square** and a **triangle** overlapping to reflect their combined influence.

Definition: These individuals hold formal leadership positions and also possess significant informal influence through personal relationships.

Look-fors:

- **Combination of Traits:** Demonstrates behaviors characteristic of both formal and informal leaders.
- **Dual Influence:** Exercises formal authority while also being a trusted and influential colleague.
- **Holistic Leadership:** Balances official responsibilities with nurturing strong informal networks.

- **Broad Impact:** Influences both the organizational structure and the cultural dynamics.

Representation: An **overlapping square and triangle** with initials inside.

Typical Members (Circle)

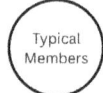

Definition: Members of the organization who do not display significant formal or informal influence.

Look-fors:

- **Standard Participation:** Carries out typical professional duties without notable influence beyond their role.
- **Routine Communication:** Communicates mainly through standard channels and usual interactions with colleagues.
- **Limited Network:** Engages with peers as needed for job responsibilities but lacks a strong influence network.
- **Limited Influence:** Generally looks to formal leaders for direction and informal leaders for social cues, without significantly impacting the broader organization.

Representation: Circle with initials inside.

Formal vs. Informal Influences

Leadership is a complex process that requires understanding the people you lead, the ability to build capacity, and applying systems-thinking. A critical aspect of leadership is identifying the individuals within the system who are "influencers"—those whose voices significantly impact the organization's culture, vision, and the work of others around them

CREATING A CULTURAL MAP

(Burt, 2005). Both formal and informal influencers can be recognized through careful observation of relationships and interactions.

Formal influence among peers exists within hierarchical structures of organizations, such as departmental leadership roles, established policies and procedures, and committee work. These formal positions can significantly impact others' decision-making and overall perspectives. In the workplace, formal influence refers to the official capacity through which individuals, like managers or department chairs, guide behavior—by setting goals, assigning tasks, and providing feedback.

Informal influence is often where the "magic" happens. It refers to the unofficial channels of influence—those formed through casual conversations, friendships, and social networks that operate outside formal structures. For instance, an employee may hold informal influence simply by offering advice or encouragement, thanks to strong personal relationships with colleagues.

- **Social Networks:** Connections formed outside of formal meetings, such as during lunch breaks or social gatherings.
- **Personal Relationships:** Friendships or mentorships that develop regardless of job titles or roles.
- **Informal Communication:** The everyday, spontaneous conversations and exchanges of advice that occur naturally among coworkers.

The key difference between formal and informal influence is that formal influence stems from positional authority, while informal influence arises from trust and personal relationships. Formal influence is typically visible and direct, whereas informal influence can be equally—if not more—powerful, as it operates through social connections and is often less predictable or easily controlled. Both types of influence play essential roles in shaping an organization's culture. Understanding this distinction enables leaders to leverage both channels effectively to achieve goals and foster a positive work environment. As leaders, it's important to intentionally recognize and harness both formal and informal influence when working to strengthen culture and implement new initiatives.

Mapping Connectivity through Proximity

When mapping your team, consider how closely you place individuals to reflect the strength of their work-related and personal connections. Proximity between members' shapes is used to indicate the quality and closeness of their relationships. Closer placement suggests shared experiences or interests within work, social, or even familial contexts. Influential individuals are typically positioned at the center of the network, symbolizing their broad connections and their role in influencing the flow of information and ideas across the team.

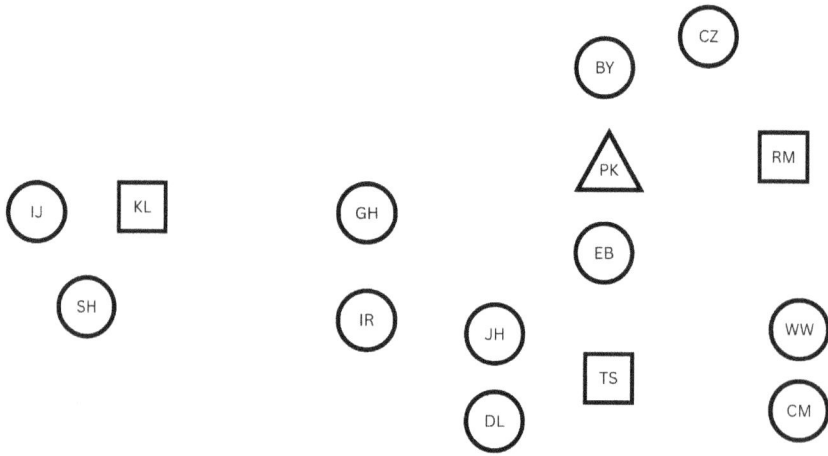

Figure - Cultural Map

Step 2: Categorize Commitment Levels

In this step, the goal is to assess each individual's level of support for the cultural direction the leader is working to establish. By categorizing individuals' commitment levels, leaders gain a clearer understanding of how aligned and invested team members are in the desired cultural shift. The five levels of commitment to consider are:

1. **Committed**
2. **Nearly Committed**
3. **Compliant**
4. **Disengaged**
5. **Resister**

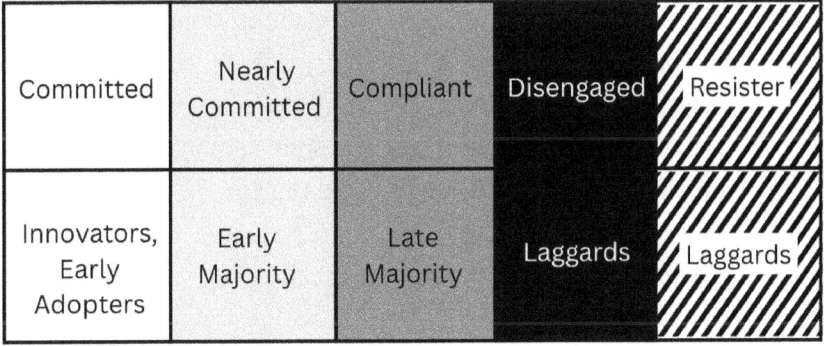

Figure - Continuum of Commitment

Understanding where each team member falls in terms of their level of commitment is essential. To accurately categorize an individual's commitment level, leaders must assess whether their beliefs and values align with the organization's desired culture and practices. Insights gathered during the reflective process of identifying an individual's influence can also inform their level of commitment.

Let's break down the different levels of commitment, along with key "look-fors" to determine where each person fits:

1. **Committed**

These individuals are fully aligned with the organization's mission, values, and beliefs. They are driven by purpose and consistently go above and beyond their job responsibilities to support the organization's success.

Look-fors:

- **Proactive Engagement:** Frequently takes initiative and seeks out additional responsibilities.
- **Advocacy:** Speaks positively about the organization internally and externally.
- **Ownership:** Takes personal responsibility for organizational success.
- **High Performance:** Regularly exceeds performance expectations.
- **Collaboration:** Actively participates in teams and initiatives.
- **Continuous Improvement:** Suggests and implements enhancements to practices.
- **Mentorship:** Supports and guides colleagues, fostering a positive culture.

2. **Nearly Committed**

These individuals support many aspects of the organization's mission but may not be fully aligned. While they generally perform well, their engagement is more selective, often based on personal interests.

Look-fors:

- **Reliable Performance:** Consistently meets and occasionally exceeds expectations.
- **Positive Attitude:** Shows general support for the organization.
- **Selective Engagement:** Participates in initiatives aligned with their interests.

- **Constructive Feedback:** Offers helpful suggestions for improvement.
- **Occasional Initiative:** Takes on extra tasks when personally motivated.
- **Partial Advocacy:** Promotes aspects they agree with, but less vocal otherwise.

3. **Compliant**

Compliant individuals follow rules and meet expectations, but without deep alignment to the mission. They fulfill their responsibilities but show little initiative or passion beyond assigned duties.

Look-fors:

- **Rule Following:** Adheres to guidelines with minimal prompting.
- **Basic Participation:** Engages as required, but not enthusiastically.
- **Task-Oriented:** Focused on completing assignments efficiently.
- **Limited Initiative:** Rarely volunteers beyond core responsibilities.
- **Neutral Attitude:** Neither strongly supports nor opposes the mission.
- **Dependability:** Reliable, though not particularly invested.

4. **Disengaged**

These individuals are disconnected from the organization's mission and values. They fulfill basic duties but lack motivation or emotional investment.

Look-fors:

- **Minimal Effort:** Performs only what is required.
- **Lack of Interest:** Uninterested in broader goals or values.
- **Isolation:** Avoids collaboration or team activities.

- **Passive Behavior:** Rarely contributes ideas or feedback.
- **Frequent Absence:** Tends to be absent or disengaged in meetings.
- **Disinterested Demeanor:** Displays low energy and enthusiasm.

5. **Resisters**

Resisters actively oppose the organization's direction. They disagree with its mission and may work against its efforts, influencing others negatively.

Look-fors:

- **Active Opposition:** Vocal in their criticism of leadership or initiatives.
- **Undermining Behavior:** Engages in actions that hinder progress.
- **Negative Attitude:** Consistently expresses dissatisfaction.
- **Conflict:** Frequently in tension with colleagues or leadership.
- **Non-Compliance:** Disregards rules and procedures.
- **Influence:** May persuade others to adopt a resistant mindset.

Understanding where individuals fall on this commitment continuum allows leaders to more effectively support, engage, and influence their teams. By identifying commitment levels, leaders can design targeted strategies to increase alignment, motivation, and overall cultural strength.

CREATING A CULTURAL MAP

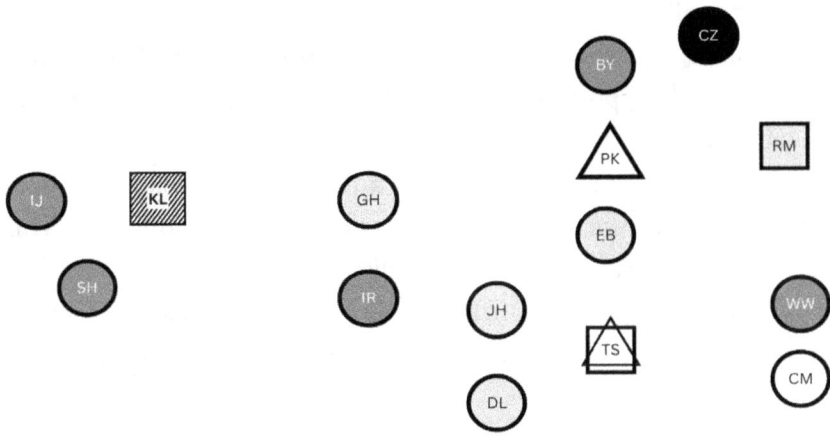

Figure - Cultural Map

Step 3: Map the Relational Connectivity and Influence

Relational influence refers to the extent to which an individual's social or professional capital can be leveraged to shape culture and facilitate the flow of ideas and perspectives about an initiative within the organization. However, proximity does not always equate to influence; people may be physically or socially close but not necessarily exert relational influence over one another. The arrows indicate the direction and magnitude of relational influence from one member to another.

When mapping the relationship between members of an organization leaders should consider the magnitude of the relationships between members. Another consideration when mapping relational connections is determining the directional flow of the influence between members. Does the influence between members flow **one-way,** or does the influence flow both ways (i.e. **reciprocal influence**)? If the influence is **one-way,** it will be characterized by a directional line with an arrow originating from one member towards the member they influence. This indicates that one person predominantly influences the other without reciprocal influence.

Example: Teacher A frequently mentors Teacher B, providing guidance and support, but Teacher B does not significantly influence Teacher A.

If the relationship has **reciprocal influence,** there will be *two* lines flowing between the individuals with arrows pointing both ways. This indicates that both individuals mutually influence each other.

Example: Two department heads collaborate closely, sharing ideas and strategies, each influencing the other's approach and decision-making.

Strong Degree of Professional Influence:

When a **strong degree** of professional influence exists, individuals actively engage in shaping culture and exchanging ideas. Their opinions carry significant weight, and they often collaborate effectively with one another. We represent this strong relational influence with a **thicker solid line**, indicating a higher level of connection between members.

- **Regular and Effective Communication:** Maintains consistent, open communication and frequently engages in meaningful discussions and idea sharing.
- **Consistent and Effective Collaboration:** Works closely on projects, often taking a lead or coordinating role, demonstrating a strong partnership.
- **Frequent Feedback:** Actively provides constructive feedback to the other individual.
- **Highly Valued Input:** Their advice is regularly sought and respected.
- **Mentorship and Guidance:** Often serves as a mentor or guide, supporting the other's professional growth and decision-making.

- **Significant Decision Influence:** Has a notable impact on the other person's opinions, decisions, and actions.

Moderate Degree of Professional Influence:

When there is a **moderate degree** of professional influence, individuals show some impact on others' perceptions and beliefs. This level of connectivity indicates engagement in cultural influence and participation in idea sharing. Moderate relational influence is represented by a **dotted line** with an arrow pointing from the influencer to the other member.

- **Moderate Frequency of Engagement:** Occasionally engages in meaningful conversations and/or collaborates with the other individual.
- **Selective/Periodic Collaboration:** Works together on specific projects or tasks, but not as consistently or deeply as in strong influence relationships.
- **Intermittent Feedback:** Sometimes provides feedback or is sought out for feedback by the other person.
- **Valued Opinions:** Opinions are respected and considered important, though not always actively sought.
- **Support Role:** Offers support and assistance, but not typically in a formal mentorship role.
- **Some Decision Influence:** Has a noticeable, though moderate, impact on the other person's perceptions and decisions.

Additionally, we color-code the lines to indicate the **type of influence** flowing from an individual. This color corresponds to the originator's level of commitment and support for a specific initiative or the overall culture. When there is no connection or ongoing influence between individuals, it reflects a lack of evidence of professional

INTENTIONAL INFLUENCE

influence, suggesting **no or weak influence**. To reduce distractions and visual noise, **weak levels** of influence are not represented by lines on the map.

Organizing the Relational Influence Connections

Depending on an organization's size and scope, leaders can optionally use a matrix (figure) to represent connections between individuals. In this matrix, rows and columns illustrate members, with colors corresponding to their commitment levels and types of commitment. As with the Cultural Map, weak relationships and connections are not shown, to avoid diluting the impact of the visualized relationships.

		Person 1	Person 2	Person 3	Person 4	Person 5
	Person 1	-	None	Strong	Strong	Moderate
Influencer	Person 2	None	-	Moderate	None	Strong
	Person 3	Strong	Strong	-	None	None
	Person 4	Moderate	None	None	-	Moderate
	Person 5	Moderate	Moderate	None	Strong	-

Figure - Degree of Influence Amongst a Team

Note: In this example, the origin of influence is color-coded from the first column (Commitment Levels) toward the columns on the right. One may also choose to include indicators for the presence of Formal or Informal influence.

Emergence of the Cultural Map:

By following the prescribed steps, leaders can begin effectively crafting a Cultural Map. In these maps, arrows visually represent the flow and direction of influence between members, while colors and symbols indicate commitment levels and types of influence. As the Cultural Map

CREATING A CULTURAL MAP

takes shape, it provides leaders with a visual representation of relationships within the organization, identifying both formal and informal leaders and highlighting individuals with high levels of commitment. Once analyzed, the Cultural Map offers valuable insights that leaders can use to shape organizational culture, develop targeted strategies, and drive change to scale key initiatives.

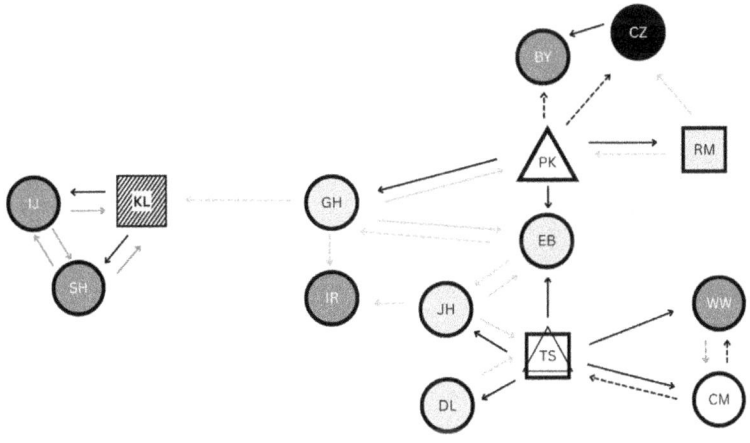

Figure - Cultural Map

At-a-Glance Guide: Getting Started with Creating a Cultural Map

Step 1: Map Your People – Categorize Members' Influence

- Identify Formal and/or Informal Influence (use shapes)
- Represent Proximity of Relationships

Step 2: Categorize Commitment Levels

- Assign each individual a level of commitment to the organization's culture and initiatives

Step 3: Map the Relational Connectivity and Influence

- Identify Key Relationships: Pinpoint relationships that significantly impact culture and information flow
- Determine Direction of Influence: One-way or two-way influence
- Assess Strength of Influence: Use bold lines for strong influence; dotted lines for moderate influence

CHAPTER 8

Cultural Mapping Reflections

Phase 2: Cultural Mapping Reflections – Influence and Commitment

After completing the Cultural Map, leaders are presented with an opportunity to pause, reflect, and develop actionable next steps. This visual representation of commitment levels, relational influence, and leadership roles across various subcultures offers invaluable insight into how members interact and connect. Cultural Mapping provides a powerful lens through which to examine the complex web of relationships within a social system. By analyzing these connections, we gain a deeper understanding of the dynamics that influence behavior, decision-making, and the overall culture of the organization. With these insights, leaders can identify key individuals—both formal and informal—who hold influence within the system and strategically leverage their leadership to shape cultural direction. Additionally, areas of tension or disconnection can be surfaced, allowing for the development of targeted strategies to address challenges and foster a more cohesive, aligned culture.

During the reflection phase, examining the organization as a whole—or from the perspective of an individual member—can help identify key influencers and the positive factors shaping behavior. Understanding these dynamics is essential for guiding individuals toward desired outcomes. Another effective approach is to focus on a specific team or group. Driving change at a smaller scale can create a "ripple effect" that influences other individuals and groups across the organization. Successful leadership requires a systemic, multifaceted strategy of intentional influence to guide individuals and teams in ways that support strategic and sustainable transformation. Cultural Mapping offers a deeper understanding of influence dynamics, helping leaders foster meaningful relationships, strengthen capacity, and implement more effective change strategies. A Cultural Map is not a static snapshot—it is a dynamic tool that can successfully guide cultural cascades.

The hands-on process of creating Cultural Maps engages individuals and teams in actively visualizing professional networks by illustrating levels of commitment and influence—an essential step in building a culture of influence within an organization. This process offers valuable insights into the strength of connections and the flow of influence, while also revealing opportunities for capacity building and strategic partnerships. Leaders can use this information to identify individuals with varying levels of commitment and support their development. Facilitating collaboration between highly committed individuals and those seeking guidance helps strengthen the network and fosters shared ownership and growth. Ultimately, this comprehensive and creative approach not only provides a tangible representation of relational dynamics, but also lays the groundwork for deeper engagement and a sustained culture of intentional influence across the organization.

CULTURAL MAPPING REFLECTIONS

Step 1: Map the Community Groups

Investing time in identifying and labeling tightly knit social groups or communities within an organization is critically important. These groups often span across departments, teams, or grade levels and are frequently connected by external social factors that bring them together. These groups have the power to influence each other positively or negatively. Staff who share similar perspectives naturally gravitate toward one another. When these groups demonstrate high levels of commitment, they can become powerful forces for promoting or sustaining positive cultural change and help introduce new initiatives into the organization.

Recognizing the collective influence of these groups can advance initiatives and improve the overall culture. However, if these positive groups become isolated "islands of excellence," disconnected from the broader organizational network, their influence weakens without relational connectivity. As a leader, it's essential to identify these high-functioning groups and create opportunities for their positive influence to intentionally spread across other groups, ensuring their impact is sustained throughout the organizational culture.

To identify where these groups exist within an organization, leaders should examine the number of influential relational connections among members and look for tight group clusters (circle the groups). This analysis reveals which groups are closely connected and have the potential to influence others. Such understanding enables leaders to foster positive change by promoting a more cohesive organizational culture. By clearly identifying these groups within the Cultural Map, leaders can pinpoint informal leaders who hold significant influence over their peers and gain a deeper understanding of their roles and their impact within the organization. This insight provides a valuable foundation for developing targeted strategies to strengthen positive group dynamics and address potential challenges or conflicts. By engaging these influential individuals and leveraging their social capital, leaders can foster meaningful change within the group—ultimately creating ripple effects that shape and strengthen the broader organizational culture.

Step 2: Assess Commitment Levels

Awareness of commitment and influence levels within an organization is essential for leaders seeking to advance a culture of influence. By analyzing the color-coded Cultural Map, leaders can identify members who are truly committed to the organization's objectives and understand their relational connections throughout the organization. This initial evaluation is crucial for spotting individuals with the potential to significantly influence cultural initiatives. To build a culture of influence, leaders must recognize and understand the existing commitment and varying levels of influence within the organization, creating a foundation for nurturing that culture. This enables leaders to strategically focus their efforts, resources, and time on nurturing key influencers, fostering capacity building, and driving positive organizational change. By identifying individuals who are close to full commitment and creating opportunities to engage others, leaders can help elevate overall commitment. Striking a balance between individual investment and collective capacity-building fosters a cascading effect of cultural influence. Cultural Mapping and its analysis become a reflective process that helps leaders amplify their impact and guide their organization toward achieving its goals.

Step 3: Evaluate Relational Connectivity and Influence

In a culture of influence, understanding the strength of relationships and levels of connectivity is invaluable for driving professional growth and fostering collaboration. Relational connectivity and influence can be categorized into three levels: no degree, moderate degree, and strong degree. Reflecting on the presence or absence of professional influence encourages leaders to evaluate and strengthen communication channels and collaboration opportunities. Leaders who harness connectivity, tap into collective wisdom, and nurture strong professional influence help cultivate a positive culture that supports a thriving, impactful work environment.

Assessing connectivity involves examining the number of connections within an individual's network, considering both outgoing and incoming connections. Understanding existing connectivity helps leaders gauge the level of interconnectedness and the collaborative potential within teams and across the organization, reinforcing a culture of influence. Leaders can use these connectivity patterns to identify communication gaps and areas where relationships need strengthening, thereby maximizing opportunities for idea sharing. The plan developed through the Cultural Mapping process enables leaders to make strategic decisions, foster relationships that accelerate innovation and shared learning, and create targeted action plans for support. Reflection might center around questions such as:

Number and Strength of Connections

- **Quantitative Analysis**: How many connections does an individual have? Count the number of direct relationships each person maintains within the organization.
- **Qualitative Analysis**: Who are they connected with, and what is the quality of those relationships? Assess the strength of connections based on the frequency, depth, and nature of interactions. Consider the characteristics of the relationship and the degree of influence the individual holds.

Intentional Influence

Nature of Connections

+ **Professional vs. Personal**: Determine whether connections are primarily rooted in professional collaboration or personal rapport.
+ **Formal vs. Informal**: Identify whether connections stem from official roles and responsibilities or from informal social networks and peer interactions.

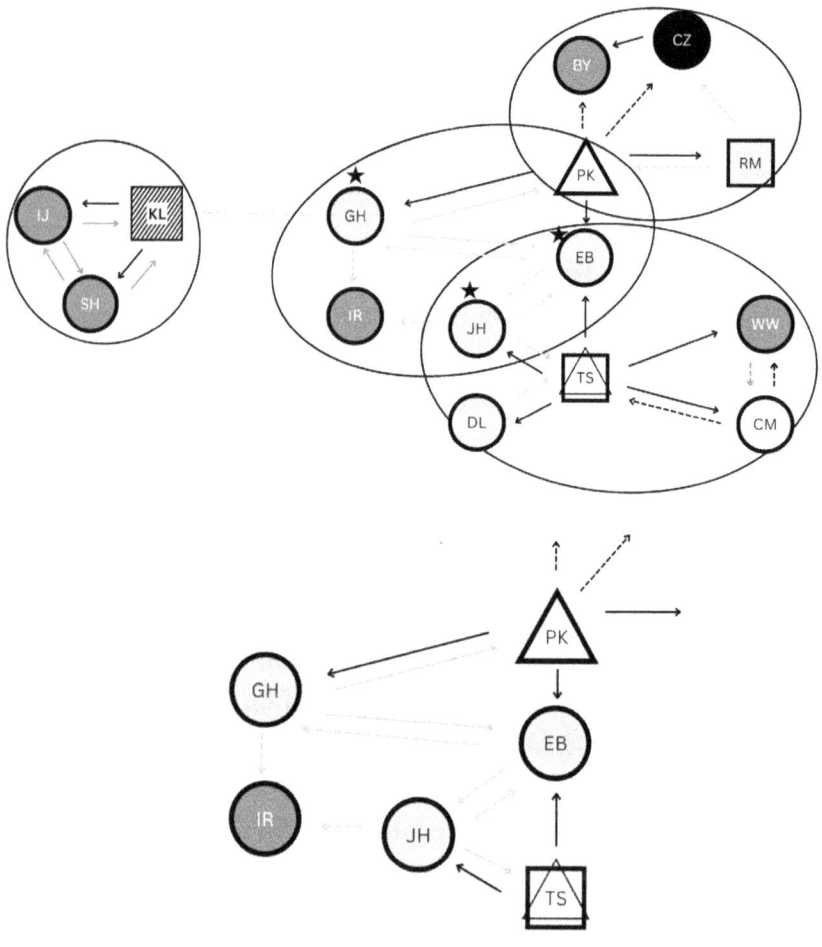

Figure - Cultural Map

No Degree of Professional Influence

- **Characteristics:** A lack of connection and communication among individuals results in minimal professional influence within the organization.
- **Remedies:** Encourage collaboration, open communication, and opportunities for idea sharing. This can be supported through team-building activities, regular meetings, and collaborative projects that help build relationships and trust.

Moderate Degree of Professional Influence

- **Characteristics:** Individuals with moderate influence can shape perceptions and beliefs within their immediate circles.
- **Enhancement Strategies:** Strengthen this influence by fostering collaboration, facilitating meaningful dialogue, and encouraging active participation. Initiatives such as professional development workshops, cross-functional projects, and discussion forums can help deepen connections and promote shared learning.

Strong Degree of Professional Influence

- **Characteristics:** Individuals with strong influence are key drivers of collaboration, innovation, and positive change.
- **Leverage Strategies:** Empower these individuals by giving them platforms to share their expertise and lead initiatives. This fosters a culture where influence is used constructively, and individuals are inspired to contribute meaningfully. Examples include leadership opportunities, mentorship roles, and highlighting their successes.

Cultural Mapping Reflections

As we approach organizational transformation, building a culture of influence brings us to a pivotal point where reflection can naturally evolve into action. The insights uncovered through the Cultural Mapping process have revealed the hidden web of connections, commitments, and influences that shape our organization. Much like a treasure map, the Cultural Map exposes untapped potential and offers a strategic roadmap for driving meaningful change.

At the heart of this understanding is the ability to gauge varying levels of commitment and influence among team members. Through thoughtful analysis, we can identify individuals who hold both professional and social influence—key figures who are well-positioned to shape the direction and culture of the organization. Leaders are uniquely positioned to engage these individuals and collaborate with them to spark transformative momentum.

Additionally, Cultural Mapping underscores the importance of strong professional networks and relationships. In the chapter ahead, we will explore the next phase of the process, offering a framework to guide planning and action based on insights from the Cultural Map. In our quest to cultivate a culture of influence, we will harness the untapped energy within these relational connections—empowering individuals, deepening commitment, and strengthening the cultural fabric of the organization.

At-a-Glance Guide: Getting Started with Creating a Cultural Map

Step 1: Map the Community Groups

- Identify and circle the distinct groups or subcultures within your organization.

CULTURAL MAPPING REFLECTIONS

Step 2: Assess Commitment Levels

- Understand each individual's current level of commitment.
- Identify the committed leaders within each subculture.

Step 3: Evaluate Relational Connectivity and Influence

- Assess the strength and nature of relationships.
- Pinpoint where to build capacity and strengthen influence networks.

CHAPTER 9

Cultural Mapping Planning

Phase 3: Cultural Mapping Planning – Using the Framework

In the intricate tapestry of organizational culture, effective leadership goes beyond top-down directives—it evolves into a nuanced process of understanding influence and leveraging relational connectivity. Cultural Mapping serves not merely as a tool, but as a compass, guiding leaders through the complex web of interpersonal relationships and group dynamics that shape the core of an organization. As we deepen our insights into the sources of influence within our system, it becomes essential to examine the varied types of connections that form these relational networks. This includes identifying strategic entry points to elevate commitment levels and recognizing the value of truly understanding your people. By doing so, leaders can effectively use Cultural Mapping to strengthen cultural commitment and foster lasting organizational growth.

Embarking on this journey, leaders are equipped not only with tools but with a vision—a vision to transform organizational culture through the careful mapping of influence, commitment, and connections. In the first step, the focus turns to how insights into influence can propel the culture forward. Through the lens of Cultural Mapping, leaders seek out isolated pockets and opportunities to bridge gaps, fostering a more interconnected community. The second and third steps build a strategic roadmap—identifying entry points for influence and leveraging a deep understanding of your people to cultivate a culture of empowerment. This approach enables leaders to develop actionable steps that increase connectivity and influence. The emphasis lies in recognizing the key conduits of influence—both formal leaders and informal influencers—whose commitment and relational connections act as catalysts, sparking cultural cascades throughout the organization.

Step 1: Gain Insights Into Influence

Grouping Smaller Communities

When analyzing a large group, it's important to identify the subgroups that naturally form within it. These subgroups may emerge based on factors such as department, grade level, team affiliation, or social relationships. For leaders aiming to foster a culture of influence, understanding the dynamics of these smaller communities is essential. Individuals are typically grouped based on observed relationships, interactions, and shared activities. It is also important to recognize that individuals may belong to more than one subgroup.

Reflecting on these subgroups allows leaders to uncover the hidden structure of the organization and gain insights into how members interact and influence one another. For instance, a group of athletic coaches may span multiple departments, or a close-knit social group may regularly connect outside of school hours. Leaders should look for opportunities to build new connections across these communities to promote positive influence and collaboration.

In the process of Cultural Mapping, educational leaders might

CULTURAL MAPPING PLANNING

find that some groups—such as special education departments—are tightly bonded internally but have limited relational connections with the broader faculty. Recognizing and addressing these gaps can create valuable opportunities to strengthen cultural cohesion and influence across the organization.

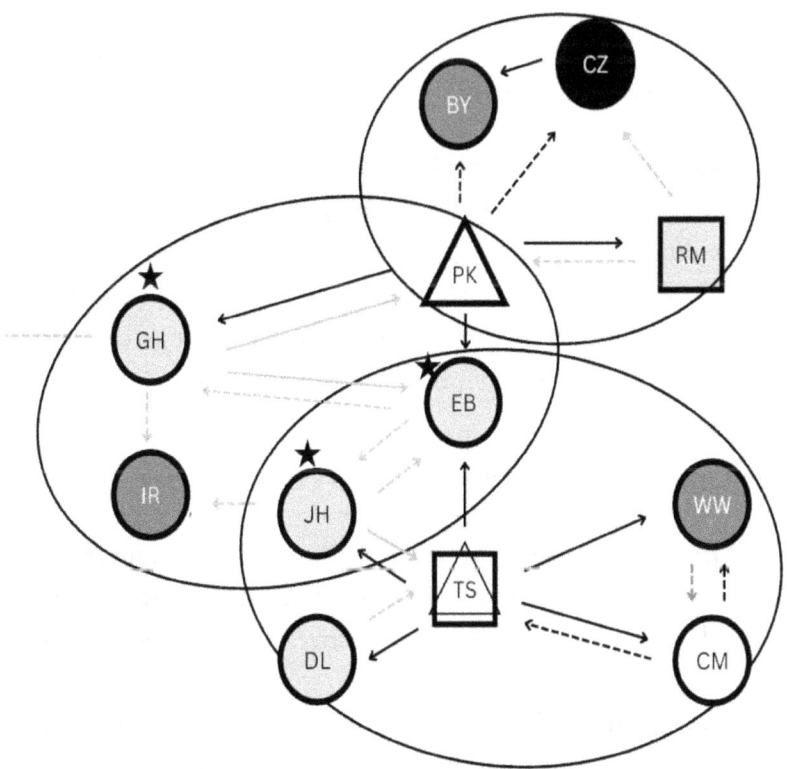

Figure -Cultural Map

Key Questions for Community Analysis

Identifying Subgroups and Connections

- **Professional or Personal:** What similarities exist among this group of individuals? Are their connections primarily

professional (e.g., based on roles, departments, or teams) or personal (e.g., friendships outside of work)?
- **Nature of Connections:** How would you describe the basis of their connections? Are they rooted in work responsibilities, social relationships, family ties, or other factors? How much social interaction occurs outside the professional setting?

Diversity and Dominance

- **Connection Diversity:** How varied are the connections within the group? Are interactions evenly distributed, or do a few individuals dominate the group dynamic?
- **Commitment Levels:** Is there a consistent level of commitment or energy among group members? What range of commitment exists within the group?

Echo Chambers vs. Interconnected Communities

- **Echo Chambers:** Are there groups or communities within the organization that appear isolated? Do you notice any "echo chambers" where limited perspectives circulate without external input?
- **Interconnected Perspectives:** Are diverse viewpoints encouraged and valued within and across groups? What barriers, if any, might be preventing open dialogue and inclusion of different perspectives?

Patterns and Themes

- **Diversity Considerations:** Are there emerging patterns or themes related to race, ethnicity, or other dimensions of diversity and inclusion?

- **Generational Silos:** Are generational divides present that may hinder collaboration or understanding across age groups? What steps could help bridge these gaps and foster a more inclusive, connected culture?

Engaging Formal and Informal Influencers

Identifying both formal and informal influencers enables leaders to better understand the varied sources of influence within an organization. Formal leaders hold authority through their designated roles, while informal leaders—often less visible—exert social influence through relationships, credibility, and expertise within their networks. Recognizing and strategically leveraging both types of influencers empowers leaders to engage individuals and groups more effectively. By aligning influence with commitment levels and relational dynamics, leaders can foster cultural shifts and initiative cascades that build momentum across the organization.

From the perspective of cultivating a culture of influence grounded in mapped relationships, consider how your leaders are directing energy into various groups across the organization. Where are your *leaders* and members of the building leadership team positioned within the Cultural Map? What is their current level of commitment—are they highly committed, compliant, or disengaged? Reflect on the implications of their commitment levels and the impact this has on the broader organizational culture. Their influence—positive or negative—can significantly shape the momentum and direction of your school or organization.

Who are your key *influencers*, and how are they connected to others within your system? What type of influence are they bringing into their groups—positive, negative, or neutral? Who are the *most connected individuals* in your organization, and who are the *"bridgers"* that link one community or group to another? Once influencers are identified, leaders should develop intentional strategies to gain their support and actively engage them in the change process. This can involve providing them with targeted information or resources, involving them in decision-making, or positioning them in leadership roles within the initiative to help shape attitudes and actions across their networks.

Individual Considerations for Connections of Influence

When examining and reflecting on a specific individual within the Cultural Map, consider the following guiding questions: What is their current level of commitment? How many relationship connections do they have? What is the strength of those relationships? It's also helpful to consider key connectivity metrics—such as centrality, density, and betweenness—which each provide valuable insights into how influence flows through the organization. Once the Cultural Map is established, leaders can apply concepts from Freeman's (1978) work on social networks to assess an individual's position and potential impact within the system using a range of these considerations.

Centrality

- *Degree Centrality*: Refers to the number of direct connections an individual has within the network. A high degree of centrality indicates strong connectivity and potential influence.
- *Closeness Centrality*: Measures how close an individual is to all other members in the network. Individuals with high closeness centrality are well-positioned to quickly disseminate information or ideas across the organization.

Density

- *Network Density*: This refers to the overall level of connectivity within the network, calculated as the proportion of actual connections relative to all possible connections. A high network density indicates a tightly knit, collaborative community.

Betweenness

- *Betweenness Centrality*: Measures how often an individual acts as a bridge between different groups within the network. Individuals with high betweenness centrality serve as key connectors, facilitating communication and influence across subgroups.

Degree of Influence

- *Connection Analysis*: Examines the number and quality of an individual's connections within the group or organization. Consider where they are positioned in the network, how connected they are to others—particularly to those with influence—and the strength of those connections.

Centrality and Connectivity of Connectors

Understanding the connectivity of key individuals within an organization is essential for facilitating the spread of influence and ideas. *Centrality* refers to how actively an individual participates in the interactions of the broader group, indicating their level of influence within the network. Those with high centrality are often positioned at the core of where influence and communication occur. Because they are well-connected, these individuals can reach a wider audience and exert a greater impact across the organization.

Central connectors play a vital role not only in spreading information and ideas but also in linking different subgroups. It's important for leaders to assess both the number and strength of each individual's connections, as well as the nature of those relationships. In smaller organizations, relational ties often run deeper, yet some influential connections may remain unnoticed. While visible roles of authority are easier to recognize, quiet connectors can hold significant professional capital.

Leaders must be intentional in evaluating both the social and professional dynamics of all members. Paying close attention to highly central individuals—and ensuring they are aligned with the organization's goals—can help leaders strategically leverage their influence to drive positive cultural momentum and support key initiatives.

High Centrality and Critical Connectors

- **Role:** Individuals with high centrality often serve as influential conduits for spreading information and ideas. They also play a key role in bridging different groups within the organization.
- **Engagement:** It is essential to ensure these individuals are aligned with the organization's goals and understand how their unique position can be leveraged to support and advance the cultural vision or key initiatives.

Reciprocal Relationships and Influence

Cultural Maps help leaders visually identify reciprocal relationships—those where influence flows in both directions. A *dyad* refers to two individuals connected by a relationship, which often serves as a foundation for trust, collaboration, and shared influence within the network. Understanding the strength of these connections—whether moderate or strong—provides valuable insights into the health and potential of the organizational culture. By recognizing and nurturing these relational bonds, leaders can foster mutual growth and strategically leverage them to support collective progress.

- **Reciprocal Influence:** Look for relationships where influence moves both ways. These tend to be stronger, more resilient, and mutually supportive.
- **Moderate vs. Strong Influence:** Evaluate the strength of these reciprocal connections to determine their potential for driving meaningful impact.

Identifying Isolation and Bridging Gaps

The process involves a critical examination of isolation within organizations—identifying groups or smaller communities that, while possibly thriving in their own silos, remain disconnected from the broader organizational narrative. *Bridgers* play a vital role in connecting these subgroups by facilitating communication and collaboration across the organization (Burt, 2005). These individuals are essential for scaling influence throughout the entire organization. They often understand the dynamics of different groups and work to minimize the potentially negative impact of individuals who are not aligned with the organization's direction.

Identifying Bridgers:

- **Cross-Group Connections:** Identify individuals who link different social groups or clusters within the organization.
- **Facilitation Role:** These individuals enhance organizational cohesion by sharing information and bridging gaps between subgroups.

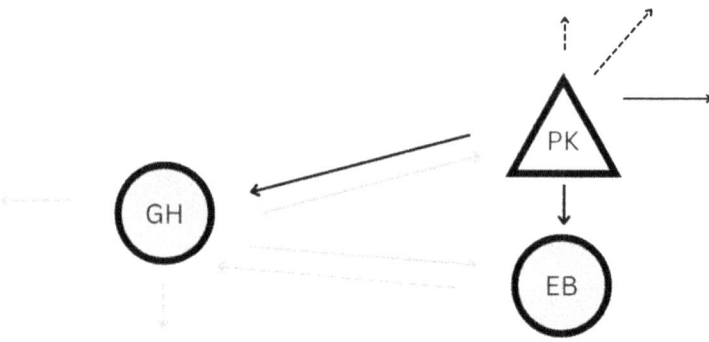

Figure - Cultural Map

Note: Bridgers and triads play important roles in facilitating influence across the organization.

Triads

It is important to recognize tight groups of three members—triads—within an organization. A triad consists of three individuals, each interconnected with the others. The triangular shape is fundamental in engineering due to its inherent structural stability, distributing forces evenly across each joint, which makes it ideal for bridges, trusses, and frameworks. Similarly, in sports formations like the defensive triangle in soccer or basketball, this setup maximizes coverage and support, enabling players to cover more ground and respond quickly to opponents' movements.

Identifying triads offers valuable insights into group dynamics, including how influence and information flow within small groups. Triads serve as key leverage points for leaders to understand resistance and opportunities to strengthen existing connections. When a triad is committed, leaders should explore ways to extend relational ties from that group to other communities within the organization.

Furthermore, leaders should intentionally create new connections or foster deeper ties within existing triads. For example, if two members of a triad share a strong connection, there's a significant opportunity to strengthen the third individual's relationship with the other two. This deepens social and professional capital among members and enhances the overall influence within the organization.

Examining Relationship Dynamics

Visualizing professional networks enables leaders to examine the closeness of connections within dyads, triads, and other group structures. By assessing the proximity and influence of these relationships, leaders can identify in-group dynamics or echo chambers—highlighting how overlapping relationships shape the flow of influence and information (Granovetter, 1973). Reflecting on these relational forces prompts leaders to consider their effects on collaboration and organizational influence. Leaders should intentionally guide and strengthen connections within and across teams to encourage diverse perspectives and build a more cohesive, connected staff.

Larger Cliques: Groups of four or more individuals where all members are closely connected to one another. These clusters reflect high levels of interconnectedness and often resemble social cliques found in other settings.

In-Group Dynamics: These are the strong internal bonds within a specific group that can promote trust, collaboration, and cohesion. However, they may also create insular environments that exclude outside perspectives and limit broader engagement.

Echo Chambers: These form when a group's interactions primarily reinforce shared beliefs, with little exposure to differing viewpoints.

Echo chambers can hinder innovation and contribute to groupthink, reducing critical thinking and the consideration of alternative ideas.

Step 2: Identify Entry Points to Moving Forward

Creating a Cultural Map is just the first step for leaders—it serves as a tool to identify key entry points: individuals you aim to influence and move toward deeper commitment within your staff. Since Cultural Mapping is not a static process, the ultimate goal is to increase the number of committed members across the map each time it is revisited.

Each year, leaders should set strategic targets for growing their cadre of committed individuals, aiming to intentionally influence two to five staff members with the goal of guiding them toward full commitment. A good starting point is identifying individuals with whom the leader already has a relationship—potential entry points. Place a star next to their initials to mark them as priority focus areas.

After selecting your focus individuals, the next step is determining how to move them forward. Cultivating a culture of influence also requires identifying others with significant relational capital—those connected to your target individuals—and leveraging their influence to create momentum. As previously discussed, "bridgers" naturally connect groups and individuals. Leaders can use these relational connectors to close gaps and expand influence.

Additionally, leaders can tap into their own professional capital and existing relationships to indirectly impact the commitment level of others and build overall capacity. In a school setting, this responsibility should not rest solely on the principal. It should involve collaboration with assistant principals, instructional coaches, or a few highly respected staff members who are seen as informal leaders.

Leaders must plan specific, intentional actions to grow a more committed staff and, over time, strengthen the organization's cultural

CULTURAL MAPPING PLANNING

fabric. Throughout the book, you'll find practical strategies for expanding your influence and deepening commitment across your team.

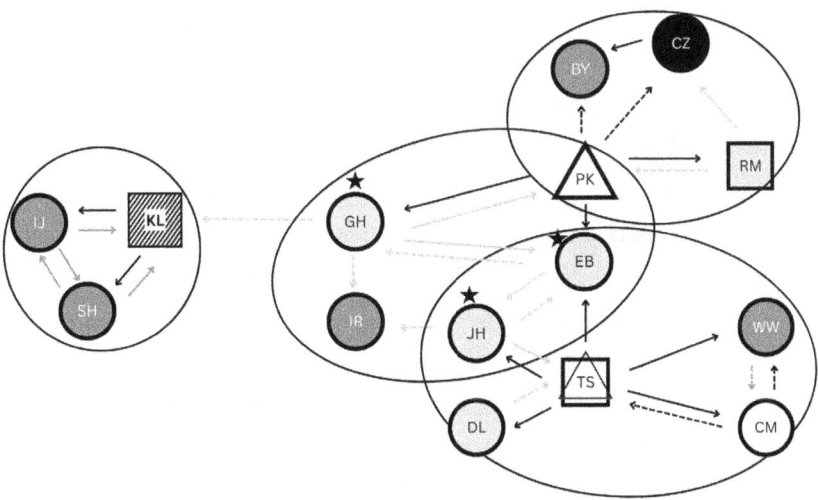

Figure - Cultural Map

Note: Stars indicate individuals identified for targeted capacity building and intentional investment.

Step 3: Understand Your People – Show What You Know

Reflection spreadsheets are valuable tools for organizing information about individuals within an organization. Leaders should establish intentional practices that help them better understand team members' strengths and identify areas where they can contribute their expertise. Collaborating with a small leadership team to create these spreadsheets can also foster alignment and capture meaningful insights into the personal and professional lives of staff members.

One practical approach is to develop a spreadsheet listing each staff member's name and identifying their current level of commitment (see Table below). Next, record three personal details about each individual that can be used to build or strengthen relationships, enhancing collaboration and trust across the team. Finally, include any recent professional development experiences, specific areas of expertise, committee involvement, or leadership roles. This structured reflection helps leaders make informed decisions when leveraging individuals' strengths and fostering a more connected, collaborative culture.

Leveraging reflection spreadsheets with insights from your Cultural Map helps leaders make informed decisions about future team assignments, professional development opportunities, and collaborative projects. Aligning individual expertise with organizational goals not only fosters a culture of empowerment but also strengthens collective efficacy. To cultivate a culture of influence, leaders can use this combined data to provide targeted support, mentoring, and coaching—strategies that can further enhance team members' commitment and engagement.

Teacher Name	Commitment Level	1st Personal Info.	2nd Personal Info.	3rd Personal Info.	Professional Development Experiences	Formal Committees/ Leadership Experiences
John Doe	Committed	Loves hiking	Plays guitar	Volunteers at a shelter	Attended Ed-Tech Conference 2022 PBL 2023	Department Chair
Jane Smith	Nearly Committed	Enjoys painting	Speaks French	Coaches children's soccer	Participated in PBIS Training 2023	PBIS Committee

Every individual is unique and complex. As a leader, it's important to invest in your people and understand them beyond their professional roles. Engaging in meaningful conversations that uncover insights into their personal lives and stories is essential. While leadership teams may compile lists of personal details about staff, they often find it difficult to recall deeper insights—even after years of working together. When people feel unknown or unseen by those leading them, it can diminish trust, loyalty, and commitment.

Effective leadership calls us back to our core values, reminding us to prioritize time and energy in building authentic relationships. Getting to know others on a deeper level not only strengthens connection and trust, it also allows leaders to experience the joy and responsibility that comes with being truly entrusted to lead their people.

Investing in Staff Members

When was the last time you had a one-on-one conversation to better understand and invest in your staff members? A leader's investment in their team is crucial. Too often, it's easy to rely repeatedly on the same individuals to build capacity and implement new initiatives. However, an overreliance on a small group can lead to disengagement among other team members, distancing them from the broader organizational culture and shared vision.

As John Kotter (1996) advocates, deliberately selecting staff for opportunities fosters short-term successes and builds momentum. Leaders should seek occasions to intentionally bring colleagues together in safe settings where they can ask critical questions and voice concerns. This supports collaborative problem-solving and strengthens team success.

Understanding your team's strengths and interests can inform future committee involvement—such as PBIS teams, building leadership, or department chairs—and contributes to the intentional development of new leaders. Inviting staff to external conferences or professional development events can boost collective efficacy. Shared meals or travel time provide valuable moments for meaningful conversations that deepen relationships. Do not overlook these opportunities to invest intentionally in your staff. Helping them feel valued and connected ensures that everyone plays a role in achieving the organization's goals.

Stories From the Field

Ron sent Jacob and Matt—the choir teacher and a counselor—to a professional development conference. During the trip, these two educators connected and had meaningful conversations that strengthened their working relationship. This connection also benefited Jacob, who gained an advocate during the ninth-grade registration process. While the choir teacher's efforts were commendable, having a supportive colleague was crucial—like a Scottie Pippen to your Michael Jordan. Ron recognized the power of understanding his team members and intentionally creating opportunities for relational connections as key to cultivating a sense of collective efficacy.

Cultural Mapping for Organizational Improvement

Upon completing a Cultural Mapping analysis cycle, leaders can leverage the insights gained through the reflective process to develop actionable steps aimed at positively influencing individuals, departments or grade levels within a school, and even across a district. This practice is essential, as it encourages leaders to critically examine the emerging picture in order to shape culture and strengthen the implementation of initiatives. Leaders can then engage their administrative team, the full faculty, small groups, or individual teachers in purposeful conversations about the current cultural dynamics and the professional development needed to advance the organization.

Coaching leaders to interpret insights from their Cultural Map and leverage this information is where the art of leadership truly emerges in cultivating a culture of influence within an organization. There is no one-size-fits-all approach to next steps or specific strategies, as each organization has unique relational connections, commitment levels, and varying degrees of influence. For example, leaders must consider the impact of a member's departure on the Cultural Map—how it affects existing connections, the flow of influence, and overall commitment levels. Since turnover is constant, leaders need to continuously focus on capacity building and developing leadership qualities in others to fill potential gaps, especially within smaller groups. At the same time, turnover presents an opportunity to bring in new individuals who align with the organization's vision, ensuring that personnel changes serve to maintain or enhance commitment levels within the cultural landscape.

Employing Cultural Mapping as a catalyst for cultural advancement equips leaders with a process to build a culture of intentional influence through rapid, continuous cycles of reflection and impact. Cultural Mapping illuminates a path forward by highlighting organizational strengths and diagnosing areas needing attention. The insights are visually presented, enabling leaders to guide individuals, groups, and the organization on a journey from their current state to a desired future through strategic actions.

The destination? A culture of influence, where leaders use their strategic insights to shape staff members' relational connections, commitment levels, and individual capacity to leverage influence. This process allows leaders to use their reflections, analysis, and planning as a compass to guide strategic actions toward cultivating intentional influence.

At a Glance Guide: Getting started in Creating a Cultural Map

Step 1: Gain Insights Into Influence

- Groups and Smaller Communities
- Individual Considerations

Step 2: Identify Entry Points to Move Forward

Step 3: Understand Your People – Show What You Know

- Leveraging Reflection Spreadsheets
- Investing in Organizational Improvement

CHAPTER 10

Moving Forward: 10 Practical Applications of Cultural Mapping

Cultural Mapping is a vital process for leaders seeking to build a pervasive culture of influence by revealing the complex web of relationships, commitment levels, and spheres of influence within an organization. Adopting the Cultural Mapping process, supported by executive coaching, acts as a catalyst that equips leaders with the insights needed to leverage relational connections and influences for transformational change—boosting staff engagement, driving key initiatives, and strengthening commitment across the school culture.

The following section explores ten practical applications for leaders to leverage the rich insights gained from Cultural Mapping and shows how this reflective process can help build a thriving culture where intentional influence spreads at all levels, shaping individuals, transforming teams, and reshaping the broader organization.

1. Understanding Cultural Influence and Connections

The Cultural Mapping process analyzes the social fabric of an organization by examining communication, collaboration, and influence patterns among staff. It reveals the complex network of relationships, uncovering social forces and power structures that shape the culture. By mapping these connections, leaders can identify both formal and informal influencers who impact organizational culture and learning. Recognizing key figures—those driving positive change as well as those who are resistant or disengaged—is essential. Understanding their motivations allows for tailored interactions aimed at building constructive relationships and mitigating negative influences. Leaders must grasp commitment levels and relational influence dynamics across the organization to effectively navigate and leverage influence for growth. Essentially, Cultural Mapping gives leaders a strategic lens to view their organization and guide cultural and professional practices.

2. Visualizing Professional Networks

Cultural Mapping provides a visual insight into the intricate relationships and networks within an organization, highlighting the distribution of social and professional capital. It showcases the formal and informal leadership roles, influence levels, and commitment of individuals, revealing key influencers and the underlying forces of their interactions. Visualizing this information enables leaders to strategically navigate and leverage these networks to foster cultural shifts and enhance the implementation of professional initiatives. This approach to mapping out influence and collaboration pathways, allows leaders to spot collaboration opportunities, identify potential obstacles and address silos, gaps, or even bottlenecks to facilitate a smoother flow of influence. Through this process leaders are aided in creating an environment within their respective subcultures that is conducive to collaboration and the successful adoption of new initiatives.

3. Assessing Communication and the Flow of Influence

Cultural Mapping uncovers communication channels and spots where information flow may be interrupted or inefficient. It helps leaders identify key communicators and those who are out of the loop, enabling focused strategies to bridge gaps or bottlenecks. Strategic communication planning with key influencers enhances information spread and nurtures a culture of influence and adaptability. This approach ensures team members feel connected, informed, and empowered, improving overall organizational synergy.

4. Uncovering the Power of Influencers

Cultural Maps go beyond the formal hierarchies depicted in traditional organizational charts. They offer leaders a visual representation of the organization's relational web, revealing informal influence, social structures, and the complex connections among members. Cultural Mapping helps leaders identify key influencers—both formal leaders with positional authority and informal leaders with strong social capital—who play a critical role in shaping cultural outcomes. Understanding and strategically engaging these individuals is essential for driving positive cultural change and advancing meaningful initiatives.

Leaders can engage these influencers in meaningful dialogue and include them in planning and helping to build buy-in throughout each step of system change—from communication to implementation. Involving them in this way not only helps address concerns early, but also boosts overall commitment which transforms them into key allies by leveraging their collective expertise and influence within the network. This approach underscores the importance of targeted coaching to harness the influence of key individuals, enabling them to become champions who drive cultural change and contribute to a more cohesive and committed organization.

5. Building a Coalition of Committed

When influential individuals are identified and brought together, leaders can cultivate a culture of commitment and collaboration by rallying them around the organization's mission to form a guiding coalition (Kotter, 1996). Through Cultural Mapping, leaders can pinpoint those with significant influence who are genuinely aligned with organizational goals. Assembling these committed individuals into a guiding coalition enables leaders to leverage their collective influence to drive change. This strategic alignment taps into their potential as change agents, allowing for more effective decision-making and accelerating organizational transformation.

Cultivating this coalition fosters a deep sense of ownership and motivates these key individuals to advocate passionately for the organization's goals. Leaders can further strengthen these bonds by creating opportunities for collaboration, shared experiences, and ongoing professional development. These intentional efforts to build and nurture professional relationships not only enhance the organization's capacity for change but also provide valuable insight into each member's contributions and alignment with the desired culture.

6. Multiplying Positive Effects Throughout the Organization

Leaders can amplify an organization's success by harnessing the professional capital and influence of key members, as revealed through

Cultural Mapping. This process uncovers not only who the influencers are but also the depth of their expertise and the collaborative impact they have within their networks. By understanding these individuals' professional capital, leaders can empower them to encourage collaboration among peers and advance initiatives aligned with organizational goals.

Visualizing professional networks reveals opportunities to build capacity in others and create partnerships through strategic relationship building. Leaders can identify individuals with varying levels of commitment and intentionally develop their skills. This encourages collaborations between the highly committed and others.

In essence, Cultural Mapping provides a roadmap for leaders to mobilize the collective power of their teams, cultivating an environment where collaboration, commitment, and professional growth thrive, thus ensuring a strong organizational culture. Strategically leveraging these insights empowers committed members to lead efforts that not only deepen commitment but also generate "ripple effects" of influence throughout their networks, enriching the organization's culture.

7. Scaling Professional Development and Implementing Initiatives

Through Cultural Mapping, leaders gain a powerful strategy for enhancing the implementation of professional development initiatives by leveraging the natural cultural networks within their organization. By identifying linchpins—individuals who play pivotal roles in aligning strategies, guiding action steps, and scaling efforts—leaders can embed programs more deeply and sustainably. This approach is rooted in a leader's ability to recognize who the influential and committed members are and understand the relational connections that can be strategically leveraged to catalyze change and foster a culture of professional learning.

Armed with insights from Cultural Mapping, leaders can more effectively cultivate an innovative climate by spotlighting collaborative, well-connected individuals who can serve as catalysts for supporting the successful execution of professional development efforts. Empowering these individuals to lead innovation nurtures an environment of creative experimentation and calculated risk-taking. This focused approach not only ensures that initiatives take root but also aligns them with broader school and district goals.

8. Addressing Disengagement and Active Resisters

Cultural Mapping helps leaders identify disengaged or resistant individuals or groups who may hinder cultural efforts or initiative implementation. Engaging these members directly enables leaders to understand their concerns and motivations, crafting targeted strategies to shift their commitment levels. The goal is to transform resistance into alignment and reduce opposition. This may involve fostering connections with isolated individuals or groups to better integrate them into the organizational fabric. Addressing resistance proactively cultivates a more inclusive and cooperative culture, smoothing initiative implementation and unifying the organization's direction.

9. Amplifying the Unheard: Empowering Voices

Cultural Mapping allows leaders to examine and strengthen inclusivity by identifying marginalized groups and power imbalances within the organization. This process highlights individuals whose voices may be underrepresented, giving leaders the opportunity to intentionally develop strategies to increase their engagement.

By recognizing groups that are often sidelined in key conversations or decision-making processes, leaders can tailor their efforts to foster a more inclusive and collaborative culture. Ensuring representation requires reconfiguring communication pathways and deliberately incorporating input from those who may be outside a leader's immediate "spheres of influence."

Leaders can dismantle barriers that hinder connection and influence across the cultural landscape by encouraging interactions among diverse groups and proactively addressing conflict. These intentional actions not only promote inclusivity but also amplify underrepresented voices, cultivating a culture where all members feel valued and diverse perspectives shape the organization's direction.

10. Strategically Investing Your Time and Effort

Cultural Mapping equips leaders with insights to efficiently invest their time and energy in building relationships, leadership capacity, and commitment. This strategic approach focuses on developing key influencers who can catalyze change. Leaders should identify staff with professional capital to influence cultural values, foster collaboration, and champion initiatives. Empowering these individuals to assume leadership roles amplifies their impact, spreading commitment and support. This targeted investment maximizes efforts on those most likely to drive positive change. While it may be tempting to devote extensive resources to resisters, leaders should weigh benefits carefully, prioritizing those with growth potential. This mindful allocation accelerates the growth of collective efficacy and an influential culture.

SECTION IV

Leading Organizations

CHAPTER 11

Leading Teams: Collaborative Cultures of Influence

Three Rings of Influence

While watching *Footloose* starring Kevin Bacon, Ron was reminded of a game he used to play, similar to "Six Degrees of Separation," which illustrates how individuals are interconnected within a network. Recently, he had read about the power of social networks and how our connections with others significantly influence our behaviors and attitudes (Christakis & Fowler, 2009). The authors showed how networks can propagate everything from happiness to obesity, demonstrating the profound impact that social ties have on our lives.

Similarly, Ron reflected on the Cultural Mapping process he had started, which revealed how influence spreads through networks and creates far-reaching "ripple effects" within organizations. It's important to recognize that while we may be connected to many people, the first three rings of social influence hold the greatest potential for sparking cascades of change (Christakis & Fowler, 2009). When leaders focus on these close connections within their "circle of influence," they can foster positive "spheres of influence" across teams, groups, and the organization as a whole. Additionally, leaders must build capacity in others throughout the organization to effectively leverage influence within various subcultures.

Whether we hold formal leadership positions or not, we all serve as leaders and should recognize that the heart of our work takes place within team settings—such as grade-level professional learning communities, middle school teams, departments, administrative groups, or project teams. The power of learning together becomes especially important when we understand that learning is fundamentally a social act, not just an individual endeavor. As leaders, it is crucial to leverage our time as a key factor in influencing learning and to treat it as a resource that reflects our system's values and beliefs, all aimed at achieving our mission and vision. Too often, we become narrowly focused on managerial tasks or consumed by direct services to students—whether teaching in the classroom, coaching athletic teams, or leading performances on stage. Yet, the true joy and satisfaction of our work comes from the collaborative process of leading and working with others to align our efforts toward the purpose and mission of our organizations.

Our focus on relational connections is reflected in intentionally cultivating a culture of collaboration and teamwork. This fosters an environment where individuals feel valued for their contributions and connected to their colleagues. Everyone desires a sense of belonging—to feel connected with others at work—and leaders must actively create conditions that enhance these relational connections among team members. When people not only feel supported but also have a true colleague and friend at work, engagement, retention, and commitment to the organization all increase. By prioritizing relational connections and improving the microenvironment within teams, leaders can create changes that resonate throughout the entire organization.

Subcultures: Teams within Organizations

Subcultures and their leaders play a critical role in shaping individuals, teams, and the broader organization (Schein, 2010). Subcultures are smaller groups within the larger culture that share a distinct set of values, priorities, or behaviors separate from the dominant culture. These subcultures often reinforce shared perspectives through relational influence emerging from formal or informal role connections. For example, a subculture that values innovation may consist of individuals inspired by peer leaders who actively embrace innovative practices. Subcultures can develop naturally or be intentionally cultivated to support specific organizational goals. However, there is also a risk in ignoring or dismissing the influence embedded in subcultures' professional capital which can negatively affect team cohesion and the overall culture by creating divisions within the organization.

Subcultures and their leaders play a symbiotic role in shaping an organization's culture. Leaders can leverage existing relational connections and the influence of individuals within subcultures to foster a sense of belonging and community among members. To advance the organization's vision, leaders must understand and embrace the power of subcultures and harness the influence of key staff to grow commitment and impact throughout the organization.

Leaders must identify the "central players" within the organization's subcultures—those perceived as critical to its success. When your influence is felt through your actions, behaviors, and words, you are a leader in every meaningful sense, regardless of title. These influencers may hold formal leadership roles or wield significant power through informal connections and relationships. By developing relationships and building capacity in these key influencers, leaders can enlist their support to drive cultural change—helping to spread messages, model desired behaviors, and influence peers' attitudes and actions toward the culture's intended direction.

Subgroup leaders play a crucial role in shaping and influencing a collaborative culture among their peers. Empowering and equipping them with the right skills unlocks their potential to drive commitment and positively impact the broader organization through their connections within teams. These purposeful conversations with subgroup leaders also help identify and address issues affecting team performance. It's important to remember that each team member's background and circumstances are unique, so guidance that works for one may not apply to another. Leaders should remain flexible and adapt their approaches to meet individual needs and specific situations. When multiplied across the organization, this impact creates a transformative ripple effect—cascading leadership capacity throughout teams.

Building Collaborative Cultures of Commitment

Engaging in Cultural Mapping helps leaders better understand the formal and informal influences within subcultures and the relational connections throughout the organization. This insight allows leaders to identify gaps in cultural networks and opportunities to influence individuals, move teams forward, and ultimately shape the broader organizational culture. For example, mapping can identify "bridgers"—individuals in brokerage positions who connect people and ideas that might otherwise remain isolated. As leaders deepen their understanding of these connections, they can create opportunities to bring together members with diverse perspectives and expertise. To accelerate initiative implementation, leaders can intentionally break down cultural silos by encouraging collaboration across departments and teams. Cultural Mapping can also highlight areas where teams or departments are not collaborating effectively. When leaders identify "bottlenecks," they can develop targeted strategies to facilitate better collaboration by mapping professional and social networks within and between groups. By intentionally creating opportunities to link members, leaders increase pathways for connection, enhance collaboration, and improve the overall connectivity of the organization.

This highlights the importance of understanding the social networks and professional capital within our teams, as well as being intentional about exerting influence within these systems. The popular phrase by Jim Rohn states that "we are the sum of the five individuals closest to us in our personal and professional lives." By examining commitment levels within teams, leaders can identify "Entry Points"—opportunities to build capacity directly or by influencing the growth of others. Leaders are continually striving to encourage the sharing of best practices among team members. This, in turn, sets the stage for advancing the effectiveness of a Professional Learning Community (PLC). Periodic assessment of individuals' commitment levels within the PLC enables leaders to reflect on how best to support members and make necessary adjustments to implement instructional initiatives effectively.

The "Pinging Effect"

We've all had that one friend or colleague who just "gets us." When we're together or collaborating, ideas seem to flow effortlessly, bouncing back and forth like a "ping." The "Pinging Effect" describes how committed individuals, when working as a team, can exponentially boost each other's dedication and drive to implement initiatives. Through teamwork, they uplift and energize their colleagues, leading to greater overall success. This effect highlights the transformative power of collaboration and is critical for effective teams. When committed individuals collaborate closely, their relational synergy propels the team forward.

Cultivating this effect rarely happens by accident—a leader can intentionally create conditions for meaningful conversations and connections among members. This dynamic builds trust, makes members feel valued, and increases the frequency of collaboration, which leads to more idea-sharing and calculated risk-taking. On the other hand, working in isolation can lead to feelings of loneliness, diminished passion, and burnout. Without peer support and encouragement, sustaining commitment over time becomes difficult. Therefore, it's vital for leaders to foster a collaborative environment where team members exchange ideas, provide feedback, and celebrate each other's successes. This approach encourages individuals to reach new heights and achieve more collectively than they ever could alone.

Critical Connectors within Teams

1. **Unveiling the Hidden Influence of Critical Connectors**

In creating a culture of influence, it's essential to recognize the presence and importance of critical connectors within professional networks. These individuals often act as gatekeepers, holding unique relationships and connections that significantly impact the flow of information and influence within an organization (Burt, 2005). While their authority within a team may not be immediately visible, these connectors possess social power and a keen awareness of others, enabling them to exert influence beyond what is initially apparent.

2. **Moving Beyond Positional Authority: The Power of Influence**

The influence of critical connectors often extends beyond their formal roles. While they may be highly connected across the organization, it's important to distinguish between simple connectivity and true influence. These individuals often serve as trusted sources of insight, offering leadership a clearer understanding of the day-to-day realities within the organization. Leaders can leverage the unique relationships and professional capital of critical connectors to drive meaningful change and shape a culture of influence, making them valuable allies.

3. **Leveraging Critical Connectors for Cultural Transformation**

To foster a culture of influence, leaders must harness the potential of critical connectors as catalysts for change. These individuals bridge gaps between team members, facilitating the flow of information and shaping how others think and act. Their insights and feedback provide a deeper understanding of the organization's levels of commitment and engagement. By actively engaging and empowering critical connectors as "bridgers," leaders can tap into their network influence to promote collaboration around key initiatives and spark cascading influence across the organization.

People and Subcultures

As leaders, it's important to recognize that we cannot do everything alone. Part of our responsibility is to move people forward, both as individuals and as collective groups. We must leverage the strengths of subculture leaders within our organization to help guide teams through challenges and create opportunities for deeper connection and commitment. Whether it's addressing relationship issues or fixing broken systems, every challenge presents an opportunity to strengthen our culture and build a more resilient organization. To achieve this, leaders should pause and reflect on their priorities, taking time to fully understand the current state in order to effectively plan and drive action toward the desired future state.

The Cultural Mapping process helps leaders understand the relationships and dynamics at play, allowing them to strategically build capacity within individuals on teams which in turn propels the organization. By defining subcultures through this process, leaders can more effectively determine how to exert cultural influence and cultivate leadership within their spheres of influence. Cultural Mapping helps strengthen networks, promote collaboration, and identify critical connectors who are instrumental in scaling initiatives. This process empowers leaders to drive cultural change, build more engaged teams, and proactively anticipate resistance or emerging undercurrents. In doing so, leaders can more effectively shape their microenvironments, moving the organization toward success by investing in people and deepening connections that leverage cascades of professional capital across the organization.

CHAPTER 12

Leading Cultural Cascades: Cultivating an Organization of Influence

R*on's evolution in leadership, driven by the strategic use of Cultural Mapping, was pivotal in cultivating a culture of intentional influence within his school. As a visionary principal, Ron understood the power of creating cultural cascades and the compounding effect they had on commitment levels. He believed that a school's culture was not simply built through top-down hierarchical control via rules and regulations.*

Instead, Ron was committed to fostering an environment where every student and staff member felt a sense of belonging—where they were valued, connected, and inspired to thrive. By understanding the intricate web of cultural connections that formed the organization's network, Ron identified key influencers, anticipated potential bottlenecks, and laid the groundwork for a resilient professional community—one capable of withstanding the departure of key members over time.

Ron was fascinated by the concept of cultural cascades and how individuals within an organization could shape its culture through their everyday actions and behaviors. Ron saw a unique opportunity to harness these principles to build a more positive and sustainable culture in his school. Through intentional connections, he nurtured a network of support and collaboration, distributing leadership and influence across the school. This approach ensured that ownership of the culture was shared and that commitment extended beyond a few individuals, embedding resilience and continuity throughout the school community.

Ron's efforts to build deep relationships and a guiding coalition were central to fostering a culture of engaged investment. He recognized that the strength of an organization's culture lies not only in its structures but in the quality of the connections among its members. He began by identifying a group of committed staff—individuals who consistently demonstrated positivity, engagement, and a belief in the school's mission. Ron made time to understand their origin stories, motivations, and perspectives. Through workshops, retreats, and one-on-one meetings, he influenced their approaches to leadership and collaboration.

Ron viewed these committed individuals as catalysts for change and inspired them to lead others in building a stronger school culture. He celebrated their contributions not only through recognition but through meaningful actions—highlighting their successes in meetings, showcasing their implementation of new initiatives, and empowering them to take on leadership roles.

One such individual, Sarah, was a passionate teacher who emerged as a subculture leader within her department. Her enthusiasm was contagious—encouraging her colleagues to adopt new teaching strategies and work more collaboratively. Recognizing her impact, Ron appointed her as department team lead. Sarah embraced her role wholeheartedly, mentoring peers and cultivating a sense of purpose within her team. Over time, the culture within her department transformed: teacher engagement increased, instructional strategies improved, and a strong sense of collective efficacy took root.

Ron continued to identify and support other committed individuals across the school. He believed that strategically positioning them in leadership roles—such as department chairs or team leads—would amplify their influence. He also invested in their professional development to ensure they had the necessary tools to lead with confidence and clarity. For Ron, committed leadership at every level was essential to the school's success.

The results were remarkable. Staff began to experience a compounding effect on their commitment as the school became a vibrant community where individuals grew together, collaboration, and shared purpose. Ron was crafting a legacy—not through mandates, but by strategically nurturing relational connections that would outlast his tenure.

Ron was not focused on short-term gains. His leadership ensured the school was not just surviving, but thriving. His strategic actions and relational depth made the school a place where transformative change was possible—and sustainable. The culture of influence he cultivated was defined by a shared vision and collective commitment to the school's mission, demonstrating the profound impact of leadership that is both visionary and deeply human.

Guided by the principles of cultural cascades and compounding influence, Ron empowered committed members to transform the school from within. He led others to embrace the school's vision for positive change while remaining grounded in authentic relationships and purposeful action. Under his leadership, the school became a place where students thrived and educators felt empowered to fulfill their calling. The ripple effects of this cultural shift extended far beyond the school's walls—impacting the wider community and serving as an inspiring model for other organizations.

Cultural Cascades: Compounding Effect of Commitment

Cultural cascades are processes that harness the power of social and professional influence, where individuals adopt the opinions, actions, or behaviors of others within their networks. In organizational settings, these cascades can have significant implications for the spread of cultural norms and the successful scaling of initiatives. Both cultural and initiative cascades can generate "ripple effects" that occur at multiple levels—from small teams and subgroups to the broader organization.

A defining characteristic of cultural cascades is their tendency to be "self-reinforcing," particularly through the influence of subculture leaders and peer groups. Staff members often have varying threshold levels for how much peer commitment they need to observe before adopting a behavior or initiative themselves. As more individuals commit to a specific belief or practice, others within their subculture or sphere of influence are increasingly likely to follow, triggering a cascade of cultural alignment. This phenomenon can rapidly accelerate the transfer of knowledge, beliefs, and practices throughout the organization.

This threshold effect—similar to the idea that "a rising tide lifts all boats"—illustrates how individual growth contributes to collective advancement through enhanced collaboration. Building a culture of cooperation requires intentionally cultivating staff members who demonstrate positive commitment and form meaningful partnerships that reinforce a shared sense of purpose. These connections help align individual contributions with the organization's broader vision.

Leaders must trust in the capabilities and mindsets of subculture leaders to influence others within their unique spheres of influence. These intentional opportunities for peer collaboration not only strengthen relationships but also create a supportive community where members grow together, exchange insights, and celebrate one another's successes. Ultimately, fostering these connections enhances the team's sense of collective efficacy, reinforcing the belief that, together, they can achieve shared goals.

Leadership is fundamentally about inspiring and aligning collective action toward shared goals, which requires identifying and mobilizing committed individuals to help reinforce the organization's cultural direction. Recognizing those who are genuinely invested in the organization's values is essential for fostering a compounding effect of commitment. By intentionally recognizing and elevating these individuals, leaders can create "ripple effects" that bring others' commitment into alignment with the organization's core values. Actions such as highlighting early adopters and celebrating implementation milestones help reinforce desired behaviors and accelerate the spread of positive cultural norms. These efforts embed cultural commitments across the organization, ensuring that change is not only effective but also sustainable.

The presence of committed peers creates a powerful conduit for supporting those who may be uncertain in their commitment, offering mentorship and collaboration as pathways to growth. Strategically positioning committed individuals in formal leadership roles (e.g., department chairs or team leads) is essential, but it must be paired with intentional support and a focus on leadership development. By investing in professional learning opportunities for emerging leaders, organizations ensure they are equipped with the skills and confidence to lead effectively and positively influence others within their sphere of influence.

Leadership Cascades: Leading Others, Teams, and Organizations

The ecological impacts of the removal and reintroduction of wolves in Yellowstone National Park serve as a powerful metaphor: without systematic and intentional leadership, the fabric of an organization can begin to unravel, leading to cultural decay. Dysfunctional leadership erodes members' cultural commitment, often resulting in a fragmented and counterproductive culture. In contrast, systematic leadership can renew and restore an organization's culture through a deliberate effort to align individual commitment with the organization's core values—amplifying relational influence across the system. The trophic cascades observed in Yellowstone highlight the powerful lesson that even seemingly minor or unseen elements—much like individual behaviors within organizations—can significantly disrupt or stabilize an entire ecosystem.

Natural scientists often describe a healthy ecosystem as one marked by numerous symbiotic relationships between species. Similarly, in our organizational ecosystem, ideal collaboration between individuals and teams reflects a form of symbiosis—positive relationships that benefit both the individual and the broader system. Through intentional collaboration, we can create cultural cascades by building leadership capacity in others and fostering professional connections that deepen commitment, ultimately triggering further cascades of influence within subcultures.

Throughout the previous chapters, we have shared examples of how intentionally fostering successful collaborations—between individuals, within teams and departments, and across groups—can create a vibrant culture of influence. Cultural Mapping enables leaders to cultivate this culture of collaboration and leverage the professional capital that arises from the collective expertise of their members. As a result, workplace ecosystems can experience transformative change by building aligned teams united around a shared vision for the organization's future. We have provided practical strategies for leaders to develop professional capital within their team by intentionally expanding relational connections and building influential bridges across the entire organizational ecosystem.

Cultural Mapping within organizations is a complex and dynamic process that goes well beyond individual actions. It involves the cascading effects that begin with a single member's behavior, spreading from their immediate "circle of influence" through wider "rings of influence," forming complex webs throughout their broader "sphere of influence." These interactions create cultural and initiative cascades across the entire organization. This lesson highlights the interdependence between individual actions and the overall organizational culture. Leaders seeking to nurture professional capital and foster a positive workplace culture recognize that understanding this interplay is essential for aligning influence and implementing cohesive strategies through relational connections that reinforce desired cultural commitments.

Within an ecosystem, trophic cascades illustrate how the influence of one species can have profound direct and indirect effects on the entire web of life. This lesson underscores the interconnectedness and sensitivity of our own systems, where small actions by one individual can lead to significant consequences across an organization. In terms of individual influence, our behaviors create far-reaching "ripple effects" on others. Leaders must remain mindful of these potential impacts and strive to foster positive ripple effects throughout their organizations. Using Cultural Mapping, leaders can intentionally leverage relational connections and the power of committed influencers to shape and sustain a healthy organizational culture. By embracing the principles of trophic cascades applied to leadership, we cultivate a culture that supports the collective commitment of our ecosystem.

Promoting organizational success requires leaders to navigate a complex process that involves managing their time and energy to support their people and align systems effectively. Leaders can foster a relational culture of collaboration and influence that propels the organization forward. Through intentional and systemic efforts, leaders can build commitment by leveraging areas of strength while addressing challenges to sustain change (Schein, 2010). It is essential for leaders to work simultaneously on the overall culture and on shifting dynamics within subcultures. By focusing on strategies that encourage others to invest in the organization's culture, leaders can generate strong support for implementing initiatives (Kotter, 1996). Cultivating a culture of investment involves leveraging the power of relationships and empowering those in positions of influence. When leaders intentionally develop and support individuals aligned with the organization's values and goals, motivated team members emerge who make meaningful impacts on the lives of others.

To achieve an organization's collective goals, it is essential for leaders to deepen members' commitment to the vision, culture, and implementation of initiatives. Leaders can influence others to embrace the culture and advance initiatives by leveraging relationships and positions of influence, aligning outcomes with values, empowering individuals, building capacity, and providing resources and opportunities for professional growth. Ultimately, as leaders, we are in the relationship-building business and must be seen walking alongside our team members to cultivate a culture of investment—where individuals are motivated to contribute and grow.

Leadership is not just about managing tasks; it's about inspiring and empowering the people we aspire to lead. When leaders focus on capacity-building strategies, they can cultivate a positive organizational culture where individuals are motivated to commit and grow as professionals. This intentional approach to creating a culture of influence not only drives organizational success but also reconnects leaders to the joy and fulfillment of their role, allowing them to live vicariously through the impact of their team members.

The Power of Positive Stories

Our internal and external narratives shape the culture of our institutions, highlighting the importance of mindful storytelling for retention, recruitment, and influencing the community's perceptions. By deliberately promoting positive narratives and celebrating successes, we can cultivate a culture of excellence that inspires others to join our mission.

As principal, Ron was determined to create a warm and welcoming environment for both staff and students. He deeply believed in the transformative power of positive communication and instilled the belief that every positive interaction shapes the school's culture. Inspired by a leadership seminar, he introduced an initiative encouraging staff to make five positive calls a week to parents, celebrating their students' achievements and behavior. This approach aimed not only to share good news but to nurture relationships and nurture a culture of positivity.

Although initially met with some hesitation about the practicality of making these calls, Ron led by example to demonstrate the power of positive outreach. Following this initiative, the school experienced a remarkable shift as staff, parents, and students were moved by the ripple effects created by waves of praise and gratitude.

Encouraged by this success, Ron expanded his practice of gratitude. He believed it was equally important to celebrate staff by reaching out to those who supported them behind the scenes—their families and friends. One day, Ron wrote heartfelt handwritten notes to relatives and close friends of several staff members, expressing gratitude for their support and acknowledging their contributions to the school's mission to educate and inspire students. The response was overwhelming.

One letter was sent to Frank's parents just before Christmas break. On Christmas Eve, as Frank's family gathered around the dinner table, his father read Ron's words aloud. Tears of pride were shared by everyone that night. Through Ron's affirmation, staff members felt appreciated, and Frank felt truly part of the school family. The bonds within the community grew stronger, and the culture of excellence Ron envisioned soon became a reality.

Looking back at the impact, Ron couldn't help but smile. He had witnessed firsthand how intentional storytelling, positive communication, and *celebrating one another's successes could shape a school's culture. By promoting a positive narrative and honoring achievements, they had created a community where a thriving sense of belonging prevailed. Ron's simple yet powerful commitment to making five positive calls a week sparked cultural cascades and ripple effects that strengthened relationships throughout the school.*

Cultivating Intentional Influence

In the journey to lead cultural cascades and cultivate a culture of intentional influence, leaders often embark on a transformative effort to shape the very relational fabric of their organizations. Creating a culture of influence requires leaders to use the Cultural Mapping process to understand and navigate the dynamics of their professional networks. This involves assessing the commitment levels of various members and identifying key influencers—whether champions, resisters, or those who may be disengaged.

A culture of influence is not built by chance; it is intentionally cultivated. When leaders take the time to explore individuals' origin stories, motives, and perspectives, they can build strong relational connections that form committed clusters within the professional network. This enables leaders to create a guiding coalition that fosters positive momentum and influences others within their "spheres of influence." By strategically building capacity among members of this coalition, leaders support subculture leadership and activate the alignment necessary for transformative change.

> A culture of influence is not built by chance; it is intentionally cultivated.

Ultimately, leading cultural cascades is not just about achieving organizational goals but about creating environments where members feel empowered to collectively pursue excellence. At its core, Cultural Mapping enables leaders to understand the cultural network and staff connections, unlocking the power of professional capital to intentionally cultivate cultural cascades. By empowering committed members, leaders can build a culture of collective influence. Cultural cascades remind us that every action, no matter how small, has the potential to spark significant change. As leaders navigate these complexities and foster a community of influence, they pave the way for ripple effects that spread throughout the organization, enabling all members to thrive.

CHAPTER 13

Leading Initiative Cascades: Organizational Learning

Creating an Ecosystem for Learning

Organizational culture is often defined as the set of shared values, beliefs, and practices that shape individuals' behavior within an organization (Schein, 2010). Leaders can strategically leverage initiative cascades to significantly influence organizational culture by encouraging the adoption of new initiatives and the spread of cultural norms. When a leader introduces a new initiative, it may initially be met with skepticism or resistance (Kotter, 1996). However, if a few influential individuals adopt and advocate for the initiative, they can inspire others to follow. As more individuals adopt the initiative, the threshold for broader acceptance is lowered, creating a cascade effect that can lead to widespread implementation and cultural alignment.

Leaders must consider not only their intentional actions but also the complexity of facilitating individual choices and the cultural power generated through relational connections, which manifest as professional capital within an organization. This cultural influence and professional capital are most impactful when leaders rally key connectors—individuals who can influence those around them and across the organization. Their influence has the potential to shape the organizational culture and the implementation of initiatives, accelerating meaningful progress toward the organization's intended outcomes.

Cultural Mapping, built on the power of initiative cascades, offers a systemic framework for leaders seeking to intentionally build cohesive organizational cultures. By strategically engaging influential individuals and leveraging cultural influence, leaders can drive meaningful cultural transformation within an environment of shared learning and collaboration. This approach positions organizations for sustained success and innovation by ensuring that cultural shifts and new initiatives are widely embraced and effectively implemented across teams. Through these efforts, leaders foster a dynamic and inclusive culture that empowers all members to contribute meaningfully to the organization's goals.

Administrators as Lead Learners

During an observation in a science classroom, Ron watched students learn about how animals often exhibit allelomimetic (or contagious) behaviors.

LEADING INITIATIVE CASCADES: ORGANIZATIONAL LEARNING

Through social facilitation and imitation (modeling), groups of organisms learn together to overcome environmental limitations. This struck Ron as a powerful metaphor for administrators shaping educators' skillsets to implement initiatives aimed at improving student academic success.

As highlighted by Marzano and colleagues (2005), the quality of teaching and principal leadership are the most critical factors we can control to impact educational outcomes. Intentionally integrating leadership in learning while fostering a supportive culture enables administrators to lead effectively—both directly through their influence and indirectly by leveraging cultural networks to build professional capital among staff. Marzano and colleagues (2005) emphasized the importance of embedding school improvement initiatives within the organizational structure for sustained reform. Lead learners must effectively create a culture of continuous instructional and supervisory improvement by focusing on rigorous, relevant teaching and learning methods grounded in respect and trust (Wagner et al., 2006).

Together, these insights show that administrators must leverage influence to cultivate culture and lead learning, transitioning from traditional managerial roles to embracing their role as lead learners. This new paradigm requires leaders to evolve into lead learners who guide learning and cultural growth within their schools. Through intentional professional development, collaboration, and strategic use of tools like Cultural Mapping, administrators can foster a culture of continuous improvement and actively work toward a unified vision supporting academic excellence. Understanding teacher needs, structuring organizational systems to support learning, creating time for meaningful PLCs, and promoting collaboration for skill development are essential components of this approach (DuFour & Marzano, 2009).

Leveraging Initiative Cascades for Professional Learning

Information cascades occur when individuals in a group or network adopt the views, actions, or behaviors of their peers rather than relying on their own independent analysis or beliefs (Bikhchandani, Hirshleifer, & Welch, 1992). This phenomenon is especially relevant in organizational contexts, where it can greatly influence the adoption of new initiatives, the spread of cultural values, and the success of change efforts. A key characteristic of information cascades is their self-reinforcing nature: as more members adopt a particular behavior or belief, the likelihood that others will follow increases, creating a "cascade" effect that rapidly spreads through the community. Information cascades can be observed across many areas, from social media and workplaces to political movements. By understanding and leveraging these dynamics, leaders can strategically use members' relational influence and political capital to shape organizational culture and effectively scale initiatives.

Organizational decisions and actions are often perceived as being imposed in a "top-down" manner, overlooking the valuable insights of frontline staff. For leaders aiming to drive meaningful shifts in professional practices, a thoughtful and reflective strategy is essential to effectively scale and support new professional development initiatives. Initiative cascades offer a paradigm shift by moving away from the traditional hierarchical approach that tends to bypass critical contributions from those on the ground. To increase the likelihood of success, it is important to consider staff members' commitment levels and relational connections as foundational elements in leading change.

Cultural Mapping provides actionable strategies and a systemic process that empowers leaders to shape commitment, relationships, and influence towards the organizational goals. This approach encourages reflective and constructive dialogue among professionals on how to improve their environment and implement best practices. Without a clear understanding of influence dynamics, relational ties, and commitment levels, leaders risk losing the momentum needed for lasting change. By mapping the cultural landscape, leaders can better understand staff perspectives, identify key individuals to engage early, and address potential concerns.

Dynamics of Initiative Cascades

- **Observation and Adoption:** Individuals observe the actions or beliefs of others and often choose to adopt them, sometimes setting aside their own independent analysis.
- **Reinforcement and Propagation:** As more individuals adopt a behavior or belief, it becomes increasingly likely that others will follow, strengthening and expanding the cascade.
- **Threshold Effect:** Different individuals have varying thresholds for adoption, which affects the pace of adoption and can lead to rapid acceleration, resulting in widespread acceptance within the group or network.
- **Peer Influence:** The relational influence of peers—especially those who are committed or seen as leaders—plays a critical role in driving the cascade process.

Cultural Mapping goes beyond simple survey data collection for school leaders; it becomes a strategic process for identifying areas that need attention and fostering a culture of collaboration by creating cascades of cultural influence. This approach empowers administrators not only to cultivate a positive organizational culture but also to scale the implementation of professional learning initiatives. Professional development thrives when it is intentional, ongoing, and systematic—principles that are exemplified in effective Professional Learning Communities (PLCs) (DuFour & Eaker, 1998; Guskey, 2000). Much like contagious (allelomimetic) behaviors in nature, PLCs are groups of educators who come together to learn, collaborate, and support one another in improving student learning outcomes. Leadership plays a vital role in these communities by cultivating committed educators who actively engage in PLC activities and demonstrate a continuous willingness to learn and refine their practice.

A key strategy for cultivating a culture conducive to professional development is leveraging Cultural Mapping to uncover the informal networks that exist within the organization. By gaining insight into communication patterns and relational connections, leaders can identify key influencers who are well-positioned to drive change and foster collaboration through strategic influence. Cultural Mapping provides a valuable foundation for organizing members into PLCs and other professional development initiatives by enabling leaders to group individuals based on their levels of commitment and connectivity within the organization. These strategic groupings encourage the exchange of knowledge and best practices, ensuring that professional development efforts lead to meaningful improvements in practice. For administrators, Cultural Mapping helps foster a culture of continuous learning and growth by revealing and addressing gaps in professional capacity and collaboration.

Stories From the Field

One day, Ron sat staring at his computer screen, contemplating the myriad challenges facing his high school. As the morning sun filtered through his office window, he braced himself for another day navigating the complex demands of educational leadership. His gaze shifted to the stack of papers on his desk—each folder representing a different initiative or issue awaiting his attention. Despite the weight of responsibility, Ron remained grounded in his belief in collaboration and continuous improvement. He knew that meaningful change could not be achieved in isolation; transforming his school would require the collective expertise and shared effort of his staff.

LEADING INITIATIVE CASCADES: ORGANIZATIONAL LEARNING

Recently, Ron had begun exploring Cultural Mapping and found himself intrigued by the concept of allelomimetic behavior—a type of contagious behavior that often occurs unconsciously. As he studied the stack of initiatives before him, he began to see how Cultural Mapping could help identify key stakeholders and reveal the potential for influence through networks of relational connections. As a leader, he understood that people often mirror the actions and beliefs of their peers—frequently without deep analysis or questioning. Within the school context, this meant that initiatives introduced by administration were far more likely to gain traction if they were embraced and championed by influential staff members.

Ron saw the potential to create a supportive framework that encouraged these contagious behaviors by fostering collaboration among educators. At the heart of his leadership philosophy was a belief in continuous growth and the idea that every staff member possessed unique strengths that could elevate the team. His recognition of each individual's expertise helped build a culture of collective efficacy, where staff felt empowered to strive for excellence together. He prioritized creating a culture where experimentation and learning were encouraged, not feared—where mistakes were viewed as opportunities for growth and invitations to tap into the expertise of others.

Ron was also attuned to the emotional landscape of his school. He understood the isolation and imposter syndrome that many educators, especially those new to the profession, often experienced. To combat this, he focused on building additional layers of support, knowing that a strong sense of belonging and collaboration could reduce turnover and help create a more resilient and connected staff. He recalled a recent conversation with his instructional coach about implementing project-based learning. By recognizing individual strengths and providing targeted support, they had already begun to shift the school's culture toward one of ongoing collaboration and improvement. Cultural Mapping had served as a strategic lens to guide their efforts and they planned to continue using it to deepen instructional practice and professional learning.

That afternoon, Ron met with his leadership team to explore how they might further apply the principles of initiative cascades and Cultural Mapping to address the school's most pressing challenges. Together, they developed a plan to identify other committed influencers within the staff and empower them to champion new initiatives. Through targeted professional learning, this core group would be connected with others to reinforce a culture of continuous improvement and expand relational influence across the school.

As the day came to a close, Ron felt a renewed sense of optimism. He knew the road ahead would be demanding, but he was confident that, by channeling initiative cascades and the insights of Cultural Mapping, he could lead his school toward meaningful, sustainable change. With this clarity of purpose, he closed his laptop, ready to face whatever challenges tomorrow might bring.

Sustainability of the Profession and Initiatives

The journey for many educators often begins in an environment that demands immediate "survival of the fittest," as new teachers frequently start their careers without adequate support, leading to high turnover rates. It is essential for educational systems to dismantle the barriers that contribute to teacher isolation. Ingersoll (2001) highlighted that teacher attrition is especially severe among newcomers, a challenge that has since been exacerbated, including difficulties in retaining seasoned educators who may lack the contemporary skills needed for today's learning environments. This shortfall threatens the development of a competent workforce capable of thriving in a global economy. Therefore, it is critical for school leaders to spearhead professional learning efforts to ensure every classroom embodies a learner-centered approach.

The school environment reflects its culture, which can drift and evolve over time. Leaders play a crucial role in guiding these shifts, as they are best positioned to influence and activate multiple positive cascades within the organization. Cultural Mapping offers administrators a pathway to foster systematic collaboration among educators, positively impacting the creation of a connected culture that supports initiative implementation. It also serves as an essential strategy to counteract the widespread isolation common in the teaching profession while easing members as they transition into their roles and navigate their complex professional responsibilities. Administrators thus serve multifaceted roles—as managers, leaders, coaches, and mentors—striving to improve classroom practices and equip teachers with the skills essential for implementing educational initiatives.

Change initiatives often begin with strong momentum but can quickly lose traction if not properly supported to ensure long-term sustainability (Hargreaves & Fink, 2006). The responsibility of leadership is to guide from a foundation rooted in core values while simultaneously building systems and developing the capacity of their people to ensure that the work and implemented changes endure over time. A cornerstone of Ron's leadership journey in transforming school culture was his recognition of the complexities involved in maintaining momentum as a critical factor in deepening the commitment levels necessary for lasting change. To sustain these efforts, Ron began to view both budgetary resources and the allocation of his time as a "moral document" reflecting his values and priorities. This intentional approach emphasized the importance of generating influence through leadership that actively supports and nurtures the organizational culture, enabling members to engage in meaningful, systemic improvement.

Ron's story exemplifies that sustaining change initiatives is not merely about introducing new policies or programs, but about cultivating a workplace ecosystem where people can truly thrive. Commitment is built through cascades of influence—by fostering relational connections and leveraging the expertise within our staff. The Cultural Mapping process has the potential to drive positive transformations that become embedded in the fabric of the organization, resulting in lasting change that benefits the entire school community.

Stories From the Field

The shift toward a more inclusive and supportive culture at Ron's school had a profound impact on student performance and engagement. This transformation was driven by several interconnected factors that collectively enhanced the educational environment for everyone while significantly improving student well-being. The inclusive culture cultivated by leadership created a cascade of positive effects throughout the school. As teachers began to feel more valued and connected, they became better equipped to tailor their instructional approaches to meet students' needs—leading to improved academic outcomes and higher levels of student engagement.

Survey data collected afterward revealed measurable improvements that reflected the tangible impact of these efforts. Staff morale rose significantly, coinciding with a notable decrease in turnover. Likewise, students reported experiencing a more inclusive and connected learning environment. This cultural shift also had a ripple effect through its emphasis on belonging and relational support, fostering a safer environment that positively impacted students' mental health and contributed to a reduction in bullying incidents. One of the most meaningful changes for Ron was the shift in perception of the school's administration. Staff and students began to view school leaders not as distant managers, but as engaged and empathetic partners invested in shaping the daily life of the school.

Leading Organizational Learning

Accountability mandates and evolving social expectations place significant responsibility on school leaders to improve student outcomes—requiring schools not only to educate but to ensure student proficiency. Initiative cascades, facilitated through the use of Cultural

LEADING INITIATIVE CASCADES: ORGANIZATIONAL LEARNING

Mapping, offer a systemic and strategic process that enables leaders to scale initiatives by creating a culture of influence and activating cultural cascades across the organization. Leaders serving as the "Leader of the Learning" must leverage collective professional capital among key influencers to lay the foundation for effective Professional Learning Communities (PLCs). Simultaneously, acting as the "Cultivator of the Culture" requires leaders to align the organizational culture in ways that support the implementation and sustainability of professional learning initiatives.

Through intentional, strategic engagement, leaders can move beyond traditional top-down models and adopt a more reflective and inclusive strategy—harnessing staff influence, relational connections, and commitment to drive meaningful, lasting change. In the end, leaders must skillfully navigate initiative cascades to maximize the power of professional capital, cultivating a thriving culture grounded in collective efficacy and empowered relationships.

CHAPTER 14

Ron's Journey of Cultural Transformation

How Can I Be Ron?

Ron's story is a powerful testament to the impact of authentic leadership and the enduring strength of creating cascades of intentional influence. School leaders play a pivotal role in guiding their institutions through continuous improvement efforts by leading strategically and fostering cultural transformation. At some point in our leadership journey, we must recognize that it is our responsibility to become the kind of leader we once hoped to be guided by. In essence, we must grow into the best version of ourselves and reconnect with the true joy of our work—leading and serving our people.

As you continue to grow into the leader your team needs work intentionally to create a culture of influence by following the key practices outlined throughout this book:

C – Create a Culture of Intentional Influence and Commitment
U – Understand Influence
L – Leverage Relationships
T – Target Individuals and Teams
U – Uncover Resistance
R – Reflect on Relationships
A – Activate Commitment
L – Lead Oneself, Others, Teams, and the Organization

M – Map Your People
A – Analyze and Reflect
P – Plan for Purposeful Action
P – Propel Cascades
I – Influence Individuals
N – Navigate Disengagement and Resistance
G – Grow Others and the Organization

With determination, Ron embarked on a mission to revitalize the school's culture. His leadership style underwent a profound evolution as he shifted from a top-down approach to one that fostered cascades of intentional cultural influence and prioritized collaboration. Ron realized that as a relational leader he must lead from within and operate from his core values to build a culture of connection and belonging. He became a model of authentic leadership by embracing vulnerability—openly sharing his challenges and aspirations, seeking input from his team and the wider community, and encouraging others to do the same. Through this on-going journey, Ron not only transformed the school culture but also rediscovered himself—finding joy in leadership and passion in creating a culture where everyone could thrive.

Using insights from the three phases of Culture Mapping, Ron and his team developed a roadmap for change that emphasized fostering positive relationships and building a strong network of intentional influence. Ron's narrative shows that organizational resilience is about more than just survival—it's about creating a thriving environment. His leadership approach secured the lasting impact and sustained success of the cultural transformation by creating conditions for empowerment at all levels through deepening relational connections and strengthening commitment. Over time, the school's culture began to shift, as reflected in survey data showing an increased sense of connection and belonging. Ron's story serves as a beacon of hope, inspiring leaders to embrace their authentic selves and leverage strategic insights to drive lasting change by shaping the culture within their organizations.

Process for Cultural Mapping

	Creating a Cultural Map	Cultural Mapping Reflections	Cultural Mapping Planning
Step 1:	Map Your People - Categorize Members' Influence	Map the Community Groups	Gain Insights Into Influence
Step 2:	Categorize Commitment Levels	Assess Commitment Levels	Identify Entry Points to Moving Forward
Step 3:	Map the Relational Connectivity and Influence	Evaluate Relational Connectivity and Influence	Understand Your People – Show What You Know

Embracing the Joy of the Leadership Journey: Engaging in the Right Work

In Ron's leadership journey, he discovered the profound joy of driving systemic change through an unconventional path. Ron's leadership philosophy was simple yet powerful: **Be the best version of yourself** and focus on doing the ***Right Work***, for the ***Right Reasons***, with the ***Right People***, and a leader will achieve the ***Right Results***. This credo became the foundation of his approach, guiding his decisions and actions throughout the cultural transformation of individuals and teams across the school.

As educators, we enter this profession with the intention to serve—not only to make a difference in the lives of our students but also within our communities. Leadership is a craft that develops over time through intentional effort and skill-building. It calls on each of us to be authentic and to tailor our actions to the unique circumstances of our organizations. The deepest joy for a leader comes from connecting with people—whether students, staff, faculty, parents, or community members. In making these connections, it is essential to pause and reflect, finding ways to reconnect with the joy of serving and leading others. Ron understood that true leadership joy doesn't come from accolades or achievements, but from witnessing and celebrating the success of his team and students. He believed that by intentionally influencing relational connections, leaders can create a committed culture that drives success for everyone involved. Ron cultivated a workplace where everyone could thrive and contribute to the school's vision by placing the right people in roles aligned with their strengths and passions.

Ron's story teaches us that leadership is an ongoing journey of self-improvement and a life of service—one where he gave himself and his team permission to rediscover joy in their work and prioritize the development of their collective capabilities. Ron sought to identify common themes behind challenges and responded by creating plans aimed at deeply influencing the school's culture through strengthening relational connections, building leadership capacity, and increasing initiative implementation. He worked to understand the nuances of staff members' relationships and their commitment to the organization's goals while developing intentional actions to support leaders in positively shaping both culture and initiative outcomes. Throughout this work, Ron discovered that the true joy of leadership lies in the journey itself—engaging in meaningful relational work alongside a team of passionate individuals.

Ron worked tirelessly to harness the leadership potential within his organization, embracing his roles as both cultivator of culture and lead learner. His commitment to creating cultural cascades through relationships became the foundation for continuous improvement—an approach that was contagious and inspired those around him to strive for excellence while serving their community with dedication.

Building the Culture We Want: Transforming Organizational Culture

As leaders, we must remember that creating the culture we envision requires intentional effort. *We get the culture we BUILD, not just the one we merely WISH for.* Cultural Mapping is a process of understanding the relational connections that shape our professional lives and of creating a culture of intentional influence that fosters a supportive community. Collaboration has the power to transform organizations by leveraging members' professional capital to generate cultural cascades. We trust that you now appreciate the significance of using Cultural Mapping for leaders—to drive positive cultural change, identify opportunities for new connections, and strengthen relationships—providing you with a roadmap for reflection and actionable steps to enhance influence.

> We get the culture we BUILD, not just the one we merely WISH for.

Leading through Cultural Mapping offers an inspiring blueprint for leaders seeking to cultivate a culture of continuous improvement. Ron leveraged this process to understand and unleash cultural cascades of influence by examining relational connections, identifying key influencers, and assessing commitment levels—ultimately leveraging strategic insights to shape a thriving environment where members of the school community felt valued and empowered.

The Cultural Mapping process is a game-changer for leaders striving to build a culture of influence. It offers deep insights into the importance of our social and professional networks, enabling leaders to foster meaningful relationships that act as catalysts for positive influence among colleagues, students, and families. This process helps leaders monitor commitment levels and the implementation of professional initiatives. When school leaders systematically utilize Cultural Mapping, they can serve as catalysts for creating a supportive culture and enhancing teaching and learning by engaging individuals in reflective conversations that accelerate school improvement efforts. Embracing Cultural Mapping as a proactive leadership approach unlocks vast opportunities for building professional and personal capacity, ultimately shaping the transformation of the entire community. To harness the power of our networks in driving transformative change, we must embrace our strengths, reflect on our insights, and recognize the significance of relational connections. In doing so, we enhance our ability to create an environment that nurtures commitment and empowers others to thrive.

Leading change in any organization is complex and challenging, yet essential for meeting the evolving needs of staff. Throughout these chapters, we have explored several key strategies to help leaders create cultural cascades:

- Create a Cultural Map of the network to visualize relationships, commitment levels, and influence.
- Harness commitment and collaboration that foster trust and collective efficacy.
- Build capacity in your key committed influencers to empower others and multiply their positive impact in creating a culture of influence.
- Address disengagement and resistance with empathy and strategy.
- Sustain commitment over time through reflection and intentional actions.

Regardless of your position or title within an organization, you must believe and know that you are a leader capable of successfully guiding change and making a positive impact on those you serve. While the strategies presented in this book are important, remember that leading change is not a one-size-fits-all approach. Through intentional actions focused on building relationships and strategically scaling capacity for initiatives, leaders can create environments where every member feels valued and empowered to contribute their best. These strategies must be interconnected and supported by leaders who deeply understand their organization, its culture, and its people. To leave a lasting legacy as a leader, you must embrace your authentic self and foster a collaborative culture that enables others to help you lead through cultural cascades of influence.

Your Leadership Journey

As you continue on your leadership journey, we encourage you to take what you have learned from this book and apply it in your daily work to make a meaningful impact on your organization and those you lead. As leaders, it is essential to continually learn and evolve our practices to effectively influence the culture within our organizations. We hope this book has challenged you to think differently about your approach to intentional influence and reconnecting with the *"Joy of the Work"* in leading and serving your people.

As you strive to better lead your teams, remember to reflect on the concepts presented here to better equip you in creating a culture of intentional influence that builds a stronger, more cohesive organization. Become the leader your organization needs. Build the culture you want. Whether you lead a classroom, a club or activity, a small team, or an entire organization, the principles explored in this process apply across all levels of leadership. Leadership isn't about titles — it's about creating intentional influence. Through deliberate action and sustained support, we can transform our communities into vibrant hubs of intentional influence by fostering collaborative environments grounded in relational connections and cultural cascades of commitment.

References

Barabási, A.-L. (2003). *Linked: How everything is connected to everything else and what it means*. Plume.

Bikhchandani, S., Hirshleifer, D., & Welch, I. (1992). A theory of fads, fashion, custom, and cultural change as informational cascades. *Journal of Political Economy, 100*(5), 992-1026.

Burt, R. S. (2005). *Brokerage and closure: An introduction to social capital*. Oxford University Press.

Casas, J. (2017). *Culturize: Every student. Every day. Whatever it takes*. Dave Burgess Consulting, Inc.

Christakis, N. A., & Fowler, J. H. (2009). *Connected: The surprising power of our social networks and how they shape our lives*. Little, Brown and Company.

Collins, J. (2001). *Good to great: Why some companies make the leap... and others don't*. Harper Business.

Covey, S. R. (1989). *The 7 habits of highly effective people: Powerful lessons in personal change*. Simon & Schuster.

Cross, R., Borgatti, S. P., & Parker, A. (2002). Making invisible work visible: Using social network analysis to support strategic collaboration. *California Management Review, 44*(2), 25-46. https://doi.org/10.2307/41166121

Cross, R., & Parker, A. (2004). *The hidden power of social networks: Understanding how work really gets done in organizations*. Harvard Business School Press.

DuFour, R., & Eaker, R. (1998). *Professional learning communities at work: Best practices for enhancing student achievement*. Bloomington, IN: Solution Tree.

DuFour, R., & Marzano, R. J. (2009). High-Leverage Strategies for Principal Leadership. *Educational Leadership, 66*(5), 62 - 68.

Dweck, C. S. (2006). *Mindset: The new psychology of success*. Ballantine Books.

Freeman, L. C. (1978). Centrality in social networks: Conceptual clarification. *Social Networks, 1*(3), 215-239. https://doi.org/10.1016/0378-8733(78)90021-7

Fullan, M. (2001). *Leading in a culture of change*. Jossey-Bass.

Fullan, M., & Hargreaves, A. (2012). *Professional capital: Transforming teaching in every school*. Teachers College Press.

Gladwell, M. (2000). *The tipping point: How little things can make a big difference*. Little, Brown, and Company.

Gordon, J. (2007). *The energy bus: 10 rules to fuel your life, work, and team with positive energy*. Wiley.

Granovetter, M. (1973). The strength of weak ties. *American Journal of Sociology, 78*(6), 1360-1380. https://doi.org/10.1086/225469

Guskey, T. R. (2000). *Evaluating professional development*. Thousand Oaks, CA: Corwin Press.

Hargreaves, A., & Fink, D. (2006). *Sustainable leadership*. Jossey-Bass.

Ingersoll, R. M. (2001). *Teacher turnover and teacher shortages: An organizational analysis*. American Educational Research Journal, 38(3), 499-534. https://doi.org/10.3102/00028312038003499

Kegan, R., & Lahey, L. L. (2016). *An everyone culture: Becoming a deliberately developmental organization*. Harvard Business Review Press.

Kotter, J. P. (1996). *Leading change*. Harvard Business Review Press.

Lencioni, P. (2002). *The five dysfunctions of a team: A leadership fable*. Jossey-Bass.

Marzano, R. J., Waters, T., & McNulty, B. (2005). *School leadership that works*. Alexandria, VA: Association for Supervision and Curriculum Development.

Maxwell, J. C. (2007). *The 21 irrefutable laws of leadership: Follow them and people will follow you*. Thomas Nelson.

Milgram, S. (1967). The small-world problem. *Psychology Today, 1*(1), 60-67.

REFERENCES

Ripple, W. J., & Beschta, R. L. (2012). Trophic cascades in Yellowstone: The first 15 years after wolf reintroduction. *Biological Conservation*, 145(1), 205-213. https://doi.org/10.1016/j.biocon.2011.11.005

Rogers, E. M. (1962). *Diffusion of innovations*. Free Press.

Schein, E. H. (2010). *Organizational culture and leadership* (4th ed.). Jossey-Bass.

Scott, J. (2013). *Social network analysis* (3rd ed.). Sage Publications.

Sinek, S. (2009). *Start with why: How great leaders inspire everyone to take action*. Penguin.

Wagner, T., Kegan, R., Lahey, L., Lemons, R. W., Garnier, J., Helsing, D., et al. (2006). *Change Leadership: A Practical Guide to Transforming Our Schools*. San Francisco, CA: Jossey-Bass.

Wheatley, M. J. (2006). *Leadership and the new science: Discovering order in a chaotic world* (3rd ed.). Berrett-Koehler Publishers.

About the Authors

Dr. Ben Johnson has been the Assistant Superintendent of Secondary Schools for Bismarck Public Schools (ND) since 2014. He has a doctorate degree in Educational Leadership and Policy Studies from Iowa State University. He achieved his master's degree from The University of Iowa and his undergraduate degree is from Cornell College in Iowa.

As an executive coach, Johnson believes that organizational leaders have two primary roles: to "Create a Culture of Influence" and to be the "Lead Learner." At the core of his leadership philosophy is fostering and maintaining relationships with all stakeholders, so they feel that they are valued members of their community. He believes that as leaders, we have the power to shape culture and guide the learning that empowers others to change the trajectory of students' lives, impact their families, and redefine the potential of entire communities—ultimately becoming a destination organization where people want to live, work, and thrive.

With over two decades of experience as a teacher and administrator, Dr. Johnson is passionate about leading systems that support innovative learning practices. He fosters innovative, personalized learning environments by combining project-based learning, customized scheduling, and the effective use of technology. He champions competency-based education integrated within a Multi-Tiered System of Supports that form the cornerstone for authentic learning experiences. Dr. Johnson is committed to preparing students for personalized learning pathways by cultivating a culture of learning rooted in strong relationships and innovative practices.

Ben and his wife, Brigitte, stay busy together raising two amazing young ladies. They enjoy outdoor activities during their spare time. Website: www.cascadingsolutions.org

ABOUT THE AUTHORS

Bobby Dodd earned four degrees before discovering his true calling—dedicating his life to helping others. Driven by a passion for helping others, Bobby Dodd pursued a career in school leadership, serving as principal at three Ohio high schools. During his tenure, he championed innovative initiatives that expanded opportunities for students and staff, including the development of digital academies, college summer camps, fabrication laboratories, Early College High School programs, and redesigned bell schedules featuring "Connect-Time" to foster relationships. He also led the creation of personalized learning environments that supported both student growth and staff development.

As an educator and leader, Dodd actively communicates, collaborates, and builds connections with stakeholders to strengthen his school community and contribute to the broader field of education. He has received awards for his contributions as a connected educator, including the 2016 NASSP Digital Principal of the Year award. He was also a finalist for the 2017 Varsity Brands "Principal of Principle" award. Dodd continues to assist others in education by presenting at the local, state, and national levels.

More from ConnectEDD Publishing

Since 2015, ConnectEDD has worked to transform education by empowering educators to become better-equipped to teach, learn, and lead. What started as a small company designed to provide professional learning events for educators has grown to include a variety of services to help educators and administrators address essential challenges. ConnectEDD offers instructional and leadership coaching, professional development workshops focusing on a variety of educational topics, a roster of nationally recognized educator associates who possess hands-on knowledge and experience, educational conferences custom-designed to meet the specific needs of schools, districts, and state/national organizations, and ongoing, personalized support, both virtually and onsite. In 2020, ConnectEDD expanded to include publishing services designed to provide busy educators with books and resources consisting of practical information on a wide variety of teaching, learning, and leadership topics. Please visit us online at connecteddpublishing.com or contact us at: info@connecteddpublishing.com

Recent Publications:

Live Your Excellence: Action Guide by Jimmy Casas

Culturize: Action Guide by Jimmy Casas

Daily Inspiration for Educators: Positive Thoughts for Every Day of the Year by Jimmy Casas

Eyes on Culture: Multiply Excellence in Your School by Emily Paschall

Pause. Breathe. Flourish. Living Your Best Life as an Educator by William D. Parker

L.E.A.R.N.E.R. Finding the True, Good, and Beautiful in Education by Marita Diffenbaugh

Educator Reflection Tips Volume II: Refining Our Practice by Jami Fowler-White

Handle With Care: Managing Difficult Situations in Schools with Dignity and Respect by Jimmy Casas and Joy Kelly

Disruptive Thinking: Preparing Learners for Their Future by Eric Sheninger

Permission to be Great: Increasing Engagement in Your School by Dan Butler

Daily Inspiration for Educators: Positive Thoughts for Every Day of the Year, Volume II by Jimmy Casas

The 6 Literacy Levers: Creating a Community of Readers by Brad Gustafson

The Educator's ATLAS: Your Roadmap to Engagement by Weston Kieschnick

In This Season: Words for the Heart by Todd Nesloney, LaNesha Tabb, Tanner Olson, and Alice Lee

MORE FROM CONNECTEDD PUBLISHING

Leading with a Humble Heart: A 40-Day Devotional for Leaders by Zac Bauermaster

Recalibrate the Culture: Our Why…Our Work…Our Values by Jimmy Casas

Creating Curious Classrooms: The Beauty of Questions by Emma Chiappetta

Crafting the Culture: 45 Reflections on What Matters Most by Joe Sanfelippo and Jeffrey Zoul

Improving School Mental Health: The Thriving School Community Solution by Charle Peck and Dr. Cameron Caswell

Building Authenticity: A Blueprint for the Leader Inside You by Todd Nesloney and Tyler Cook

Connecting Through Conversation: A Playbook for Talking with Kids by Erika Bare and Tiffany Burns

The Dream Factory: Designing a Purposeful Life by Mark Trumbo

Stories Behind Stances: Creating Empathy Through Hearing "The Other Side" by Chris Singleton

Happy Eyes: Becoming All Things to All People by Ryan Tillman

The Generative Age: Artificial Intelligence and the Future of Education by Alana Winnick

Recalibrate the Culture: Action Guide by Jimmy Casas

Leading with PEOPLE: A Six Pillar Framework for Fruitful Leadership by Zac Bauermaster

A School Leader's Guide to Reclaiming Purpose by Frederick C. Buskey

Foundations of an Elite Culture: Building Success with High Standards and a Positive Environment by David Arencibia

Personalize: Meeting the Needs of All Learners by Eric Sheninger and Nicki Slaugh

The Five Principles of Educator Professionalism: Rebuilding Trust in Schools by Nason Lollar

Words on the Wall: Culturizing Your Classroom For Observable Impact by Jimmy Casas and Cale Birk

School of Engagement: 45 Activities to Ignite Student Learning by Jonathan Alsheimer

Intentional Instructional Moves: Strategic Steps to Accelerate Student Learning by Sherry St. Clair

Overcoming Education: Complex Challenges, Difficult People, and the Art of Making a Difference by Brad R. Gustafson

The Language of Behavior: A Framework to Elevate Student Success by Charle Peck and Joshua Stamper

Whose Permission Are You Waiting For? An Educator's Guide to Doing What You Love by William D. Parker

The Leader You're Not…And Why It's Just As Important As the Leader You Are by Scott Borba

The Growth-Minded Leader by Tyler Cook

When Words Come to Life by Kheila Casas

Day by Day: 180 Days of Hope and Encouragement by Zac Bauermaster

Make Your Move: For Ambitious People Ready to Live Their Aspirations by Marlon Styles, Jr.

www.ingramcontent.com/pod-product-compliance
Lightning Source LLC
Chambersburg PA
CBHW070621030426
42337CB00020B/3877